SILVER MOUNTAIN CITY:
Ghost of the Sierra

Karen Dustman

C

Clairitage Press
Markleeville, California

For Claire, for whom nothing was ever impossible.

And for Rick, who breathed life into my dreams.

With special thanks to all the people without whom this book would never have seen the light of day, including (but as lawyers say, not limited to) Wanda and Gary Coyan, the Alpine County Historical Society, Gordon Harland, David Kessler and Susan Snyder of the Bancroft Library, Pat Keats and Adriane Tafoya of the Society of California Pioneers, Naomi Saito of the Beinecke Rare Book and Manuscript Library, Karen Nicholson at Calaveras County Historical Society, Kathleen Correia of the California State Library, Erin Chase and Kadin Henningsen of the Huntington Library, Kent Stoddard of the Mono County Historical Society, Lee Brumbaugh of the Nevada Historical Society, and Carson Hendricks of the Sacramento Archives. You are the best.

Ɛ

Clairitage Press
21 Nevada Rd.
Markleeville CA 96120
www.karendustman.com

ISBN 978-0-9833331-0-4

Library of Congress Control Number: 2011902610

Proudly Printed in the United States

Table of Contents

PROLOGUE

When we first visited Silver Mountain City in 2001, the old site was both surprising and disappointing. For heaven's sake, there was nothing left! <u>This</u> was a bustling county seat? These shallow, sloughed-in holes were once the foundations of a town?

Then in 2003 I was fortunate enough to work in the District Attorney's Office in Markleeville, right next door to Alpine's tiny gem of a library. Out of curiosity I spent my lunch hours scrolling through microfilmed pages of its old newspapers. And slowly the world of Silver Mountain began to emerge. Here, still etched in the pages of the Silver Mountain Bulletin, the Chronicle, the Argus, Monitor Gazette and the Miner were all the local characters, the town's vibrant celebrations, its day-to-day tragedies.

At first, the names and some of the banter were a mystery. Who were Leggett, and McBeth, and Ogden? What was this talk about the "orange groves" of Markleeville? For that matter, what was a "relocation," and why the flurry of ads for "Grand Benefit Drawings"? Over time, bits of information began to fit together. From brief advertisements and snippets of news, some of the town's landmarks started to emerge. My husband and I were entranced! Finding those spots on the ground became like discovering hidden treasure.

The true miracle of Silver Mountain, we soon realized, is not how much is gone but how much is <u>left</u>. Beyond just amazingly-complete newspaper records, the Alpine County Museum and the Archives contain an astonishing array of pristine and largely-untapped original documents. And even more of a miracle: several years after our research began, a big-hearted gentleman from the other side of the mountain donated a large collection of Lewis Chalmers' meticulously-kept letterbooks and accounting ledgers. It was a staggering windfall of information.

Chalmers' flowery script became a learning curve of its own. There were tiny "aha!" moments as lightbulbs came on: "do" stood for "ditto." Hard-to-read mining names slowly became familiar: Adolphus and Fremont; Accacia and Franklin; and of course the legendary I.X.L. From the immersion course of Chalmers' detailed reports, I began to pick up the peculiar language of old-time mining: adits and winzes, bluerock and Giant powder, amalgamating pans and Freyburg barrels; Stetefeldt furnaces and chloridizing processes.

As time wore on, through grainy newspaper clippings, old photos, and long-unread letters, one story picked up the thread of another and Silver Mountain's people and personalities began to come to life. Chalmers became a portly ghost hovering over my computer as I typed, whispering in his Scottish brogue about the ruby ore he'd seen with his own eyes and how close he'd come to uncovering a second Comstock.

Today when Rick and I walk Silver Mountain's long-overgrown byways we hear the town's silent heartbeat: bursts of raucous saloon laughter; the shuffling of a deck of cards; the low-pitched whine of the busy lumber mill; a bleating caravan of sheep parading down Main Street. Clusters of townsfolk still linger by the old hand-dug wells, sharing gossip and mining tips – just as they did nearly a century and a half ago. It's all still there, still vibrant, still hopeful, still alive.

We hope that in this book, the town of Silver Mountain comes alive again for you, too.

INTRODUCTION

The modern historical marker proclaims it "Silver Mountain City." But a century and a half ago, the locals called their town just plain Silver Mountain, the same as the nearby cliffs.

Today, Silver Mountain is a ghost of a ghost town, with not a stick of lumber left standing. The ruts of once-bustling Main Street have been buried beneath the blacktop of modern Highway 4. A flourishing army of stately pines has invaded the cross streets and taken up residence in the pits where noisy saloons once stood. Even the old stone jail, once the proud centerpiece of town, is now just a jumble of broken blocks, sheltered from the too-curious by a chain link fence.

But not so long ago, this flat beside Silver Creek was home to thousands who lived here, loved here, or just briefly passed through: miners and merchants; murderers and mothers. For one brief, heady decade during the 1860s, Silver Mountain was a thriving incarnation of greed and muscle, silver and seduction – in short, a quintessential mining town.

And in its own ghostly way, the town of Silver Mountain has never really died. Its people and their stories remain etched in microfilm and photographs and hand-scrawled documents. With a bit of puzzling, visitors can still pick out the spot where the Fiske Hotel once stood, stop by Sauquet's Store, or pay a visit to Davidson's Saloon. Close your eyes as you stand beside Main Street and you can almost hear the clink of glasses in the saloons and feel the earth tremble as Giant Powder explodes deep inside the mines.

Silver Mountain's legacy lives on, too, in Alpine County itself. For without the impetus of this amazing town, tiny Alpine county never would have been formed.

This is the long-forgotten tale of that long-forgotten town. And as most good tales do, our story begins at the beginning – before the first foot-sore miner threw down his heavy pack, before the first square nail was pounded, before the town of Silver Mountain even had a name, with a few tantalizing hints of silver. . . .

Courtesy Nevada Historical Society.

CHAPTER 1:
FIRST FLASH OF SILVER

The year 1858 spelled hard work and unsettled fortunes for California mining hopefuls. Ten long years had elapsed since the initial Gold Rush lured so many thousands westward, and the torrent of overland migration had dwindled to a steady trickle. But by the late 1850s, easy-to-obtain placer gold was largely played out, and remaining gold-seekers were forced to employ increasingly elaborate means to reach the deposits that remained.

Then in the Spring of 1859, a scant twenty miles east of the California border in Nevada Territory, Virginia City's blue clay launched a renewed rush for riches – this time, for silver.[1] In a hasty reverse migration, miners from California's central valleys retraced the South Fork of the American River to Strawberry Flat, crossed the mountains over Echo Summit and Luther Pass, and streaked through Genoa heading for the Comstock capital of Virginia City. Others trouped to their destination over what would later be called Ebbett's Pass and down the East Fork of the Carson River. By 1860, Virginia City had become "at once the most miserable and the most exciting place on earth," with Comstock mania reaching its torrid peak around April of that year.[2]

Meanwhile, to the East, citizens began turning anxious ears to the first faint drumbeats that would become the Civil War, a cadence that in its own way helped fuel the lust for silver.[3] And so, against this backdrop, the story of Silver Mountain begins.

Sometime around 1860, two small groups of miners began plying prospecting shovels on opposite sides of Silver Creek. One trio focussed their attentions south of the creek on Silver Mountain itself. A second group comprised of 16 Norwegian miners followed traces of silver-bearing quartz or "float" up the hillside to the north, pitching their camp in what became known as Scandinavian Canyon.[4]

The Silver Mountain hopefuls were the first to spot paydirt, or more accurately, pay *rock*, spying "from a distance" what later reports would dub "the massive croppings of the celebrated Mountain lode" in the fall of 1860.[5] It seems the charms of a pot-bellied stove and a solid roof to keep out the weather trumped the prospect of squatting high on the side of craggy Silver Mountain for the winter, and the group returned to Virginia City without staking an active claim. But mining activity resumed the following spring, with the Silver Mountain Mining District officially blessed into existence on May 27, 1861;[6] and in June the unimaginatively-named "Mountain No. 1"[7] and Silver Creek companies posted hasty location notices and commenced work on their claims.[8] By July, a few lots beside the river had been "located" as homesites.[9] And even more important, a pair of Notices of Location were filed July 1, 1861 on twin Scandinavian Canyon mines destined to play a starring role in Alpine mining affairs for decades to come: the I.X.L. (a play on the words "I Excel"), and the Buckeye No. 1.[10]

Dustman collection.

Miners eagerly awaited early assay results.

Assays must have been encouraging, as fourteen hardy silver-seekers endured the particularly severe winter of 1861-2 at Silver Mountain to hold down their claims.[11] By the time the spring thaws arrived in 1862, the secret was out. Eager prospectors swarmed the Silver Mountain vicinity, encouraged by assays as high as $860 per ton.[12]

In the blink of an eye, the camp beside Silver Creek was transformed into a settlement, and by October, 1862, enterprising land barons had formally platted a townsite.[13] Though many of its initial dwellings were probably simple canvas tents, the thriving mini-metropolis soon boasted 60 spanking-new wooden

A Town By Any Other Name

When a post office was first opened at Silver Mountain on May 12, 1863, the town was officially christened "Konigsberg,"[15] perhaps a sentimental tribute by Scandinavian miners to the similarly-named mining region in Norway.[16]

It is just possible, however, that the name might also have been a pun honoring a pioneering citizen. One "W. Konig" appears in

Alpine documents as early as 1865, for example,[17] while tax records from 1879 identify "William Konig" as the wealthy owner of 160 acres in Silver King Valley, the Bagley Ranch, and three lots in Markleeville.[18]

Whatever its origins, the name "Konigsberg" did not long retain the affections of the local populace. According to one early account, the ostensible source of dissatisfaction came from residents who "believe this a most unsuitable appellation and altogether outlandish." There was speculation, however, that the "real cause of the disaffection . . . [was] a bit of jealousy toward the hardy Norsemen who pioneered the district."[19]

On March 28, 1865, the town's postal moniker was officially changed to Silver Mountain – a perfect choice to reflect its citizens' hopes that a veritable "mountain of silver" lay nearby.

structures – including three stores, two hotels, a blacksmith shop, bakery, and assay office – all serving an equally-new populace of about 300 hopeful souls.[14]

In June, 1863, while Grant was busy laying siege to Vicksburg on the other side of the continent,[20] incorporation papers were filed to form Silver Mountain's "Mountain Gold and Silver Mining Company No. 1," optimistically offering 2,750 shares at a pricey $200 apiece.[21]

When itinerant geologist William H. Brewer[22] paid Silver Mountain a flying visit that August, he found a town overrun with "hundreds of men, all active, busy, scampering like a nest of disturbed ants." According to Brewer, "One hears nothing but 'feet,' 'lode,' 'indications,' 'rich rock,' and similar mining terms. Nearly everyone is, in his belief, in the incipient stages of immense wealth."[23]

A similar description of these early days comes to us by way of mining superintendent Lewis Chalmers who, although not present at its inception, describes the I.X.L. Mine as the "pioneer" discovery of Scandinavian Canyon:

Dustman collection.

An unsmiling William Brewer (seated) with Richard Cotter, "packer" for the survey party, circa 1864.

> To the discovery of this Lode in the summer of 1861, Alpine County is indebted, I may say, for its existence. No sooner was work commenced almost in the Croppings, than the richest description of Ruby Silver ore revealed itself, and as a matter of course, created one of those "excitements" once so common in this Country.
>
> Eager prospectors covered the Mountain Sides, swarmed in the immediate vicinity of the pioneer discovery, and almost before the Year expired, nothing was left in the shape of a ledge or stain or outcrop to locate, the same ledge taken up two or three times over by a rude Notice on some of its spurs or angles, and all found a place in the Records of the then-formed "Silver Mining District."
>
> A general rush from Virginia and other mining camps was made to the new Eldorado, buildings of all kinds were erected in anxious haste, saloons drove a rushing trade, corner lots ruled high; with all this, but little useful work was done after the first coyote hole was made to hold the ground.[24]

Dustman collection

*A*dditional hopefuls streamed into town daily. From the west, the stage line ran through the settlement of Big Trees to a terminus in Silver Valley some 10 or 12 miles from Silver Mountain, with the final stretch traversed by horse or mule. Similarly arduous access was available from the east, with wagon roads reaching as far as Woodfords and Markleeville, and pack-trails completing the journey to Silver Mountain.

Markleeville, where the good wagon road ended, quickly blossomed into a freighting depot for the Silver Mountain mines. By August, 1863, Markleeville itself could boast some 100 structures, including one "euphemistically called an opera house."[25] But even this amazing building fever paled by comparison with the boomtown emerging at Silver Mountain, which proudly numbered *twice* as many structures.[26]

Alpine County Is Born

Surveying during the 1860s involved considerably more art and considerably less science than it does today. Based on the common wisdom that everything east of the Sierra summit was part of Nevada Territory, Silver Mountain was widely assumed to have been planted on the *Nevada* side of the border.[27] In 1863, however, a survey crew placed it firmly in California's domain.

With that minor detail resolved, Silver Mountain residents began to circulate a petition in the Fall of 1863 demanding their own fresh county. The "Alpine Bill" sped its way through the California Legislature and on March 16, 1864, the Legislature gave its official nod to this brash request, carving a tiny 723-square mile chunk from the junction of Amador, El Dorado, Calaveras, Mono and Tuolumne Counties.[28]

The "Alpine County Bill" adopted a colorful if somewhat imprecise boundary description for the newly-minted county.[29] Commencing at a vague spot "where the State line crosses the East summit of the Sierra Nevada mountains," the border then jogged southwest:

> *to a point two miles west of James Green's house, in Hope Valley, called Thompson's Peak; thence south westerly in a direct line to Z. Kirkwood's house on the Amador and Nevada Turnpike Road, excluding said Kirkwood's house; thence due south across the North Fork of the Mokelumne river to the road leading from West Point, in Calaveras county, to the Big Tree Road, near the Big Meadows; thence easterly along said West Point Road to the Big Tree Road; thence easterly in a direct line to where the Sonora trail strikes the Middle Fork of the Stanislaus river; thence easterly to the summit of the Sierra Nevada mountains; thence northerly along said summit to the dividing ridge between the West Walker and Carson rivers; thence northerly along said dividing ridge to the State line to the place of beginning.[30]*

The population of the new county was later estimated (perhaps somewhat optimistically) at some 11,000 souls[31] – a figure which, if accurate, it has never managed to regain in the ensuing 140 years.

The towns of Markleeville, Silver Mountain, and Monitor all vied for the plum title as the new County seat. An election held August 11, 1864 to determine the winner finally awarded that honor to Silver Mountain by less than 100 votes out of the 1,660 votes cast.[32]

It was a time of new beginnings and shifting politics. Just two months after Alpine County's creation, the State of Nevada was welcomed into the Union – a move engineered in part to increase electoral votes for Lincoln during the upcoming presidential election.[33]

There was a price to pay for Alpine's new-found independence, however; the freshly-minted county was forced to assume $10,000 of Amador County's debt,[34] an obligation which proved a nearly-unsupportable financial burden. Amador quickly lost hope of receiving prompt repayment, selling off the Alpine debt to Capital Savings Bank of Sacramento in September, 1870, for a nominal $7,700 gold coin.[35] The Bank actually "paid" for the note by redeeming the county's own heavily-discounted warrants, however, netting Amador just $2,250 in cash.[36] Even at that, *The Amador Ledger* tartly concluded that the Bank had been "badly sold," adding that "the scrip will probably be redeemed in about 99 years – if the IXL [Mine] strikes it rich."[37]

Alpine managed to scrape together a $1,113.50 payment in December 1870, and by 1871 claimed to have retired $5,000 of the debt during the previous year.[38] A proposal was floated briefly (and apparently unsuccessfully) in February, 1872 to persuade the Legislature to refinance the debt by issuing bonds.[39] By January, 1878, nearly a decade and a half after its birth, Alpine County had forked over a whopping $11,000 and still owed another $4,000 on its debt.[40]

High on optimism and low on cash: it would be a pattern that would repeat itself throughout the county's formative years. But for the new County's first decade, at least, optimism would carry the day.

Zacharius S. Kirkwood's House was such a prominent site that it was identified as a landmark in the Alpine County boundary description by the 1864 "Alpine County Bill."

Courtesy Alpine County Historical Society

8

Silver Mountain at its bustling height circa 1863, looking from west to east. The building to the right (lower foreground) is the Fiske Hotel; just across Main Street and farther right is the Mammoth Hotel with its adjacent false-fronted stable. A few trees still dot the hillside across the river, but most of the original local stands had already been converted to building lumber, firewood, and shoring timbers.

CHAPTER 2:
SILVER MOUNTAIN HEY-DAY
CANVAS, ROUGH BOARDS,
& CIVIC SPIRIT

By 1863, hopes in the new town of Silver Mountain were as lofty as the rarified mountain air. Vacant homesites were trading hands for a pricey $50 each, while prime commercial lots on Main Street commanded $1,000 and up.[1]

In 1864, barely two months after Alpine County was officially blessed into being, a pseudonymous mining newspaper correspondent calling himself "Argent" (the French word for 'silver') offered a bird's-eye view of the rough-and-tumble settlement:

> *The town of Silver Mountain is regularly and scientifically laid off into blocks and lots, all of which have long since had claimants. At the present writing it contains five stores which deal in general merchandise, one hardware store, two hotels, two blacksmith shops, one restaurant, one meat market, two sawmills, and several places where the 'poison' is dealt which 'maketh the brain mad.'*[2]

Strolling east from the three-story Fisk Hotel at the corner of Main and First, visitors during the town's first decade might catch the whirr of a printing press in the nearby *Bulletin* office or peer in the windows of Harris's Jewelry store. The next block uptown included I.S. Powers's drygoods store and, by 1867, the *Chronicle* headquarters – a composite of two early buildings remodelled to include a high false front and second-story balcony.

Many of the town's male citizens turned out in 1867 for a celebratory photo marking the Chronicle's recent move to Silver Mountain, with new headquarters at the corner of Second Street and Main.

Courtesy Alpine County Historical Society

On the south side of Main Street, a long, narrow livery stable huddled close beside the frumpy Mammoth Hotel – itself a blocky, unadorned structure which even the sugar-tongued *Chronicle* would candidly describe as an "eye sore" by 1871.[3] Farther uptown, other Main Street establishments included Jacob Struben's shoe shop, Swinerton's "Pioneer Hardware" store, and Dastague's meat market. A "drug store emporium" graced Gates's Corner at the intersection of Main and Third Streets, while physician and surgeon J.S. Adams welcomed patients at his medical office between Fifth and Sixth.[4]

Alpine County Historical Society

Swiss emigrant Jacob Struben had a shoe shop in Silver Mountain as early as 1865, but he was more than a humble cobbler; like other residents, Struben speculated in buying and selling mining stocks.

Like all good mining towns, Silver Mountain featured an assortment of saloons competing for the attentions of thirsty miners. One of the more prominent watering holes, Gibson's Fashion Billiard Saloon, was conveniently located just "a few doors below and across the street from Court House Block" at the corner of Fourth Street. The Fashion advertised not one but two "first-class" billiard tables inside its generous 25-by-40-foot edifice, touting its twelve-foot ceilings and "a finished front not excelled by any other building in Alpine County."[5] Close by and also on the north side of Courthouse block, the "Forty Drops" saloon similarly welcomed tipplers, while across the street Patterson's Saloon adjoined the court-house building itself[6] and Davidson's Saloon could be found a mere half-lot away.

Some early Silver Mountain homes were substantial wooden structures, but many abodes were far more hastily constructed affairs. Newcomers might stake out a homesite by simply throwing up a tent, while cash-starved miners with somewhat more permanent homes might make do using canvas in place of doors and windows. Still others inhabited the rudest kind of brush lean-to or log cabin.[7] Little wonder, then, that Silver Mountain visitor Addison Curtiss confided to his diary in the spring of 1864: "Awful windy all day; blew down several houses."[8]

Curtiss's diary leaves us a marvelous account of Silver Mountain life through a summer of daily entries capturing both the cost of goods and the rhythm of a miner's life. Tantalizing details like "Treated the boys [to drinks] – 50 [cents]" would be followed equally solemnly by the mundane entry: "got a pair [of] socks."[9] From Curtiss, we know that supplies were easy to come by in 1864, if not to pay for; a simple pair of duck overalls from Harris's store set him back nearly a day's wages at $2.25.[10] Curtis's diary also offers a glimpse of the physical discomforts of mining life, encapsulated in haiku-like snippets. "Got a pair of boots of Frank Smith & Co., [$]7.00" was followed a few days later in his diary by: "Feet awful sore from tight boots."[11] After three days' contract labor on a mining claim, one morose entry reads: "Cut my thumb – bad."[12] And two days of hard digging later: "nearly finished and I ain't sorry – back lame."[13]

INTERIOR OF A MINER'S CABIN.

A vivid picture of Silver Mountain night life emerges from Curtiss's diary as well, laced with visits to an "up town" watering hole known as "Billy Ryan's Exchange," later said to be the most valuable property in town,[14] and liberal consumption of cider, lager, and cigars.[15] "Played a game of billiards with Bill Hughes," one entry records saucily, adding with evident satisfaction: "– beat him."[16] Curtiss also reported the inevitable consequences of such rowdy visits. One Friday night notation "went up town evening" was followed by Saturday's: "Felt sick nearly all day."[17]

While Silver Mountain was brimming with mining excitement, however, the rest of the nation was becoming increasingly embroiled in the Union-rending Civil War. Though far removed from the actual fighting, California pioneers found themselves similarly split into cadres of Union and Confederate sympathizers. Over the crest of the Sierras in nearby Amador County, one rebel enthusiast was hauled up on criminal charges by the local district attorney for the crime of "hurrahing for Jeff Davis."[18] Within what would later become Alpine County, observers noted as early as 1863 that "[t]he Union element is powerful in these mountains," estimating generously that about 800 out of the 1,000 local voters were expected on the Union side.[19] Indeed, the following year Alpine threw its support solidly behind Abraham Lincoln by a vote of 351 to 192 in the 1864 presidential election.[20]

Despite such strong Union sentiments, the new county was home to at least a few Confederate sympathizers. As late as October, 1864, the Monitor press cautioned its readers about a possible Confederate 'rising', anxiously repeating "a seemingly well authenticated" rumor about an "attempted outbreak" in California, ostensibly being planned through "secret and suspicious gatherings of men."[21] Alpine Copperheads, if there were any, were apparently smart enough to keep a low profile, and the "attempted outbreak" never materialized. Nevertheless, Jeff Davis Peak is thought to owe its name to Southern sympathizers in nearby Summit City, while Bull Run Peak commemorates a Confederate war victory.[22]

News of wartime hostilities found its way across the country to this tiny patch of California, albeit with little detail at times. A brief entry in Curtiss's diary for May 13, 1864, for example, says simply: "Heard that Grant & Lee was having a heavy fight in Virginia."[23] Still, news filtered in during the spring of 1865 with the welcome announcement of General Lee's surrender at Appomattox, followed less than a week later by the tragic assassination of President Lincoln.[24]

Meanwhile, Silver Mountain's mining hopefuls began to discover that while hard work was plentiful, bonanzas were not. To be sure, there was silver in the local ore. But the precious metal proved difficult to extract from the highly-sulphured native rock, and high-paying deposits were spotty. Merchants, too, found local business discouraging. As early as July, 1864, one San Francisco correspondent penned a consoling letter to a Silver Mountain merchant named F.H. Smith:

I was not at all surprised at [your letter's] contents. When you have been in California as long as I have you will learn that to calculate upon favorable results here as you do in the old states is mighty hazardous business. . . . You must bear in mind that people in this country go much on excitements, and the greater the humbug the greater the excitement, and when it's all over with they neither blame nor condemn anyone for the results. Hence it is perfectly safe for bad and evil-disposed men to get up their excitement. They have all the gain, if any, and nothing to lose. You believed everything was right at your place and thought others were of the same opinion, [or] if not then soon would be, and that would bring a grand rush to your town, hence a good business season. Now you see how easy it is to be mistaken. . . . My opinion the best thing that you can do is to make your expenses as light as possible, . . .

A view of early Silver Mountain City from the north looking south across the valley, from a stereoview circa 1864. The three-section building at center of photo (just to the right of the rock) includes Ryan's Exchange.

close out your store by selling the goods when you can get the cash down for them, or closing it out altogether, . . . pay your whole attention to your Hotel and wait the result.[25]

Two months later Smith was evidently losing heart, as his correspondent was writing:

You say times are growing worse, that can't be helped. As you have got your foot into it you will have to grin and bear it until time eases you out. . . . If there is no money there to pay for goods and they give you much trouble about trying to get credit I would shut the store up and not sell any goods at all.[26]

By 1867, the town of Silver Mountain had settled from a boiling cauldron of activity to a steady simmer, with about 300 tenacious citizens[27] and a mere 109 registered voters.[28] The townsite had become an official fixture on the banks of Silver Creek with a formal plat of its city lots,[29] and the local mining districts had been memorialized in a map drawn up by none other than the district court judge, Theron Reed.[30] The early flurry of prospecting activity had died off, but active mining claims close to town included the I.X.L., Lady Franklin, Mammoth, Buckeye No. 1 and 2, and George Washington.[31] The nearby mining communities of Monitor and Mogul, too, had morphed into small but well-established towns, with smaller offshoots at Silver King and Bulliona.

To the north, the "mushroom town" of Reno soon amounted to a bustling metropolis of 600 or more inhabitants, thanks to its railway hub. Haste overtook taste in driving its development, unfortunately; one Reno visitor in 1869 described the town as "extemporized of canvas and rough boards . . . [and] built without much regard to order."[32]

Canvas and rough boards: it was a description fit for Silver Mountain, too, albeit on a smaller scale. But the city fathers had far grander things in mind.

Laying Down the Law

When the newly-appointed Alpine County Board of Supervisors initially convened in August, 1864, one of their first items of business was the weighty matter of providing the new county with a proper court-room. Rather than stretching the already-thin budget to purchase a building, the Board opted instead to solicit bids to rent an existing one.

J.A. Goodwin, owner of the Mammoth Hotel, offered his building at the south end of town for $200 per month in paper scrip for six months.[33] W.H. Ryan countered with a proposal to rent Ryan's Exchange, a three-story structure nearer the center of town, for a similar six-month period at just $190. Ryan's low bid was naturally accepted.[34] But when the initial contract expired in March, 1865, competition for the next rental period was keen. The county eventually renewed its lease on Ryan's building at the greatly reduced

Ryan's Exchange was once called "the most valuable building in town," and doubled as the Court House. The sign over the doorway to the right indicates that the County Recorder's Office was located next door.

Courtesy of California History Room, California State Library, Sacramento CA

sum of just 50 cents per month. In March, 1866, the lease was again renewed, with a monthly rent of $25. Thomas Ogden tendered his saloon building at Fourth and Main for courtroom purposes in January, 1867. But Ryan again was the winning bidder, this time for $30 per month.

In a diatribe published in the Markleeville-based *Alpine Chronicle*, Ogden accused the Supervisors of being "owned by some whisky shops" – a thinly-veiled jab at Ryan. Complained Ogden:

> *Before making my bid I was informed by [Supervisors] Calhoun and Dake that there was no [other] bid in, and immediately after making mine I was coolly informed that there was one for Ryan's building at $50 per month. I then lowered mine to $40; Ryan's went to $40; I to $35; Ryan's to $35, Dake then moved that Ryan's bid be accepted; I immediately told them to hold on, that I would come to $30 and a good deal less than that, but Calhoun said I will record the motion of Dake; we will stop this contention right here. Now let the people fully understand this business. Ryan's building at no time was offered at less than mine – if it had been but one cent less it should have been accepted, but in every case the preference was given to Ryan.[35]*

To settle such "petty strife" and free the Supervisors "from further annoyance in this matter," the Board determined that in the future it would thereafter "compel all persons who send in proposals to furnish buildings, suitable for county purposes, to remove the fixtures of each particular office, and the archives of the county, and to replace them in as good condition as before their removal."[36] Moving expenses were estimated at $300 in gold coin, a shockingly high estimate that no doubt served to deter future competing bids.

But the tenacious Ogden apparently enjoyed the last laugh, if not the loftiest remuneration. In March, 1871, the Supervisors finally "leased" Ogden's Building to serve as the County Court House for the next two years, *rent-free*. Cinching the vote, the local newspaper reported: "the archives are to be removed without expense to the dear people."[37]

Ogden's two-story structure was apparently well-suited for its new purpose, being large enough to house not only the court but also the county clerk and sheriff in a one-stop-shopping model of governmental efficiency. Raved the local press:

> *The Clerk's office is in the front room on the second floor, and the Sheriff has his office in the adjoining room, fronting on Fourth street. The Court Room will be in the building in the rear of, and adjoining the main building. The new offices are much more comfortable and pleasant than any the County has heretofore occupied.*[38]

In its free-rent quarters, the District Court held regular sessions the first Monday of April and October, while the County Court convened the first Monday of February, June, and October.[39] Judges presided over the usual array of civil disputes[40] and, despite the social strictures of the time, even a divorce or two.[41]

On occasion judges were also called upon to resolve more esoteric issues. In 1871, a vagrant who had been found "prowling about this county and Carson Valley" was hauled before Judge Goff, the presiding magistrate, to be examined. Determining the suspect to be "more of a vagrant than an insane man," the judge freed him with a stern admonition that "unless he left the county immediately he would be arrested." Hardly surprisingly, the culprit "left immediately."[42]

The court at Siver Mountain was also charged with granting citizenship, a function it apparently exercised liberally. Citizenship was encouraged by punitive legislation providing that aliens could be "excluded as trespassers or required to pay a license by law, for the privilege of occupying and working the mines."[43] Many of those naturalized at Silver Mountain were Norwegians or Swedes, like Peter Vollem,[44] Torgrim Olson, and John Johnson. Others who swore the oath of citizenship before the Alpine County court included Canadian Thomas Hay[45] and Scotsman Daniel Davidson.[46]

Courtesy of Alpine County Historical Society

Sealed bids to construct the new stone jail were solicited by the Board of Supervisors in early 1867. Specifications included four wooden cells, two lined with iron plate 1/8-inch thick, and grated doors. The gloomy cells faced toward the outer stone walls, leaving narrow passageways "lighted by small openings."

Jail Travail

Given the number of saloons in town, a fundamental accommodation for preserving the public peace was a town jail. But in a precursor of future Alpine politics, even as seemingly beneficial an endeavor as erecting a new jail sparked a flurry of controversy.

The first jail to hold prisoners at Silver Mountain was a "log house" rented by the county from its owner, William Pearson, for $15 per month.[47] Winters within this primitive jail must have been both dark and cold. Early bills presented to the Supervisors for payment included one "for making shackles" and another for "candles for jail."[48] A bid to feed prisoners for 90 cents a day was rejected, presumably as too lavish.[49] At least one inmate languished for nearly a year within these gloomy confines[50] until his doctor stepped forward in October, 1865, attesting that jail conditions were injuring his patient's health.[51]

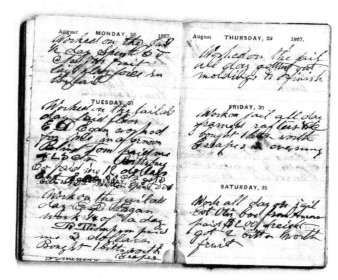

Dustman Collection

Carpenter O.S. Adams recorded his daily expenses in Silver Mountain in 1867, including purchases of twenty pounds of potatoes for 75 cents; five pounds of beans for 50 cents; and a steak for 25 cents.

By January, 1867, after a prisoner's attempt to burn the wooden jail down,[52] the Supervisors began advertising for bids to construct a new *stone* jail. Public-spirited citizens R. Thompson and D. Davidson had already donated a pair of lots in the center of town "for County buildings."[53] But the projected cost for the new jail building quickly exceeded expectations. Finding that the lowest bid for the structure was $4,270, the Board rejected all bids and went back to the drawing board,[54] modifying the plans to decrease the amount of iron to be used in reinforcing the cells. Even with that concession, however, the requirements remained daunting. "We made an attempt on Tuesday to wade through the plans and specifications on file; but finding them so voluminous, abandoned it," confessed the editor of the *Silver Mountain Bulletin*.[55] Unable to attract any more-appealing bid, the Board finally awarded the jail-building contract to E.D. Egan for a flat fee of $4,000.[56]

Egan wasted little time setting to work. With snow still deep on the surrounding mountainsides, Egan "commenced quarrying the stone for the walls on Tuesday of this week," reported the *Bulletin* of April 6, 1867. The cornerstone-laying ceremony a month later was attended by some fifty public-spirited citizens, "including the three Supervisors and most of our county officials."[57] Within two more weeks, sufficient progress had been made on the jail building to entitle Egan to two draws.[58]

Even as the work progressed, however, public sentiment against the lavish stone building was growing, stirred up by taxpayers "in the northern portion of the county." Objections included "that the county is too poor to meet the expense" of the new jail and that the bidding process had been illegal. Perhaps most tellingly, detractors pointed out that the County's Building Fund did not contain funds to cover the proposed price. The Supervisors deftly surmounted this financial hurdle by pilfering the county's Hospital Fund to pay for the new jail's construction.[59] It was rumored that such indifference to price was itself suspicious, with at least two reports suggesting (probably accurately) that one of the Supervisors had a personal interest in the contract.[60]

Public grumbling culminated in an Anti-Jail Meeting on May 11, 1867, held at the discreet distance of Markleeville, where dissenters contemplated hiring a lawyer to seek an injunction to halt the work.

One Captain Smith was elected chair of the malcontents, and the *Chronicle*'s own editor, R.M. Folger, served as secretary for the gathering.[61] Nevertheless, attendance was smugly described by the Silver Mountain-based *Bulletin* as "slim," the result of "so many farmers being busy putting in their crops."[62]

Egan continued to make progress on the jail, subcontracting the woodwork from floor joists to finish trim to carpenter O.S. Adams for a flat fee of $165, with $100 to be paid in gold coin when the work was completed, and the balance within sixty days.[63]

Courtesy of the Society of California Pioneers, San Francisco
(Gift of Florence V. Flinn)

The road leading into Silver Mountain from Markleeville, circa 1870. The building in the center foreground is a mill. The creek is visible to the right and jogs left near the large tree in the center. The bridge today would be beyond the far left side of the photo.

Again foretelling the County's future experience, the jail's construction budget fell far shy of the actual cost. Thanks to ups, extras, and over-runs, the sturdy stone edifice when finished carried an astonishing price tag of $7,000 – nearly twice the original bid.[64] By September, 1867, the newspaper glumly advised that this "much abused institution is rapidly approaching completion, and will be ready for occupancy by the 20th of next month."[65] Even as late as December, however, the Board of Supervisors failed to formally accept the completed jail building, with the newspaper observing that the structure required "extra work" to finish it to the Board's satisfaction.

In its final form, the 24- by 30-foot jail featured 18-inch-thick stone walls "laid in cement." A stoutly-timbered "under roof" was covered with a foot of dirt, a precaution intended to render the building "outwardly fireproof." Inside walls were neatly plastered and accented by painted woodwork. Twin flues allowed for a stove on each side, and – apparently in preparation for a crime wave – six stout cells stood ready for prisoners. Of these, two high-security cells were constructed of solid iron plate. These were located in the rear of the building and secured to the stone structure with angle-iron. The four additional wooden cells, presumably for less fearsome criminals, faced outward towards the side walls, leaving narrow passageways "lighted by small openings" along the walls. Each cell featured grated iron doors weighing 500 pounds each, and a 27-inch security chain fastened to the floor. In the front of the building was a stove and the jailer's bed, plus two "heavily barred" windows on either side of the main door. Other amenities included a "patent" jail lock and iron exterior shutters.[66]

The *Chronicle* coolly pronounced the edifice "ill advised and uncalled for," observing that "if the 'county comes out [grows],' the jail is too small, and if the 'county don't come out,' it is too large."[67] Even after its completion, the magnificent stone jail was both a continuing source of irritation and a drain on County finances. The *Chronicle* pointedly observed in May, 1868, that the new jail had "never had an occupant."[68] During its entire first five years of operation it would house a mere four criminals – at a cost to the County averaging $2,000 per prisoner, as the *Chronicle* tartly noted.[69] Despite this dearth of inmates, the Sheriff nevertheless was granted a new deputy for the jail in May, 1870, at a salary of $30 per month.[70] Not surprisingly, the jailer's fees were roundly criticized.[71]

History has largely erased the identities of the miscreants who languished within the jail's cheerless stone walls. But at least one minor villain's story has survived. The local paper reported that "Doctor" R.W.T. George was serving a four-month term of imprisonment when he attempted to bludgeon his jailer, Charles Sanders, with a metal leg pilfered from the jail's wood-stove.[72] Luckily, Deputy Sanders was able to overpower the inmate, and no lasting harm was done. The woodstove was no doubt moved safely out of inmates' reach thereafter.

Over time, Silver Mountain's much-maligned jail went from being a focus of opprobrium to a source of local pride. By the time talk began circulating of moving the County seat to Markleeville in 1872, the *Chronicle* had come full circle in the debate, bolstering opposition to the move by touting Silver Mountain's sturdy $7,000 edifice.[73]

Schooling for Tomorrow:

Even in the town's infancy, Silver Mountainites demonstrated their commitment to public education by reserving three full blocks above Main Street as the "School Block" – a civic indulgence representing a $600 investment at the going rate for lots.

Courtesy of Alpine County Historical Society

This Markleeville schoolroom in 1903 was likely similar to what schoolchildren experienced in Silver Mountain – complete with a prominent woodstove for heat.

The city fathers' academic ambitions were soon tested by would-be squatters, who laid claim to the school parcel and erected a fence to underscore their intentions. Outraged townsfolk assembled to pitch out the interlopers, erecting a new split-rail fence of their own to ward off future incursions.[74]

By September of 1864, Alpine County had three separate school districts (dubbed the Franklin, Webster, and Everett Districts), serving the children of Silver Mountain, Markleeville, and Monitor respectively. The Lincoln District and Clay District were soon added for students at Woodfords and Fredericksburg.

Schooling was not yet compulsory. So of the 99 school-age children living at Silver Mountain in 1864-65, only 38 were enrolled at its local Franklin School. Nevertheless, the tiny school managed to deliver an impressive seven months of instruction to its pupils that year, compared with only three months at both the Everett School at Monitor and the Lincoln School at Woodfords.

From a peak of 324 total school children in 1864-5,[75] Alpine County's school-age population plummeted to just 169 in early 1867.[76] The Superintendent's compensation likewise tumbled from the lavish sum of

Courtesy of Society of California Pioneers, San Francisco
(Gift of Florence V. Flinn)

Silver Mountain City, viewed from south of Silver Creek looking northeast, circa 1863. The toll road leading up Scandinavian Canyon to mines such as the I.X.L. and Buckeye is visible in the center. This early view shows that homes were scattered on both sides of Silver Creek.

$400 per year in 1864 to a mere $80 per annum in 1879.[77] A quick succession of county school superintendents ensued, one lasting just seven months. Teachers came and left even faster, with a revolving-door count of ten teachers serving the five schools during one particularly bad school year.[78] Failing to so much as mention of the region's harsh climate and comparative isolation, the School Superintendent's report of 1871-72 laid the blame for teacher-retention squarely on the parents:

> *There are many parents who do not* <u>*train*</u> *their children to habits of Obedience: They let them 'come up' as they (the children) like. As a matter of course, such children are totally opposed to any law, rule, regulation or authority whatever; both in school and out of School. And what is worse still: such children are supported in their opposition by their parents....A teacher with a* <u>*star*</u> *on his breast would suit many of them best.*[79]

Perhaps equally at the root of the teacher-retention problem were salaries that one later report candidly termed "starvation prices." Thus in 1865-66, for example, male teachers' salaries averaged $70 per month; female teachers could expect just $62.80. By comparison, an uneducated miner could earn close to $100 a month.

The fortunes of the schools mirrored the success of the local mines. Thus when mining prospects picked up in 1870-71, Superintendent Joseph Uncapher could find little to complain about beyond pupils' "slack attendance." Some six years later after the demonetization of silver eviscerated the *raison d'être* of the local mines, Alpine's schools were politely described as "much reduced and somewhat demoralized, consequent on the depression of the business interests of the county."[80]

In 1878, the county's first woman superintendent Anna L. Spencer summed up the school situation in just four words: "Progress slow; condition poor." Spencer herself took a sixty-day leave of absence from her post, ostensibly to visit her mother in Kansas, and apparently never returned.[81] By 1879-80, her successor described Silver Mountain's once-promising Franklin School District as "lapsed."

The town of Silver Mountain, looking east, about 1867. The prominent building in the center (with windows) is the Fiske Hotel.

Alpine County Historical Society

CHAPTER 3:
BED, BOARD & BLANKET

From its inception, Silver Mountain's population was rarely static. Tidal waves of immigrants swept in each time the mines looked promising – and swept out again with equal vigor when the glitter seemed to fade.

Newly-arriving miners found ready lodging in private homes doing double-duty as hotels. For a pricey $8 per week, better-heeled silver seekers could take their room and board at William Kent's boarding house, with a dollar off for "persons furnishing their own blankets."[1] Less-affluent miners like Addison Curtiss, whose diary chronicles his brief sojourn in the Silver Mountain mines over the summer of 1864, might take supper at Treat's Hotel and breakfast at Mrs. Scott's "French Hotel," but avoided upscale sleeping accommodations. Curtiss simply got his "bundle" and meandered "down to Jim Jacob's cabin" to sleep.[2]

Perhaps no building dominated the Silver Mountain landscape quite as prominently or for as long as the elegant Fisk Hotel. Towering some three stories over the northeast corner of Main and First Street, this stately wooden structure was built about 1863 by Charles Fisk (or Fiske)[3] and – given his flock of 13 children – may originally have been intended as a single-family home.

With wife Mary Ann and children in tow, Fisk had made the arduous journal westward from Old Town, Maine across Panama to California about the time of the gold rush. The family initially settled near Sacramento, where Charles operated a flour mill for several years.[4] But if the California gold bug had originally bitten him, the silver bug soon took its place. By 1864, Fisk and his family

FISK'S HOTEL,

Corner of Main and First streets,

SILVER MOUNTAIN.

THE Proprietor of this well known House takes this method of informing his friends and the public generally that he is prepared to accommodate the traveler with all the conveniences and comforts of a home, in a style not to be surpassed. The table will be furnished with all the substantials and luxuries of the market. The sleeping apartments are neat, airy, and furnished with good beds, and the proprietor hopes by strict attention to the comforts of his guests, to merit and receive a fair share of public patronage.

CHARLES FISK.

Silver Mountain, March 24, 1865.   43tf

Courtesy of Calaveras County Historical Society

A rare early view of the Fisk Hotel, showing a gentleman in a high top hat by the front door. Note the tiny smokestack emerging from the roof where a chimney would later stand.

Courtesy of Alpine County Histsorical Society

Mary Jane Fisk, Charles Fisk's daughter, was called the "presiding genius of the establish- ment" by the local newspaper in February, 1865, perhaps because her mother had fled to Murphys to escape the brutal Silver Mountain winter. Mary Jane would marry George Mauk in 1866.

had moved to Silver Mountain,[5] where the tax rolls identify him as the owner of a "house and other improvements" at the prime commercial corner of First and Main, assessed at a pricey $1,250[6] – ten times the value of an average Silver Mountain home.

Early advertisements for the Fisk Hotel promised travelers "all the convenience and comforts of home, in a style not to be surpassed," with the proprietor's personal assurance of good beds and "strict attention to the comfort of his guests."[7] Amenities included lavish oyster suppers, with fresh oysters shipped to town by wagon, and shells still scattered about the site testify to the popularity of this treat.[8]

Despite professed concern for the comfort of guests, the builder ignored such niceties as insulation in the hotel's exterior walls. It was a not-uncommon omission for the period; guests at the nearby Oriental Hotel apparently endured similarly drafty discomfort. A blaze inside the Oriental in 1867, for example, was blamed on a spark from a neighboring chimney which managed to catch the room's cloth lining on fire, "as the roof is not tight."[9]

Fisk liked to dabble in local mining stocks, acquiring shares in the I.X.L. and other mines. But his relative, San Francisco merchant Royal Fisk, wrote with what would turn out to be prophetic advice:

> *I think you should go out of mining stocks and mining at the earliest opportunity. If there should be any rush in the spring do not fail to take advantage of it. When there is not more than one in a hundred that makes anything by it we must make up our minds that it [is] unprofitable business.*[10]

Charles Fisk was active in Silver Mountain community affairs, serving as a member of the school board for the Franklin School District in 1868-69,[11] and helping solicit "subscriptions in work" to build a bridge at Centerville.[12] And apparently ignoring his relative's advice, he

Courtesy of Calaveras County Historical Society

Four generations of Fisks in later years in Murphys, California. Charles Fisk may be the elderly gentleman, second from right, leaning on a cane.

acquired interests in several local mining claims, including the Mountain Company and the Onondaga Gold & Silver Mining Company.[13] Whether hedging his bets or simply becoming more enthralled with the County's agricultural prospects than its mining future, Fisk also purchased the Burnside Ranch (including all of Burnside Valley), about one-half mile south of Hope Valley.[14]

But Silver Mountain life evidently did not hold the same charm for Mrs. Fisk. She was reportedly "ill a good deal of the time."[15] After enduring seven dismal winters at Silver Mountain, the Fisk family evidently left town in the fall of 1869 to spend winter months in Murphys on the warmer side of the mountain,[16] and before long, moved to Murphys for good. There, Fisk opened a series of mercantile stores, continuing to indulge his mining interests by placer mining at Oro Plata.[17]

Other prominent Silver Mountain hotels included the Mammoth Hotel, diagonally across Main Street from the Fisk. Completed in June, 1864, the Mammoth may have acquired its name, in part, for its size; the Mammoth was touted as "*by far* the largest and most commodious of any in Alpine county," with furniture alone costing an estimated $16,000.[18] The building itself commanded a staggering $4,000 mortgage in 1864.[19] All that glory tarnished quickly, however. Less than a decade later, the local paper would snippily suggest that the Mammoth had had its origins as a stable.[20] And by April, 1871, the Mammoth Hotel was frankly considered an "eye sore," with the *Chronicle* commenting approvingly on plans to demolish the structure to make way for a new brick edifice (a scheme that failed to materialize).[21]

When photographer Eliza Withington visited Silver Mountain in mid-1876 to capture the sights and perhaps dip in the healing waters of the nearby hot springs, she took rooms at the competing Ford's Hotel,[22] located two blocks north of the Fisk between Third and Fourth Streets. Known alternatively as the "Alpine House" and the "Silver Mountain Hotel," Ford's Hotel served as the town's stage stop, telegraph office, polling place, and post office. Proprietor R.H. Ford wore an appropriately diverse group of titles, including "Reverend," postmaster, and Justice of the Peace. At Ford's Hotel, townsfolk could purchase steamer tickets to New York or Europe,[23] or partake in a "Down East" Thanksgiving dinner.[24] And when the town needed an acting coroner or a pinch-hitting superintendent for its schools, it was Ford who filled in.[25]

Dustman Collection

The Isabella Boarding House, circa 1910. The boarding house was built to provide housing for Chalmers's workers at his Isabella Tunnel, on the other side of Silver Creek. To the right can be seen piles of the waste rock from the tunnel.

In addition to lodgings available in town, boarding houses were frequently erected close to the individual mines. These not only permitted mine owners to wring an additional bit of profit from their operation but also increased the distance between thirsty workmen and the local pubs. Mining mogul Lewis Chalmers operated at least two such boarding houses for his workers: one near the Exchequer Company's mines in I.X.L. Canyon, and the other below town near the Isabella Tunnel.

Chalmers boasted that his boarders enjoyed "the very best table ever set in a mining Camp," with turkey at Christmas and on the Fourth of July,[26] and pastry, corned beef and cabbage for Sunday dinner.[27] Coffee and "coffee sugar" were ordered by the sack and barrel-full from San Francisco,[28] winter flour was laid in in quantities of 4,000 pounds at a time from Stockton,[29] and the "beef bill" for a boarding house could run as much as $235 for roughly two months' supply.[30] Chalmers's boarding house cook was expected to furnish three meals a day to as many as fifty hungry miners, with the aid of a pair of Chinese assistants.[31] The cook also served as boarding house operator, as Chalmers penned the job description:

> *He must be able to keep accounts, the number of meals each man has, his washing, casual meals, provisions on hand & required each month, and has full charge of the Boarding House: keep men in order & report transgressors. Bedrooms as well as Dining Room, kitchen & Sitting rooms [must be] kept clean, windows washed when required, kitchen & sitting room stoves kept black-leaded. He will be kind to, & yet firm with the men and treat all civilly. Wages: $50 per month. He will bring his own blankets & bed.[32]*

Chalmers was a tough taskmaster at home as well. Complaining about his Irish servants, he wrote for replacements in 1881, specifying that he desired "a middle-aged, strong Scotch or German steady woman, . . . widow preferred, no Irish nor American."[33] Also on his wish list was:

> *an A-1 Scotch or English middle-aged groom: but he must be a thorough groom and a little of a gardener. Duties: Care of 2 or 3 horses, harness, saddle, & 2 carriages, milk & feed 1 or 2 cows, do chores, carry in wood &tc. to kitchen, work in & keep garden & approaches, brush my clothes & blacken boots, & generally do just what I tell him . . . He must be civil and respectful to Mrs. C & myself and must stay at home and not go to Silver Mountain without leave. Should carriage or work of any kind be required on Sunday, he must not object.[34]*

Room and board for miners was not cheap, even in such communal accomodations. Chalmers charged his workmen $1 per day at the boarding house – a significant sum for a hardworking miner, whose wages could be as low as $2.50 for a ten-hour workday.[35] As late as 1873, twenty-one miners still bunked at the Exchequer Boarding House in Scandinavian Canyon, a figure Chalmers wrote home that he hoped soon to increase.[36] His correspondence indicates corporate income of $57.20 for one month from the boarding house operation,[37] but the strain of oversight was apparently wearing; Chalmers was also seeking a manager to take over the boarding house operation in exchange for a kickback to the company of 50 cents per miner each week, "for interest on money expended on the house."[38]

William Kent and his wife Mary Elizabeth ran Brown & Kent's boarding house and restaurant at Silver Mountain. They were the parents of Nevada Alpine Kent, born at Silver Mountain on May 21, 1864, and according to family history the first baby born in newly-formed Alpine County. The Kents would have three more children at Silver Mountain: Abigail, born in 1866; Argus in 1868; and Mary Jane in 1870, and would eventually be parents to a total of seven children.

For Silver Mountain residents, "home sweet home" might be anything from a tent to a fairly substantial wooden dwelling. Most dwellings were diminutive by modern standards. At just 50 feet wide by 80 feet long, building lots were not overly generous to begin with, and prime lots in the center of town were often split down the middle, permitting buildings no wider than 25 feet.

Foundations – where builders bothered with them – typically consisted of dry-laid local rock, with an excavated basement beneath the town's more substantial structures. Smaller pits at a distance from the center of town suggest that typical dwellings consisted of just a single room or two. And an abundance of rusty tin cans flattened into shingles testify that roofs tended to be rudimentary affairs.

As the initial silver rush of 1863-64 began to ebb, many of Silver Mountain's quickly thrown up buildings were simply abandoned, at least during the hostile winter months – fair game for newcomers seeking shelter. The newpaper gently chided a lack of manners sometimes exhibited by more recent visitors:

> *We would suggest to outsiders that when they visit our town and are allowed the temporary use of a building, that when they get ready to return home it would be proper for them to see that the doors of the building aforesaid are properly secured and everything left as found. If this shoe fits any of our readers, we hope it will be put on.*[39]

Winter posed other sorts of building risks as well. Creosote-laden woodstoves, imperfectly-chinked stone chimneys, and ubiquitous kerosene lanterns created all-too-common fire hazards. It didn't help that thoughtless citizens sometimes borrowed but failed to replace the town's communal fire ladders.[40]

Unlike many of its contemporaries, the town of Silver Mountain managed to escape an all-consuming fire for much of its history. Occasional blazes such as the one at the drafty Oriental Hotel were apparently quickly extinguished.[41] An official fire brigade was organized as early as 1866 in neighboring Markleeville.[42] Nevertheless, Silver Mountain citizens would read with alarm reports of the great Chicago fire of 1871.[43] Pandering to local fire-fighting concerns, newspaper pages prominently featured advertisements for "Babcock" fire-fighting equipment.[44]

With fire an ever-present danger, the *Chronicle* extolled the virtues of a new and improved lamp fuel known as "Danforth's Non Explosive Petroleum Fluid," which promised "lighting homes with no danger of explosion."[45] As an added benefit, this miracle liquid promised to leave "no ugly grease spot if spilled on the carpet or on your clothing" and cost no more than its counterpart, "death-dealing kerosene."

By the early 1870s, Silver Mountainites – like consumers elsewhere – began to be inundated with advertisements promoting a wide assortment of newly-available consumer goods. If tinkling the ivories was your

Readers of the Alpine Chronicle were regaled with advertisements for a variety of consumer goods, including the "unequalled" Weber square piano.

passion, a Chickering Piano could be purchased through an agent in San Francisco.[46] Sewing machines, too, were heavily marketed, with ads touting the labor-saving advantages over old-fashioned hand-stitchery. A man's shirt could now be created in just over an hour using the new-fangled Elliptic Sewing Machine, compared with 15 tedious hours using an old-fashioned needle and thimble – an argument that undoubtedly made its way from newspaper page to breakfast table in more than one Silver Mountain household.[47] Newspaper editors themselves received incentives from the sewing manufacturers for running such early info-mercials, and apparently bought and then re-sold a small inventory of these marvelous inventions on a profit-sharing basis. Column-space was devoted on more than one occasion to fortunate Silver Mountain matrons who now owned a new Weed, Florence, or Wheeler & Wilson sewing machine,[48] suggesting heavy-handedly that the publishers had "a few more of the same sort left" for sale.[49]

On matters of health, however, scientific technology remained primitive. One 1871 newspaper article recited with blissful innocence a recipe for preserving fruit using an all-purpose paste of lime and creosote.[50] Patent medicines were all the rage, and ads with glowing testimonials promised sufferers that Dr. Kissner's Celebrated Consumptive Powders would "positively cure" consumption[51] or touted "Richard's Remedy" for rheumatism.[52] Holloway's Pills and Ointment vowed to make "every man his own physician."[53] And Dr. Ayer offered a complete line of products with "wonderful cures" for everything from tumors to ringworm, heart disease to "female weakness."[54]

Patients were well-acquainted with taking health care matters into their own hands, and whiskey was liberally embraced for "medicinal" use. After a tiring journey from Silver Mountain to Big Meadows, for example, one foot-sore traveler confided to his journal, "Took something to stimulate, .25 (cents). Washed my feet in whiskey and went to bed early, awful tired."[55] Herbal folk remedies were both affordable and popular. The same traveler's diary records a purchase of "boneset" – a multi-purpose remedy which, for 25 cents, promised relief from such diverse ailments as fever, tapeworm, colds, and indigestion.[56] Similarly, when carpenter O.S. Adams fell ill, he "[t]ook a rum sweat" and "got some gruel at Kent's restaurant."[57]

A variety of popular "cure-alls" were advertised in the Silver Mountain Chronicle, promising fast relief for a wide range of ailments from toothaches to cancer. Holloway's ad was unintentionally humorous. Instead of "effecting thousands of cures," it misspelled its claim as "affecting thousands of curse."

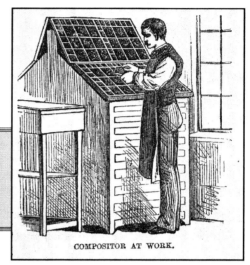

COMPOSITOR AT WORK.

CHAPTER 4:
CHRONICLING THE ORANGE GROVES

lpine County's earliest newspaper (and likely the first newspaper ever published on California's Eastern Slope)[1] was the Markleeville *Alpine Chronicle*, which began

For over a decade, brothers Robert and Alex Folger detailed the goings-on of Silver Mountain in the pages of their newspaper, mixing humor with fervent hope that the mines would someday allow the county to "come out."

rolling off a Montgomery Street press in April, 1864.[2] Within months, the little *Chronicle* would face competition from an upstart in Monitor known as the *Monitor Gazette*.[3] A fresh Silver Mountain-based newcomer, *The Bulletin*, appeared about the same time, only to fold after about a year and then re-debut in November 1866, under publisher W.O. Hayes.[4]

The mining towns of Markleeville, Silver Mountain, and Monitor enjoyed a friendly (and occasionally not-so-friendly) rivalry that was mirrored by the pages of their respective newspapers. Barbs were traded over everything from whose mines were "bilks" to which town offered the better weather. Exaggerated references to the "orange groves" of Markleeville became a running joke. Following one particularly severe snowstorm, for example, the *Chronicle* taunted:

> *Come down, Brother Hayes and take a spanking sleigh ride to Woodfords ... the snow is just deep enough to allow us to pluck the oranges with little trouble.*[5]

For the most part, sparring between the local papers remained good-natured. But Silver Mountain's *Bulletin* indulged in occasional tart exchanges with its rival in the competing mining camp of Monitor, including the following blast:

> *The Alpine Miner of last week ... attempts to criticise some remarks made by us, in our issue of the 19th of January, concerning the working of Morning Star ores at the Washington Mill.... In the first place, we would state that if there are any grievances to heal between ourselves and the stockholders of the Morning Star residing at Mogul, we can settle them without the meddlesome interference of outsiders residing at Monitor... The Alpine Miner, as usual, has gone off half-cocked, and does not comprehend what it is talking about.*[6]

Local editors were only too aware that their town's prosperity turned on the success of its mines, making them hardly disinterested observers when it came to reporting on local mining events. Story after story featured news like the following excerpts from the *Silver Mountain Bulletin*:

> *George Washington Co. – Early next week, a force will be put at work in the ledge in the main tunnel, running south in the mountain. The ledge at the bottom of the shaft is widening – the pay streak having increased one foot over its former width.*[7]

> *'Rich strikes' are heard of in places long looked upon as 'played out.' Returning miners from Montana, Idaho and British Columbia, begin to look upon California as <u>the</u> place, after all . . .*[8]

When there was good news to report, the headlines held nothing back. "Glorious News For Mogul" blared one early caption, detailing the recent production of a brick of silver measuring six inches long by two and a half inches square from Morning Star ore.[9] Even as the years piled on the mining disappointments, newspapers continued to remind their readers that the next foot of hard rock tunnel could uncover a glittering bonanza, and editors eagerly seized upon any indication that confidence in the local mines had not been misplaced:

> *The mining prospects of Alpine county never appeared so bright as now. With the results obtained from 3-1/2 tons of Tarshish ore, we demonstrate as fact what has been heretofore deemed mere assertion, that Alpine county is the richest silver bearing region on the Pacific coast. There is but one regret connected with this certain success now demonstrated, which is, that many of those who have remained here for years, and borne the beat and burden of reaching this point of success, find themselves forced to go elsewhere to recuperate financially, allowing the stranger to come in and reap where others have sown.*[10]

Courtesy of Mono County Historical Society

A.C. Folger, the younger of the two Folger brothers.

Editorial interest in the local silver mines transcended mere reporting. Alex Folger served as the Secretary/Treasurer for the Pennsylvania Mining Co.[11] and Secretary of the Mountain Gold & Silver Mining Co.[12] and was an investor in the Buckeye No. One.[13] Brother and co-publisher Robert Folger similarly held office as a trustee and director for the Mountain Mine,[14] a post which failed to deter him from writing an encouraging news note about his inspection of its tunnel, after a "resting spell of about eight years."[15] Robert also served as a director for the Pennsylvania mine,[16] and once applied for a mining patent for the Globe Mine as its "attorney in fact."[17]

In 1864 when the county was first formed, the town of Markleeville had its vocal supporters (the *Chronicle* likely among them), eager to promote Markleeville as the most logical and accessible choice for Alpine's official county seat.[18] But once the competing *Bulletin* folded its Silver Mountain newspaper in mid-1867,[19] the *Chronicle* eagerly seized the opening. A brief notice

Courtesy of Alpine County Historical Society

The Chronicle's new office at Silver Mountain, in 1867. Its letterhead (previous page) reflects the recent move from Markleeville to the new County seat with a hand-written change, and displays a romantic image of a hard-working miner.

in the *Chronicle's* August 31, 1867 issue advised: "The Chronicle after this date will be published at the county seat. Exchanges will please forward to Silver Mountain."[20] And once firmly ensconced at Silver Mountain, the editors would vigorously oppose later efforts to strip Silver Mountain of its official position as County seat.[21]

The *Chronicle* settled into distinctly upscale new quarters at the corner of Main and Second Streets, just a block north of the prominent Fisk Hotel.[22] Publisher R.M. Folger was soon joined in the new *Chronicle* offices and on the masthead by his brother, Alex C. Folger.[23] Together, the enterprising brothers hand-set four tedious pages of metal type to roll out a fresh issue of the *Alpine Chronicle* each week for the next decade.

The Brothers Folger

Twenty-nine-year-old Robert Folger was one of the early Gold Rush argonauts, leaving New York for California aboard the *Anthem* in January, 1849. The 200-ton schooner took the difficult route through the Straits of Magellan for the newly-discovered gold fields of California.[24] During the journey, Folger and nine cabin-mates formed themselves into the Winfield Scott Mining Company, in preparation for the riches they hoped awaited them in California.

Upon reaching California some six months later, however, Robert quickly realized that his fortune was unlikely to be made in gold. After trying his hand at more practical endeavors such as selling quartz-milling machinery and working for the Sacramento Fire Department, he returned to New York in 1850 (by way of Panama this time), bringing his wife back with him to Sacramento in 1852.[25] He eventually opened a newspaper business in Sacramento with his brother Frank in 1861, followed by another publishing venture in Ione in 1863.[26]

Whether drawn by the lure of the recently-booming Alpine mines or simply its beautiful mountains, Robert made his way to Markleeville about 1864. There he launched the *Alpine Chronicle* in a rented office on Montgomery Street across from the city hall,[27] using an $800 printing press he had lugged with him.[28]

Alexander C. Folger, roughly a dozen years younger than his brother, burst on the local scene about 1866 as Markleeville's first postmaster,[29] and in 1867 was serving as "host" of the Crystal Falls House, a Hope Valley hotel also known as Steven's Station.[30] Before long, Alex (or "A.C." as he frequently signed his name) joined Robert as a co-publisher of the *Chronicle*.

Small-town newspaper publishing was hard-scrabble way to make a living, as the Folger brothers no doubt discovered. The *Chronicle* was forced to cajole delinquent subscribers and advertisers to "come and pay up like a little man ... and keep our wives and children from starvation's door."[31] Both Folgers found it necessary to supplement their meager earnings as journalists with other gainful employment.

Alex offered his services at various times as an insurance agent, notary,[32] Deputy Assessor,[33] Justice of the Peace and Deputy County Clerk.[34] Brother Robert displayed a similar entrepreneurial streak, working as a deputy county clerk to "facilitate the registration of electors,"[35] an Inspector of Elections for the Silver Mountain voting district,[36] and a member of the Board of Education for Silver Mountain's Franklin School District.[37] Both brothers also served as volunteer firemen, a post which qualified them for exemption from the military list.[38]

Staunch Republicans, the Folgers launched a "Hayes and Wheeler Club" in 1876, with the organizational meeting held at their *Chronicle* office.[39] Robert indulged a passion for horse-racing, reporting in the pages of

> *To prevent your hair from coming out, soak your upper story in a solution of vinegar and glue water, and then stand on your head for about an hour.*
>
> *--Silver Mountain Bulletin*, May 4, 1867.

the *Chronicle* on race results as far away as Alameda and once taking a spin in "a butcher wagon with uncommon high wheels" at a clip that launched his occupants five feet in the air and "planted us six inches deep in the plastic mud of Sacramento."[40]

Perhaps seeking cheaper quarters, the *Chronicle* shifted its Silver Mountain office to a new location between First and Second Streets about January 1870.[41] There the paper would remain until mid-1874,[42] when the newspaper moved yet a third time, to the corner of Fifth.[43]

With the *Bulletin* now defunct, the *Chronicle* continued a series of tart exchanges with its Monitor rival. Defending itself against the *Miner's* assertion that the *Chronicle* lacked advertisers, the Folgers claimed to have simply "laid by advertisements until the arrival of our new dress [type]," adding petulantly:

> *Will our little quarto friend at Monitor put this in his pipe and smoke it? It will be so soothing to his nervous system.*[44]

For its part, the *Chronicle* launched a return salvo pointing out that the *Miner* was three years out of date in its printed list of state dignitaries[45] and asserting (probably accurately) that its rival was "published only for the purpose of selling stock" to the mine-buying citizens of Wisconsin, Illinois, and Michigan.[46] Further bickering followed, with the *Chronicle* finally declaring in exasperation that "[s]ympathy for his family has deterred the aggrieved parties from putting [the *Miner's* editor] on trial." Notwithstanding such supposed forbearance, the *Chronicle* itemized a laundry list of potential criminal charges against the rival editor, including allegations of "embezzling a letter" while serving as postmaster and offering bribes to County officials for the privilege of becoming the official litigant newspaper.[47]

As encouraging mining news ebbed in the early 1870s, the *Chronicle* began offering how-to advice on such scintillating topics as eradicating lice in poultry houses[48] and rescuing choking cattle.[49] Other columns were devoted to weighty social issues like "Who Should Milk - Man or Woman?"[50]

> **Molasses Cup Cake**
>
> Two cups of molasses, 1 [cup] of milk, 4 eggs, two cups sugar, 1 c. butter, 1-1/2 c. lard, 1 tsp. saleratus, 5 c. flour, cloves and ginger to suit.
>
> *--Alpine Chronicle,* October 15, 1870

Through it all, the eternally-optimistic Folgers somehow kept their sense of humor intact. When Alex departed for a brief visit to Sacramento in January, 1872, brother Robert offered a tongue-in-cheek excuse for his brother's shabby clothes, explaining Alex had "worn them while waiting for the county to 'come out.'"[51] And citing a neighborly competition over whose hen could lay the bigger egg, the editors claimed that W.P. Merrill's hen had produced a whopper of an egg some 6½ by 7½ inches, "and she wasn't very well that day or she would have done better than that."[52] But by the end of 1877 the Folgers were apparently searching for ways to further bolster their income, advertising "houses to let."[53]

The brothers' decision to abandon Silver Mountain was a hasty one. As late as August, 1878, the *Chronicle* was still poking gentle fun at the recent "exodus" of its citizens to the new mining boomtown of Bodie, suggesting wryly: "We may look for a return of some of them next Spring."[54] September, too, appeared to be business as usual for the newspaper, with Alex Folger making the long journey to Sacramento "to do the State Fair and Editorial Convention."[55] But by October,1878, the long-suffering Folger brothers had apparently suffered enough. District Attorney Peter Curtz had taken issue with the Folgers' recent bill for County advertising[56] and the Folgers protested strongly in return, writing a scathing article citing the county's $280 "unnecessary expense" for a special meeting and itemizing the sum: "Stolen from Chronicle Office, $390."[57] More pointedly, they sued the County for payment.

The County retaliated by filing its own lawsuit in a different court, seeking to recover $179 previously paid to the *Chronicle*[58] and claiming that the paper had failed to publish the *complete* list of tax-defaulted properties.[59] In a scathing editorial, the Folgers branded District Attorney Curtz "a new broom – and a dirty one at that."[60] Meanwhile, as if to add insult to injury, the editors noted that a few "damphools" about town were lobbying readers to withdraw their subscriptions.[61]

The Folgers' lawsuit against the County for their advertising fees was "continued" to the following court term without a decision.[62] But by then the Folgers had evidently lost their taste for the fight – and for Silver Mountain. In mid-October, the Folgers published a bittersweet farewell, decrying the "utter stagnation of legitimate mining" and timber interests in Alpine County, and moved – lock, stock and printing press – to Bodie.[63]

In a parting shot delivered under their new banner as the *Mono Alpine Chronicle*, the Folgers had the last word:

> *Alpine is cursed with a class that is always ready to do injury to any interest calculated to benefit the county . . .; they don't want their neighbors to make one dollar unless they can make two.*[64]

The departure of the *Chronicle* stamped *finis* to Silver Mountain as a going concern. The Folgers' legacy lives on, however, memorialized not only in "Folger Peak"[65] but also in a fourteen-year treasure trove of articles chronicling the ups and downs, births and deaths, politics and humor of Alpine County's earliest years.

Courtesy of California History Room, California State Library, Sacramento CA

Main Street, Silver Mountain about 1865, shortly after it was chosen as the first County seat. Three-story Ryan's Exchange is shown on the far left, with houses and businesses along Main Street to the right.

G.G. Payne, an early property owner in the town of Monitor, ran ads in the Alpine Miner championing the town's "salubrity of climate" and other advantages for business and investment, and calling attention to lots he had for sale.

CHAPTER 5:
GETTING ABOUT

Wind & Weather

Winters at Silver Mountain City were hardly a time for quiet reflection by the fire. With temperatures dipping as low as 12 degrees below zero, heat would escape through uninsulated roofs and walls nearly as quickly as a fire could produce it, making stoking the woodstove a necessary and seemingly endless chore.[1] "We have burnt seventeen cords of wood this Winter," grumbled the *Chronicle* editor one March, "and it's lucky for us that long and warm days are at hand."[2]

One local matron, pleading "health" reasons, moved her entire family to Oakland rather than endure another Silver Mountain winter.[3] And many families took the practical step of relocating for the winter months to warmer elevations. As early as the summer of 1863, itinerant geologist Brewer mentions a family in the nearby Silver Valley that was sensibly planning to leave in the fall.[4] Even the prominent Fisks of Silver Mountain would abandon their well-established hotel to spend winters at the balmier elevation of Murphys.[5]

For those hardy souls who did remain in town year-round, winters were both long and painfully cold. Even prosperous citizens could expect to find no relief from the universal winter misery. "Thermometer, two degrees below freezing & hands so cold [I] can barely write," shivered mining magnate Lewis Chalmers one January day inside his cabin at Bulliona.[6] Conditions were similarly grim a decade later inside

The Chronicle advertised this model woodstove from VanEvery's in Sacramento. Woodstoves not only helped heat drafty cabins but also often featured tubs for heating water, a stovetop for frying, an oven for baking, and a handy lip on which to dry wet boots.

The Greatest Feat of the Age. *– Two Ladies and a Boy, Six Years of Age, Crossing the Sierras on Snow Shoes.*

On Monday evening, the 6th inst., a party arrived at Silver Mountain on snow shoes [skis], consisting of A.H. Stevens, Esq., Mrs. A.H. Stevens, their daughter – Miss Caddie Stevens, aged sixteen summers, and their son, a bright little boy of six years of age, from Cottage Springs, 39 miles from Silver Mountain, on the Big Tree Road. They were accompanied by a party of gentlemen, consisting of Messrs. A. Downing of Big Meadows, A.F. Bailey of Bear Valley, and Mr. Christie and A. Richey of Hermit Valley – also on snow shoes. Mr. Stevens and family started from Cottage Springs on Wednesday, the first day of March, and by easy sliding – stopping at Big Meadows, Bear Valley, and Hermit Valley, completed the trip by arriving at Silver Mountain on the evening of the 6th, the ladies sailing down the grade into town with all the grace and fleetness of the gazelle. Think of this, ye proud mothers and daughters of the valleys, who fear lest the winds of heaven should waft a zephyr too rudely upon you, of two of your sisters braving the tempestuous Sierras in mid winter over a "pass" 10,000 feet above the level of the sea, the snows twenty-two feet deep, and calling it a pleasure trip. . . An impromptu dance was got up in the evening in honor of the occasion ... where dancing was kept up until a late hour.

– ***Monitor Gazette***, *March 11, 1865*

Chalmers' "mansion" on Silver Creek, although by then he had at least acquired a sense of humor about the seasonal discomfort:

> *In my Office with a log fire at 8 a.m. for the last four mornings, the Thermometer stood at 20 degrees = ten degrees below freezing. Fine, salubrious kind of weather.*[7]

Three- to five-foot snows were commonplace in Silver Mountain, with even more engulfing its streets on occasion. "Snow 7 foot deep in front of door," O.S. Adams noted in his diary for April 14, 1867, "average about 5 foot deep through town."[8]

Travel over the mountains in wintertime was a hazardous affair.

The Big Tree Road was similarly obliterated each season under a dozen or more feet of snow, leaving homes in Silver Valley "entirely out of sight."[9] One 1863 visitor to Hermit Valley frankly described the local climate as "arctic," noting that a measuring pole had recorded the snow depth from the previous winter at eighteen feet.[10]

During the snowy months travel over the mountains largely ground to a halt, with only the bravest or most fool-hardy attempting the perilous winter crossing. O.S. Adams, eager to reach Silver Mountain in February of 1867, found himself enveloped in a sudden snow storm and was forced to "make the best of it" amid seven-foot drifts "by keeping awake all night and gathering limbs of dead trees to keep fire going."[11] The body of one hapless winter traveler was discovered several months later, frozen to death inside an empty barn where he had sought shelter, the rescuers speculating that his warming fire must have flickered out as he slept.[12]

For Silver Mountainites, even just getting around town became an ordeal once heavy snows arrived. Cross-country skis (or "snowshoes," as the locals called them) quickly became a favored form of transportation. Fashioned of simple wooden boards adorned with crude leather bindings, these homemade contraptions made their appearance under more than one Silver Mountain Christmas tree as a practical and welcome gift.[13] Visitor William Brewer observed as early as 1863:

> With these they go everywhere, no matter how deep the snow is, and downhill they go with frightful velocity. At a race on snowshoes at an upper town last winter the papers announced that the time made by the winner was half a mile in thirty-seven seconds! And many men tell of going a mile in less than two minutes.[14]

The length and shape of these "snowshoes" were dictated by the whims of the maker, rendering some of these primitive appliances downright unwieldy. One local resident struggled along on skis "twice as long as himself,"[15] and some racers' skis were reportedly close to 14 feet in length.[16] Most were also extremely heavy, weighing as much as 25 pounds.[17] Chalmers complained wryly of getting "many a fall" after borrowing a friend's old skis to get home from Monitor. "I made out on snow shoes wonderfully well," he wrote, "till one ... (a mended thing) broke."[18]

Dustman collection.

Shoveling off roofs was a necessary winter precaution.

As winter wore on, the town's more casually-reinforced structures became prone to collapse under the accumulated weight of the snow, forcing residents to take remedial steps or risk being crushed. One Silver Mountain news note from 1867 observed brightly: "Our citizens for the past two days have been enjoying the vigorous exercise of shoveling snow from the roofs of their houses. This timely precaution saved damage."[19]

Despite such efforts, snow-collapses did occur. During the winter of 1867-68, Pearson's vacant two-story building on Silver Mountain's Main Street caved in from the weight of the snow. That same winter, an "avalanche" sliding off the roof of the Court House crushed the unfortunate Patterson's Saloon next door, "making a complete wreck of the building and giving the visitors – ten prominent members of our town – such a scare that it will require several bottles of Hall's hair restorer to restore the original color to their youthful locks." Markleeville's Armory Hall, too, was "ruined" by the snow, the *Chronicle* sniffing unsympathetically that it had "never been considered a safe building."[20]

Local communities regularly traded good-natured jibes through the pages of their local newspapers about which town enjoyed the superior weather. While still headquartered at Markleeville, the *Chronicle* contrasted its "orange groves"[21] with the arctic conditions at Silver Mountain, asserting that its rival was suffering under "fully five feet [of snow] on a dead level, and the drifts at from 15 to 30 feet in depth."[22] Once the *Chronicle* had moved its office to Silver Mountain, however, it laughed off a similar report of seven-foot drifts, boldly asserting that "[w]hoever told such stuff is a first class liar and should be in New

Orleans to testify before the Congressional Committee." The truth, it assured readers, was a "trifling" three feet of snow.[23]

For laborers at the Silver Mountain mines, snow season brought not only extra shoveling but a potentially deadly form of winter roulette. The Silver Mountain *Bulletin* recorded one winter's woes at the George Washington claim:

> *Operations at this mine have been greatly impeded for a month or more past on account of the storm, and considerable damage has been done to the premises by snow-slides. The blacksmith shop was crushed flat to the ground; the roof of the kitchen was broken in, and the main building, where the men sleep, was carried one foot from its foundation down the mountain.*[24]

A trio of Silver Mountain miners were killed in a snow slide in Scandinavian Canyon on their way home from the I.X.L. Mine, while a fourth narrowly escaped. The entire male population of Silver Mountain turned out in response, spending two days digging in the heavy snow before finally uncovering the bodies of J.H. Williams, Harry Mercer, and Christopher Nielson.

> *The three men were among our first settlers: intelligent, energetic, composing the forefront of that rank who penetrated these rugged peaks to develop the hidden wealth concealed beneath these mountain fastnesses. We attended the funerals at Silver Mountain on Tuesday, in company with others from Monitor, and deputations were there from Markleeville and Silver King. The bodies were taken to the Court House, where after an appropriate and touching address by the Rev. Mr. Ford, a procession of over three hundred was formed, who followed them to their long home.*[25]

Another miner named Sharpe was caught up in a similar snow slide near the George Washington tunnel and carried down the mountainside some two hundred feet but managed to dig himself out, as the newspaper put it, "comparatively unharmed."[26] Even when not life-threatening, a few seconds' worth of avalanche cascading down the face of Silver Mountain could translate into days of heavy labor just to reopen a buried mineshaft entrance:

> *The snow was filled in to a great depth and packed very solid, owing to the force it had acquired in its descent from the mountain, and required over 100 feet of tuneling to open passage ways to get into the mine and buildings.*[27]

Miners' homes, too, were prone to the unpredictable peril of sudden snow deluges. One such "snow-slide" on the mesa south of Silver Creek flattened Supervisor C.W. Dake's outbuildings, stopping just short of his house.[28] Supervisor E.D. Egan was even more unlucky; his home "on the same side of the creek but more distant from the base of the mountain" was completely destroyed.[29]

Chickens provided eggs and Sunday dinner – when they survived the Silver Mountain winters.

Certain parts of town were well-known for being more dangerous than others. "There are only two main streets in town that I consider safe to live in when these thunderbolts of snow, these avalanches, come down," wrote Henry Eno in 1867. "One of the best dwelling houses in town has been crushed and knocked end ways. Fortunately no family was in it, having moved out not long ago. The house stood in a dangerous situation and I would never have lived in it in the winter."[30]

But with its usual good humor, the *Chronicle* cheerfully recorded one winter story with a happy ending. After one Silver Mountain home and outbuildings were wrecked by the snow, its resident sadly concluded many of his chickens were gone, as the newspaper so eloquently put it, to "that bourne whence no chickens return." Some 33 days later, however, the homeowner was astonished to discover one plucky hen carefully picking her way out of the rubble. Crowed the Markleevile-based paper, "She seemed to be as delighted at her release from her snowy imprisonment as our county seat friends are to reach Markleeville after being snow-bound half of the winter."[31]

Between wintertime snow drifts, spring washouts, and wheel-enveloping mud during rainy season, Silver Mountain townsfolk found themselves regularly cut off from the outside world for long stretches at a time.[32] As late as June the big-wheeled stage might be able to navigate only as far as Bear Valley, leaving the final leg into Silver Mountain to be accomplished on horseback.[33]

Roadways were sometimes opened in the spring using oxen to break the trail.

Dustman collection.

Even the happy rituals of matrimony were forced to bend to the fickle hand of the weather. In 1867, it was big news indeed when popular Sheriff "Mac" McBeth (one of Alpine County's best-paid public officials[34] and likely Silver Mountain's most eligible bachelor) announced plans to wed Miss Amanda Kittridge at Woodfords. Arrangements for March nuptials were made, and the local justice of the peace was tapped to officiate. But with five-foot drifts blocking the road between the groom at Silver Mountain and the bride in Woodfords, the eagerly-awaited event required unusually creative travel arrangements.

The intrepid bridegroom commenced his journey days in advance, leaving Silver Mountain on skis. His way was evidently eased by liberal application of "spirits" from friends along his journey. The *Chronicle* humorously recorded his adventure:

> *[Upon] his arrival at the Washington mill, [the bridegroom] was completely exhausted. Stimulants being applied freely, he soon recuperated; and by the aid of three experts on snow-shoes, managed to reach Markleeville at 1 o'clock a.m. next morning.*[35]

Following a layover at Markleeville the groom pushed onward to Woodfords the next day. Wedding successfully accomplished, the happy couple left on their triumphal return journey to Silver Mountain aboard a sled pulled by "two strange objects that boasted their descent from the pure St. Bernards." The wedding party spent a night at Markleeville, then departed again at "early dawn" on skis and sled for Silver Mountain, reaching their final destination a grueling twelve hours later. Quipped the *Bulletin* on their arrival:

> *The bride looked as fresh and fair as Eve on the morn of her presentation to Adam; but Mac, we thought, looked rather fagged, as though he would rather visit his uncle.*[36]

Roads & Other Ties That Bind

The original pioneer wagon track from the Carson Valley across the Sierra was blazed to accommodate the rush of gold-seekers in 1848. Wagons heading west along this Emigrant Road quickly encountered the "Devil's Ladder," a near-vertical ascent up rocky Carson Pass to an elevation of 8,573 feet that became legendary among early travelers. The wife of James Caples described the experience in 1849:

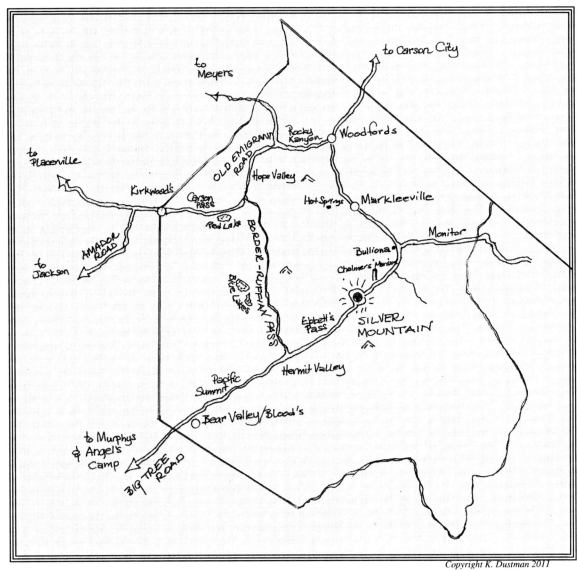

An extension of the Big Tree Toll Road was hacked over Ebbett's Pass, finally connecting with the boomtown of Silver Mountain in the summer of 1864.

After about thirty miles up the river, we came to Carson Canyon, one of the worst pieces of road on the whole route: it took us all day, with the hardest work that men and animals ever did, to make five miles. No one thought of riding; I carried my baby and walked all the way. The next day we had a beautiful drive through Hope Valley to the foot of the first summit, which we ascended with considerable difficulty by doubling teams, then down four miles to Summit Lake.[37]

This second punishing climb took travelers over 9,600-foot West Pass – called the "highest pass in the nation," by one source[38] – before the tortuous track finally dropped weary travelers down into the foothills of Placerville. Before long a cut-off was added to permit travelers to reach the Amador County seat of Jackson, a route dubbed the "Amador & Nevada Wagon Road."[39]

Wagons like this one carried a variety of freight to Silver Mountain.

The Gold Rush towns of Columbia, Sonora, and Murphys soon sought their own trading connection with the Carson Valley. By September, 1857, the "Big Trees Road" was cut over Border Ruffian Pass, permitting travelers who could afford the toll to make the journey from Stockton to Carson City in "just" five days. Eager to profit from the fresh mining excitement at Silver Mountain, road contractor James Sperry sought a franchise in 1862 to extend the Big Trees Road over what would later be called Ebbett's Pass to reach this newest mining town. By August, 1863, more than a hundred men were hard at work carving out this new roadbed with horses, mules, and black powder.[40] One exhausted Silver Mountain visitor that same month reported with chagrin that an arduous ten to twelve miles of the eagerly-awaited extension still remained unfinished:

A stage runs part of the way [from Big Trees], until the road becomes very rough; then a 'saddle train,' with a few pack animals, takes the passengers and their luggage to the promised land. . . [A]t Silver Valley the stages stop and saddle trains start . . . We arrive [in Silver Mountain] by trail, for the wagon road is left many miles back.[41]

It would be another full year before the new Big Trees Road actually reached the town of Silver Mountain. Well into April of 1864, the mining press was reporting that "six or seven weeks of work" remained to be done by a 150-man crew.[42] Even by late May, some two miles of roadway remained to be finished, suggesting that the final stretch of the new toll road was not completed until well into summer.[43]

On the Carson Valley side of the mountains, a permit was issued in 1852 for construction of a toll road up "Emigrant Kanyon" to the "top of the first summit." This franchise (issued erroneously by Utah territorial officials without benefit of an accurate survey to pinpoint the California state line) granted Israel Mott and John Reese the right to demand a dollar per wagon and 25 cents for each horse or mule using their new toll road, and required them to expend at least $1,000 on building the roadway and a new bridge by the following July.[44] A connecting toll road from Woodfords to Markleeville was similarly constructed in 1862-63 by the Carr and Harris Companies.

Courtesy of Society of California Pioneers, San Francisco
(Detail of Lawrence & Houseworth #707)
Gift of Florence V. Flinn

RATES OF TOLL.—For the information of the traveling public, below we publish the rates of toll on the Harris grade between this place and Woodford's as fixed by the Board of Supervisors on Wednesday last:

Wagon and two animals .... 50 cents.
Each additional animal .... 12½ cents.
Buggy and one animal .... 37½ cents.
Buggy and two animals .... 50 cents.
Man on horse .... 25 cents.
Pack animals .... 12½ cents.
Loose stock, per head .... 05 cents
Hogs, sheep, goats, etc., per head .... 03 cents.
Empty teams—half of above rates.

Round trip on the "Harris Grade" section of the road between Monitor and Markleeville with a two-horse buggy cost a dollar, circa 1871 – a quarter of an average day's wages. Above, the wooden sign at the west end of Silver Mountain proclaims the start of the Big Tree Toll Road.

From newly-settled Markleeville, another toll road snaked on to Silver Mountain. Ostensibly a private venture, this Silver Mountain Toll Road was so essential to the town's connection with the outside world that in February, 1864, eager residents chipped in 500 man-days of labor to finish the roadbed.[45] It was a burst of civic-mindedness they would later come to regret.

The Board of Supervisors updated its schedule of fees for the Silver Mountain Toll Road annually, and tolls were anything but cheap. Each toll-collector was allowed a five- to 10-percent commission as his incentive to keep collections high.[46] As early as 1867, local citizens were grumbling that the Board had "allow[ed] the people to be robbed of the road from Silver Mountain to Centerville,"[47] hinting darkly that graft had been involved. One toll road operator was reportedly overheard bragging that "he don't care a damn for the people of Alpine; that he feeds and clothes the Board of Supervisors, and that they belong to him."[48]

As a result, whatever direction they might choose to travel, residents of Silver Mountain had to ante up. Even would-be miners seeking employment at the I.X.L. and other Scandinavian Canyon mines found themselves faced with a toll road winding its way up the mountainside from the tail end of Silver Mountain's Third Street.

Early tolls for the Amador & Nevada Wagon Road ran as high as $2.50 for each loaded wagon and $1.25 for a man and horse.[49] Even the short trip to Monitor with a two-horse wagon cost one dollar in each direction, taking a significant bite out of a day's wages.[50] For stockmen bringing animals into Alpine pastures, the road charges could mount up quickly. One improvident stockman found himself the subject of a lawsuit for $72 in unpaid tolls accruing over a single two-month period.[51]

For the road owners, however, toll roads could be a profitable investment. A one-half interest in the four miles of toll road linking Woodfords to Fredericksburg changed hands as early as 1866 for the hefty sum of $550.[52] Precisely because they were so valuable, toll roads themselves occasionally became the subject of an execution sale for the owner's unpaid debts. Amanda E. Harris, M.H. Turrill and H.H. Hartley lost their interest in the portion of the Silver Mountain Toll Road between Markleeville and Mt. Bullion to just such a creditor's sale in 1867, for example.[53]

Adding insult to injury, the County adopted a special "road tax" in 1865, requiring "each male inhabitant of said county" between the ages of 21 and 50 to pay a tax of two dollars to help support the roads. Residents of Townships Five and Six were allowed to contribute their share "in labor" by working on the newly-surveyed road between Mount Bullion and Silver King.[54]

The unpopular tolls were roundly denounced as "exhorbitant" by some of the county's most prominent citizens. In 1867, Woodfords residents J.A. "Snowshoe" Thompson and W.P. Merrill complained that toll rates had been set by a "corrupt majority of the Board of Supervisors," and lobbied for a new "free road" from Markleeville to the Nevada border.[55]

Citizens of Monitor similarly petitioned the Board of Supervisors to declare the roadway from Monitor to Mogul a "public highway," and in September, 1866, the Board agreed.[56]

Often eroded by flooding, gullied by run-off, or blockaded by fallen trees, the humble dirt roadbeds required constant maintenance to remain passable, and the labors of local road crews were avidly followed in the local newspaper. One typical report advised readers: "Superintendent Johnson will set men to work on the toll road between here and Woodford's so that teams will be able to travel right along within a few days."[57]

Though this back-breaking work was technically the responsibility of the toll operator, snow-bound citizens often pitched in to help reopen the roadway to help the mail and supplies to get through. Applauding one such effort, the Chronicle reported:

Dustman collection.

> [T]he bone and sinew of [Markleeville] turned out and opened the road to Woodford's. Last evening a delegation from Silver Mountain arrived here, having broken a trail through to the metropolis. To-day several yoke of oxen will be put on the road, so that in a few days the stages may be able to resume their trips to the county seat [Silver Mountain].[58]

Dustman collection.

Other road-related news might include the announcement of a new cut-off eliminating the terrors of "Dead Horse Bend" between Silver Mountain and Monitor,[59] or less-upbeat reports glumly confirming that heavy storms had wiped out the road between Markleeville and Woodfords or rendered the roadway to Silver Mountain impassible until Spring.[60]

Bit by bit, thanks to the frequent attentions of sweating road crews, the roadbeds were gradually improved. By 1876, newspaperman Robert Folger was able to zoom over the Big Trees Road from Silver Mountain to Blood's Station with a light one-horse buggy in "only" eight hours.[61]

Sacramento Archives and Museum Collection Center

Driver Dick Gelatt and his team at Genoa in 1863, with the Gillman Hotel in the background. Below, Carson City's business district.

Dustman collection.

Stage Travel

Stages afforded travelers a sort of tame adventure, providing access to new places while leaving the drive to an experienced navigator. The jostling confines of the coach interior became a social venue in which to exchange gossip and strike up new acquaintances. As Brewer described one such experience in 1861:

> *There were the usual accompaniments of a stage ride – various passengers, bustling landlords running out at the stations, dust, dirt, politics, and local news.*[62]

Stages were hardly a luxurious mode of transportation, however. Travelers were bounced and jounced at every pothole, and not infrequently called upon to pitch in when the stage foundered. As Brewer recounted:

> *We . . . had gone scarcely a hundred rods when the wheels sank to their axles and the horses nearly to their bellies in the mud, [and] we unloaded. Then the usual strife on such an occasion. Horses get down, driver swears, passengers get in the mud, put shoulders to the wheels and extricate the vehicle. We walk a ways, then get in, ride two miles, then get out and walk two more in the deepest, stickiest, worst mud you ever saw, the rain pouring.*[63]

Nevada Historical Society

Old Wells Fargo safe, outside Markleeville.

Commercial stage service to Silver Mountain was available as early as June, 1864, when the firm of "Dooly, Ashly & Miller" launched a line of daily stages between Stockton and Silver Mountain over the Big Trees Road.[64] Travelers leaving Silver Mountain for the Carson Valley, however, were forced at first to make do with hired saddle horses. As one visitor to Silver Mountain described the experience:

> *The trip from [Silver Mountain] to Genoa was very pleasant with the exception of the horseback riding, that was killing to me – if the horse felt as bad as I did when he arrived at Genoa he certainly deserved pity.*[65]

As the town of Silver Mountain became more well-established, its transportation options multiplied. By 1866, a determined traveler could catch the 3 a.m. mail stage at Murphy's and arrive in Silver Mountain by dinnertime a mere 15 hours later, with stops along the way at the colorfully-named settlements of Big Trees, Cottage Springs, Big Meadows, Bear Valley, Silver Valley and Hermit Valley.[66] From Genoa, travelers that same year could board the four-horse Concord coaches of Gelatt & Moore's Pioneer Line for every-other-day service to Silver Mountain by way of Van Sickle's, Woodfords, Markleeville, Harrisburg, Mount Bullion, Monitor, and Mogul.[67]

With Genoa serving as the link to the Carson City stages, competition for the Genoa route was keen. A price war quickly ensued until in 1867, Gelatt temporarily bested his competitors by offering *free* rides between Alpine County and Genoa "so long as the opposition line continues on the route."[68] In 1870, "Snowshoe" John A. Thompson launched his own thrice-weekly stages between Genoa and Silver Mountain, charging $2 to ferry passengers from Ford's Hotel at Silver Mountain to Markleeville, and another $4 to continue on to Genoa.[69]

By April, 1871, William C. "Billy" Blackmore entered the competition, which now made three separate stage lines shuttling passengers between Genoa and Alpine.[70] Within a few short months, however, Blackmore bought out both Thompson's and Gelatt's competing lines, and by October 1871, had acquired "full control" of the Silver Mountain-to-Genoa route – after which he promptly announced plans to raise his own fare to six dollars.[71] Blackmore soon extended his stage line west to Big Trees,[72] advertising three-times-weekly service over this "short" 45-mile route "through the wildest portion of the Sierra Nevada Mountains."[73]

Snowshoe Thompson

Born about 1827 in the Telemark region of Norway, "Jon Tostensen" was the youngest of 13 children. Just two years after Jon's birth his father passed away, leaving the widow Tostensen, his second wife, with at least four remaining youngsters to raise. By the time young Jon turned ten, his mother decided to join a group of farmers heading for New York. Taking her youngest son Jon with her, she set sail for the New World, where they would later be joined by Jon's older brother and sister.

The family moved several times – first from Illinois to Missouri; then from Missouri to Iowa. Along the way, it seems, young Jon acquired a bit of a wandering spirit himself. About 1848, after his mother's death, he moved on to Wisconsin, eventually following the gold-seekers to California in 1851. At some point during his travels, young Jon Americanized his name to "John A. Thompson."

Thompson settled near the California gold-mining town of Placerville, trying his hand as a miner but finding steadier income as a wood-cutter and a farmer. Legend has it that sometime about 1855, a notice in the *Sacramento Union* caught his eye with an advertisement for contractors to carry the U.S. mail over the snowy Sierra to the Carson Valley. Fondly recalling the "snow shoes" of his Norwegian childhood, Thompson carved himself a pair of skis and began to practice skiing in the snowy foothills – and a legend was born.

For the next two decades, Thompson journeyed over the mountains about twice a month during the winter, carrying up to 100 pounds of mail, medicine, and other goods on his back. With a single wooden pole held horizontally in front of him for balance, Thompson could complete the 90-mile trek in two to three days. Some sources claim he rarely slept or rested during these journeys, "dancing a jig" to stay warm

when caught by blizzards; others suggest he used his wooden pole to probe for drifted-over cabins, breaking in through the gables to catch a good night's sleep.

The strapping six-footer must have cut quite a figure, sailing gracefully down the snowy hills clad simply in a rough Mackinaw jacket. As one historian describes it: "With his blonde hair and beard, fair skin and piercing blue eyes, he looked every bit the fierce Norseman of his ancestry."[86]

One biographer credits him as saying, "I can go anywhere in the mountains, day or night, in storm or sunshine, without becoming lost. There's something in my head that keeps me straight."[87] Another contends he advised his listeners simply to pay attention to the contours of the land: "There is no danger of getting lost if a man has his wits about him."[88]

The Eastern side of the Sierra soon captured Thompson's heart. About 1859, he hacked a dugout into the hillside of what would become his ranch at Diamond Valley, passing his first winter there in its limited comforts.[89] Despite his humble circumstances, Thompson quickly became a prominent member of the tiny Woodfords community, serving as a sponsor for the local "Christmas Ball" held that December.

Thompson soon acquired a pair of sleighs pulled by teams of mules and began operating a daily stage service, alternating trips from Lake Tahoe west to the American River and back from Lake Tahoe to Woodfords. By the summer of 1860, he had erected a log cabin on his Diamond Valley land, and in 1862 filed for a homestead on his property.

But Thompson evidently had not lost his early passion for mining. In October, 1861, he was among the earliest to claim an interest in the newly-discovered silver lodes of Scandinavian Canyon, locating the "Boone Company" lode with three friends. By 1862, the *Sacramento Daily Union*

CROSSING THE RANGE ON SNOW SKATES
Dustman collection.

reported that Thompson had "gone to work in earnest, digging for silver."

In 1866, Thompson filed a declaration of intent to become a citizen, and two years later was elected a county supervisor for the newly-formed Alpine County. He married Agnes Singleton, an Englishwoman described as "refined, attractive in appearance, even-tempered, and, like her husband, religious in outlook."[90] The Thompsons settled into a life of domesticity on their Diamond Valley ranch, harvesting oats, barley, and "more hay than any other farmer in the county." On February 11, 1867, a son, Arthur, was born at their Diamond Valley home. Legend has it that the baby's first cradle was an ore sluice box, perhaps a further hint that Thompson never entirely abandoned his love of mining.[91]

But it was Thompson's prowess on skis that would earn him his most enduring fame. He reportedly flew over a distance of 1400 feet in just 15 seconds in one timed event, and his long-jumps were measured at well over 100 feet. Snowshoe once boasted that he had entered the ski races in Sierra County to "show them how it was done."

Thompson took an active interest in local community affairs, lobbying for a free road to Woodfords and decrying the "exhorbitant" tolls exacted by the toll road companies. When a "New Hall" was built at Woodfords in 1867, Thompson was among the organizers of a Grand Dedication Ball to celebrate. And it was Thompson who, accompanied by two friends, ventured out to recover the body of a man who died trying to navigate the Big Trees Road in February,

bringing the body back to Silver Mountain for burial. Genoa postmaster S.A. Kinsey called Thompson the "most remarkable man I ever knew," adding: "He never thinks of himself, but he'd give his last breath for anyone else – even a total stranger."

Snowshoe would never receive payment for his early winter mail service. Especially during the winters of 1856 through 1858, "[i]t was the only communication between California and Utah," lamented the *Chronicle.* "The importance of this mail was well known at the time, and had it not been for the Rebellion, the Government would doubtless have recognized it."

Snowshoe passed away on May 15, 1876, at the age of 49, following a brief illness – perhaps the victim of a burst appendix. Reflecting Thompson's importance to the neighboring Nevada community, his body was carried to the graveyard in Genoa for burial, where he now lies beneath a white marble headstone featuring a pair of crossed skis, next to his wife and son. The local *Chronicle* remembered Thompson not as a famous mail carrier or county supervisor, but simply as one of two stage drivers "courageous enough to tackle a snow drift."

Legend has it that Thompson kept a chunk of ore laced with gold on his mantle, and spoke of having found a gold mine somewhere within sight of his Diamond Valley cabin.[92] But despite eager searching, no one has managed to find it since.

Given the intermittent schedules of the various stage companies, making connections with other lines could be difficult, as at least one visitor discovered to his chagrin after leaving Silver Mountain and finding himself stranded in Genoa.

I found no stage going to Carson until Wednesday. I tried to have some one to go in a buggy and take me up [to Carson], [but] they wanted $15. I would not pay no such price as that, so I walked.[74]

Another unpleasant possibility for travelers was the occasional stage robber. A rash of such crimes broke out around the region in 1866, and "the robbing of the Wells-Fargo stages became a recognized industry . . . The week that went by without one or more coaches being held up produced a feeling of dull times[;] . . . news of a robbery could be depended upon nearly every day."[75]

At least one hold-up targeted the stage betwen Hope Valley and Genoa. The would-be robber was scared off by an even more determined victim, who grabbed the robber's gun and took potshots at the fleeing culprit.[76] On another occasion, a somewhat smoother gang of highwaymen fortified with double-barreled shotguns halted a pair of Pioneer stages on their way to Virginia City, forcing the passengers to disembark. The lone female passenger at first stubbornly declined to abandon her seat, but was convinced to change her mind when the robbers expressed their intention to "blow up the coach" – a promise they promptly carried out, pouring powder into the keyhole of the Wells Fargo safe and lighting a fuse. Gallantly assisting each passenger back into the now-crowded remaining coach, the gentlemen robbers made off with $6,000 from the iron safe and an another $2,000 in loot from the passengers, including the gold watch of Comstock luminary Sandy Bowers.[77]

While relieving Wells Fargo of its cargo was one thing, pilfering passengers was viewed as quite another. According to one historian,

The general community hated the Wells-Fargo Company because of its extortions and only laughed when its stages were robbed. For a highwayman to request an express company or any other corporation to surrender a portion of its winnings would appear, in their judgment, like a mere wrangle among robbers over the division of a common spoil . . .[78]

In addition to ferrying passengers, the stage companies typically carried bullion, freight and, most important of all, mail. As early as 1867, Markleeville residents eagerly anticipated mail deliveries every Monday, Wednesday and Friday, and could post their return letters on Tuesday, Thursday, and Saturday.[79]

Mail service, too, was a frequent casualty of bad roads, bad weather, or some combination of the two. "[W]e have no later advices from the other side of the mountains than Wednesday's dailies give us," grumbled the *Chronicle* one spring, citing the "annoying" absence of Friday's mail.[80] After one particularly heavy snowstorm, the mail stage was reported to have gotten as far as Chalmers' Exchequer Mill, but "owing to one or two heavy drifts between the mill and town," opted to remain there and "did not attempt to come further."[81] On another occasion, news reports groused that the mail had become "stuck somewhere on the road, probably at Monitor."[82]

Mail contractors themselves were frequently the target of local barbs, and any tendency toward tardiness was closely watched. After repeated difficulties with previous mail carriers, the Genoa-to-Silver Mountain mail contract was eventually awarded to Snowshoe Thompson in 1870,[83] a proposition which promised an additional $256 per year for ferrying the mail to Monitor.[84] Thompson was greeted "with loud cheers" on his inaugural trip from Genoa when his mail stage arrived in Silver Mountain at 5:50 p.m., hours earlier than the previous contractor's usual appearance.[85]

Mail was also carried by the Wells Fargo cargo stages. Although the price for Wells Fargo's letter service was twice the government postal rate, its service was deemed more reliable. As one correspondent explained:

> I shall send the next [letter] by Wells & Fargo's Express. Way mails in this state are so uncertain that all important letters are carried by a private express in government envelopes. . . . Here in [California] it is used very largely, the Wells & Fargo mail being often larger than the government mail. We avail ourself of it, even on so short a distance as from [San Juan] to San Francisco, if the letter has any special importance or needs to go with certainty of dispatch. I have had letters [take] two weeks in getting where they ought to go in two days with a daily mail.[93]

Lewis Chalmers, too, preferred to use Wells Fargo's service for important deliveries, explaining to his correspondents in London the unkind treatment given to ordinary U.S. mail:

> It appears that Wells Fargo & Co. have contracted to carry the overland Mail; that [fact] notwithstanding, they still carry on their own account letters in WF & Co. envelopes, quite an institution, [and] they wish to encourage their own against the Government Postal System; & therefore when they have too heavy a load, to make time, they drop the superfluity (not their own Mail) in the nearest stream.[94]

Telegraph & Telephones

Tiny Genoa, with fewer than 200 residents, was already linked to San Francisco by telegraph as early as 1859[95] and by 1863 or so, the State Telegraph Company was racing to connect its line from Genoa through to Silver Mountain by way of Markeeville, Monitor, and Woodfords.[96] With wires simply slung from tree to tree its progress was rapid, and the telegraph service made its official debut in Monitor in June, 1864.

In Monitor, the telegraph battery was set up in S.G. Lewis's post office building by Genoa operator Alexander Bruckman, who promised to remain in town to work the system "until [some]one present is taught."[97] Markleeville, too, proudly acquired its own brand new telegraph office, operated by G.H. Shaw.

Telegraph lines were immediately pushed onward to Silver Mountain, with the final connection being made just days later and a Main Street office established at Treat's Hotel.[98] At Silver Mountain the telegraph was operated initially by H. Brownell,[99] but duties were soon assumed by DeWitte C. Riddell, a well-known local notary public and mining agent with an office in "Francis' Block"[100] also conveniently serving as the town's Wells Fargo stop.[101] The following year, Riddell would move both the telegraph and the Wells Fargo offices to new quarters in Gibson's building.[102]

Telegraph service was regularly interrupted by snowstorms and high winds, requiring frequent repair of the lines. One December, 1867 news article noted that the State Telegraph Company's "repairing train" had arrived at Silver Mountain, having successfully returned the line between Silver Mountain and Woodfords to "good order."[103] But less than a month later, fresh storms had again disrupted both telegraph and mail communications, and (wrote the editors) "considerably demoralized us."[104]

Locals decried the telegraph's monopoly,[105] which resulted in rates as high as $2 for just ten words.[106] But despite the astronomical cost, telegraph service quickly became an important part of the fabric of Silver Mountain life. Chalmers regularly fired off telegrams to his associates in London, advising them of the progress – or financial straits – of their mines, with such terse messages as: "Wire five hundred dollars for 6 months bond,"[107] or "Pluto [Lode] parties pressing."[108]

Ever the early adaptor, Chalmers expressed his desire as early as 1880 for a new-fangled invention known as a telephone to facilitate communication between his house and the Isabella Tunnel to "save us many a heavy trip to the Tunnel in winter over 6 feet of snow," estimating hopefully that "a good Bell Telephone here will cost $150."[109] But whether he ever wangled such a luxury from his London backers remains a mystery.

Railroads

With the joining of the Union Pacific and Central Pacific Railroads on May 10, 1869, the Eastern and Western sides of the country were connected as never before. Travel across the continent now took a matter of days, not months. And the era of railroad-building had only just begun.

By 1869 Reno was already linked by rail with Sacramento, thanks to over a dozen tunnels through the mountains and some 60 *miles* of protective snowsheds.[110] A survey for a proposed extension of the

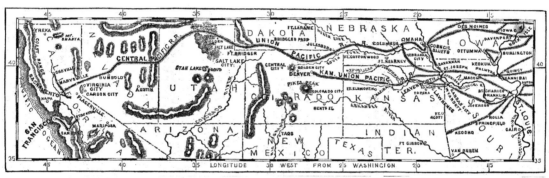

Map of Central Pacific Railroad route, circa 1869.

Dustman collection.

Virginia & Truckee Railroad designed to link Virginia City with Reno was conducted by George Hunt as early as March, 1871,[111] and by November that same year the track-laying had reached as far as Steamboat Springs.[112] By the following April, passengers could glide comfortably aboard the steam train from Carson City all the way to Virginia City for just $2.00.[113] Making progress south from Washoe City, another new rail extension was expected to stretch to Carson City by late August, 1872.[114] This new route would slice some 33 miles of "tedious staging" off the journey to Silver Mountain, leaving "but 51 miles of staging to connect with the [railroad] cars."[115] There were hints that a proposed 16-mile rail extension of the Virginia & Truckee Railroad was being surveyed from Carson City to Genoa,[116] and separate proposals circulated for a Central Pacific route between Truckee and Carson.[117]

Given such rapid rail-building, it is little wonder that the *Chronicle* speculated as early as 1872 that rail service might one day reach within three miles of Silver Mountain.[118] By 1876, the Silver Mountain newpaper was boldly proclaiming: "It is a fixed fact that the Virginia & Truckee Railroad is to be extended to Genoa," suggesting "[i]t will not be long before the Company will find it to their interest to extend the [rail]road to Alpine County."[119] Waxing poetic, a letter to the editors enthused: "We await with impatience the snort of the iron horse[,] . . . the genie that will cause Markleeville to bud and blossom as the rose."[120]

Hopes for a railroad line to Silver Mountain would, of course, prove illusory. Nevertheless by 1880, the journey to Silver Mountain had become exponentially shorter thanks to the expanded rail service connecting San Francisco to Carson City. Even so, travel to Silver Mountain was not without difficulties. Lewis Chalmers described the necessary connections to a would-be visitor from San Francisco:

> *Leave [San Francisco] by the 4:30 train for Carson on a Tuesday or Thursday. At Carson, on the arrival of the cars there on Wednesday or Friday morning, you take the bus to the Ormsby House (Carson) and get breakfast. After breakfast, take the stage for Genoa & Silver Mountain. Tell Mr. Sharp of the Ormsby you are coming here & he will show you every attention.*[121]

Careful attention to timing was necessary to avoid lengthy layovers, as Chalmers pointed out in a separate letter:

> *I omitted to mention that you ought not to leave San Francisco on a Saturday, as there is no 4 P.M. Virginia Train that day, & if you take the overland at 7 in the morning, you lay over in Reno in the middle of the night waiting [for] the Lightning Express for Virginia & Carson. Then again if you leave on Friday as proposed, you have to lay over in Carson all Saturday & Sunday as the Stage will have left Carson on Friday morning and does not go again till Monday.*[122]

Similarly, by the early 1880s the overland train had made access from the East significantly easier for those wishing to visit the local silver mines – easier, but still by no means easy. Writing to a potential visitor from London, Chalmers dispensed advice for the journey:

Courtesy of California Society of Pioneers, San Francisco
Gift of Florence V. Flinn

With horses so critical for transportation, it isn't surprising that Silver Mountain's Main Street included this stable, circa 1870. One of these gentlemen could be pioneering citizen J.J. Rice, who operated the Silver Mountain Stable at likely this location (see sign) beginning about 1871. Rice was reportedly Silver Mountain's last inhabitant. He died on March 21, 1892 in Genoa, and loyal friends brought his body back to Markleeville for burial.

I do not know any cheaper way for one to get to this place than by the regular Steamers from Liverpool to New York, emigrant class; – thence by the emigrant train (3d class) to Reno, thence to Carson by train from Reno ($21), thence by stage to Silver Mountain ($6). . . An Emigrant [Train] Ticket from New York to Reno costs $60.00 besides grub for the journey – 7 days. This [the traveller] should get put up in a basket in New York, as they charge 50 to 75 cents a meal at the stopping places along the line. A cheaper way still would be in a sailing vessel from Liverpool, round the Horn, to San Francisco, thence to Reno, Carson, & Silver Mountain, as before.[123]

The overland train pulled in at Reno in the early morning hours, permitting travelers to connect with the Virginia & Truckee from Reno to Carson. Leaving the comforts of the train behind at Carson, however, visitors faced a bone-jarring 10- or 11-hour stage journey before finally reaching Silver Mountain.[124]

Railway travel, although infinitely easier than wagon or horse, involved its own share of risk. Trains were occasionally sabotaged with objects placed on the tracks. In 1872, for example, half a dozen telephone poles were laid on the tracks near Washoe City in an effort to derail the train, though the engine managed to simply cut the poles in two.[125] Such deliberate sabotage was widespread enough, however, that a bill to punish "railroad wreckers" was introduced in the Nevada State legislature in 1877.[126] In another sign of the times, enterprising "highwaymen" largely gave up robbing stages and began robbing trains instead.[127]

Snow "blockades" regularly interrupted rail service over the mountains, holding up both passengers and mail for weeks on end. The railroads did their best to compensate by erecting elaborate systems of snow sheds. By late 1872, for example, the Union Pacific had a full 500 men at work "on the mountain division," 225 of them constructing snow sheds, and had already thrown up some 100 miles of snow fences to combat drifts.[128]

Heavy wooden snowsheds like this one helped protect the vital rail lines from heavy winter snows.

Still, on one trip East the legendary Snowshoe Thompson became so frustrated by the snow "blockade" of his Union Pacific train that he gave up waiting and proceeded on foot to Cheyenne, Wyoming. "[B]idding goodbye to the locomotives, [Thompson] traveled fifty miles the first day," reported the *Chronicle* with pride, "and we doubt not he made better time than that before he got through."[130]

Dustman collection

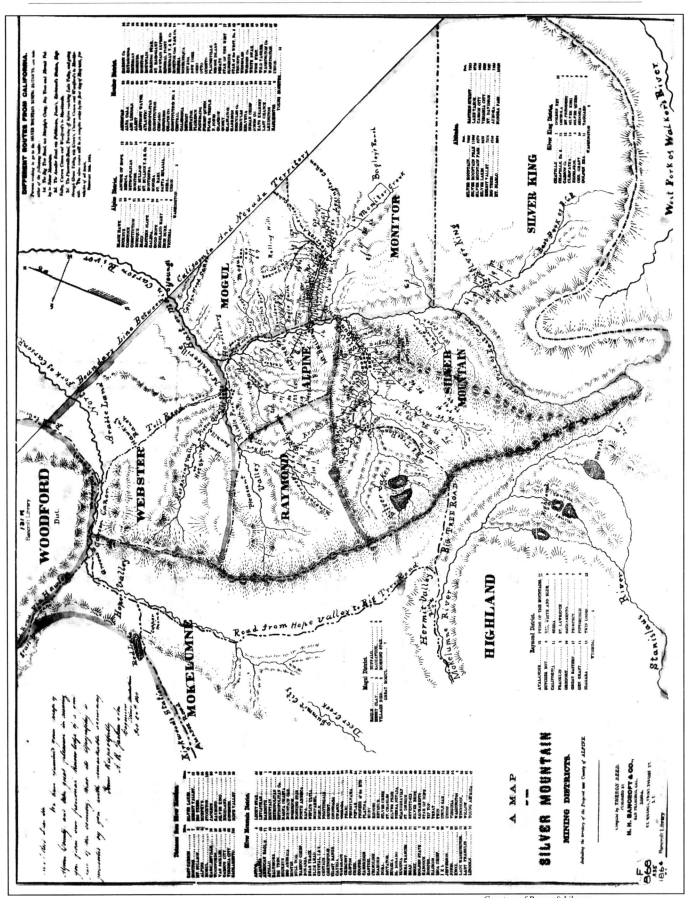

The official map of Silver Mountain's mining districts was drawn by Theron Reed in 1864. Reed would later become District Judge for Alpine County.

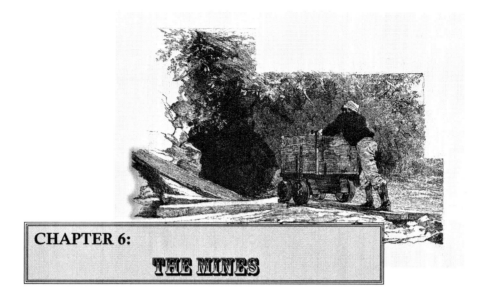

CHAPTER 6:
THE MINES

Claims & Clinkers

During the first heady days of Silver Mountain's boom, countless gopher holes were staked, claimed, and worked just long enough to re-sell the project to other eager speculators. Some but not all early claimants took formal steps to record a written location description in the books of the appropriate mining district and incorporated a "company" to work the claim. Other pioneers simply posted a scribbled "notice of location" on a stake or nearby tree, hoping to strike it rich in a few weeks, and moving on when they didn't.

Of these hundreds of early mining claims, the vast majority involved considerably more huzzah and hope than any serious digging. But pick, sweat, and muscle did produce measurable progress in at least a handful of Alpine's hard-rock tunnels. By 1867, the initial strike at the Mountain Mine on the south side of Silver Creek had inched its way 1,063 feet into the hard rocky mountainside.[1] Other eagerly-pushed claims on the Silver Mountain side of the river included the Rippon and the Lady Washington.

North of town, hopeful miners trudged up steep Scandinavian Toll Road to work at a variety of claims including the Buckeye (which later came to be known as the Exchequer), the Lady Franklin, the I.X.L., and the Accacia. Lesser-known mines in Scandinavian Canyon included the Adolphus, Gould & Curry, and Silver Prize. A canyon away to the west, the Pennsylvania Company chipped a 5-by-6½ foot tunnel over a thousand feet long into "the hardest kind of rock."[2] Meanwhile, to the east, the Mt. Bullion Company pushed its tunnel beside Monitor Creek to over 1,700 feet.[3]

The longest-worked and probably most profitable of the Alpine mines were the I.X.L. and Buckeye claims in Scandinavian Canyon, and the Tarshish (or Schenectady) in Monitor District. Exactly how much silver and gold these ventures actually managed to pull from the earth remains a mystery.[4] But reports surfaced from time to time over nearly two decades carrying tales of fabulous strikes, rich quartz specimens, and tantalizing veins.[5] In one smart marketing move, I.X.L. promoters forwarded two bars of silver bullion to San Francisco in June, 1865 with the news that they had struck a lode in their upper tunnel, described as three feet wide and "all pay rock."[6] Chalmers, too, laced his letters to England with tales of "fabulous ruby ore" and "native silver" in his company's tunnels. By 1868, ore worth $40,000 to $50,000 even without benefit of roasting had already been extracted from the I.X.L., he reported.[7] And in 1872,

Chalmers penned letters home describing a vein of "pure white gold-bearing quartz" encountered just 200 feet from the mouth of the Exchequer tunnel, assaying at over $2,500 per ton in gold.[8] No words were wasted on the unspoken corollary: What could investors expect just a few feet further in?

Progress in these hard-rock tunnels was painfully slow. Before the advent of dynamite, even relatively well-financed companies with the resources to deploy two separate shifts of 4 to 6 men each could expect progress of just seven to 10 feet of tunnel per week.[9] In the many smaller "coyote holes" worked only by their original claimants, development was sporadic at best. Virtually all of the Alpine mines were under-capitalized, making sustained development a rarity. Sighed one contemporary report, "Another evil has been the want of concentration of labor ... efforts having been spent in attempts at operating too great a number of lodes, thereby defeating the thorough development of any."[10] Recording a mining location was quick and easy; paper stock certificates were inexpensive enough to print; but laying in a supply of blasting powder took real money, and a few weeks of labor with pick and shovel quickly erased any notion of "easy" riches.

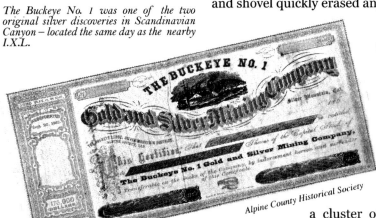

The Buckeye No. 1 was one of the two original silver discoveries in Scandinavian Canyon – located the same day as the nearby I.X.L.

Alpine County Historical Society

Of all the Alpine mining projects, the most massive was probably the Isabella Tunnel, a Sutro-inspired extravaganza fueled by Chalmers's prodigious ambitions and backed by vast sums of British capital. Situated northeast of the town of Silver Mountain with its tunnel opening just above Silver Creek, the Isabella was carefully designed to tap into a cluster of silver ledges believed to lie beneath Scandinavian Canyon, including the claims of the Exchequer, I.X.L., Buckeye, and Accacia mining companies.

Preliminary work may have begun at the site as early as 1864 under the name of the Eugenie Tunnel.[11] Once Chalmers acquired the project about 1878, however, work began in earnest on the newly-renamed "Isabella."[12] Under Chalmers' aggressive management a host of new buildings and heavy equipment quickly sprouted at the face. There was an engine room outfitted with lathe, blower, circular saw, and drill; a "tinner's" building to fabricate ventilation pipe; a stable large enough to house a dozen mules, complete with its own grain and hay loft; steam boilers; compressors; a "commodious" brick-lined powder magazine; even a tramway to ferry frozen powder from the magazine to a separate "thawing house." A sturdy 800-foot-long wooden trestle was thrown up over Silver Creek, providing easy access for supplies from the main road on the far side of the river and permitting tailings to be dumped conveniently away from the tunnel's mouth.[13]

Hacked directly into solid native rock, the Isabella Tunnel required little shoring. Its roomy 9-foot by 8-foot dimensions were wide enough to accommodate two parallel sets of rails, permitting incoming and exiting ore cars to operate simultaneously. Chalmers projected the finished length of his tunnel at 7,000 feet – well over a mile into the mountainside – and confidently predicted progress of 250 to 300 feet per month.[14] In his rosy telling, at least three mining companies would be able to profitably utilize the single tunnel to extract their ore. And perhaps most optimistic of all, he estimated that the Isabella Tunnel would tap the first ledge of silver within a mere 10 months.[15]

The Isabella never reached its projected seven thousand-foot length – a casualty of weary investors who eventually turned off the money tap. But by the time work finally ceased in January, 1881, the tunnel *had* made its way an amazing 4,429 feet into the mountainside,[16] successfully producing a three-year infusion of capital into the local economy, although no bonanza of ruby quartz.[17]

Promises, Promises

The pages of the Silver Mountain and Monitor newspapers were regularly stuffed with legal notices to mining shareholders, advising them of assessments of 50 cents to a dollar or more on each share of stock. And just as regularly, the papers would soon thereafter publish long lists of stock forfeitures, naming unhappy shareholders who had failed to pay the repeated levies. Such assessments were ostensibly imposed to raise funds to finance new work in the mines. In actuality, however, they often were used simply to "freeze out" minority shareholders, permitting large owners to confiscate shares for unpaid assessments. In one notable example, the prominent Lewis brothers of Monitor purchased a two-thirds interest in the Sam Booth mine from its original locator, Thomas W. Collins. The Lewises then promptly announced an assessment of $1,000 on each one-third share, coldly notifying poor Collins by way of a newspaper notice that his interest in the mine would be forfeited if he failed to pay the astronomical levy within eight weeks.[18]

If newspapers frequently brought bad news in the form of assessment notices, they also became eager messengers of any hint of success in the local mines. In good times, editorial enthusiasm was almost palpable. The *Chronicle*, for example, hailed a strike at the Monitor-based Tarshish as the "biggest thing in the mining line on this side of the mountains,"[19] or gleefully reported that the I.X.L. was "getting out good ore" to be worked at the local Pittsburg Mill.[20] Nevada, the editors proclaimed, "is no where."[21] The *Bulletin*, too, engaged in its share of breathless boosterism. Trumpted one upbeat news item:

> *A furnace has . . . been erected in connection with [the mill at the George Washington Gold and Silver Mining Company] for the purpose of ascertaining the feasibility of working the refractory ores from the 'Morning Star,' at Mogul, which we are happy in being able to announce was demonstrated last week to be a complete success. . . . The ledges in Scandinavian Canon, and their northern extensions, which run into Alpine District, are drawing the attention of capitalists in the East toward them.[22]*

Unhampered by truth-in-advertising laws, promotional circulars cheerfully puffed local investments to would-be investors. One prospectus unabashedly proclaimed that "the same belt of argentiferous leads [from Virginia City] continue on in a southerly course . . . through the Silver Mountain country," adding that only experts could distinguish the Comstock's ore from that of Alpine County.[23] Even mining expert Rossiter Raymond's official 1869 report confidently predicted that "many [Alpine] companies now seem to be on the eve of practical success."[24]

The bravado of the *Silver Mountain Bulletin* quickly evaporated within just a few years of the town's inception. Once-enthusiastic publisher W.O. Hayes declared himself a candidate for State Assembly in May of 1867,[25] sold off his printing equipment to a Calaveras County firm a month later and packed his bags, bidding a permanent *adieu* to Silver Mountain.[26] The ever-cheerful *Chronicle* snapped up the chance to relocate to Silver Mountain, and did its best to keep up the encouraging refrain, blithely assuring readers in 1870 that "Everything is lovely" – despite sour news about a sale of the Buckeye Mine for taxes and liens encumbering the Imperial's assets. Although refusing to lend its editorial stamp to what it called the "swindle" being perpetrated by its competitor, the ultra-rosy *Miner*,[27] the *Chronicle* steadfastly put a positive spin on local mining news with hopeful predictions such as this:

Mining operations throughout our county are progressing finely, giving our people much encouragement for an early 'coming out' of our county as a well-to-do and permanent mining county.[28]

Similarly, after reporting the gloomy news in 1871 that "several well known and valuable claims at Silver Mountain [have] this week passed into hands of English capitalists," the paper brightly observed that a new mill was starting up at Monitor's Schenectady Mine, "ensuring weekly shipment of bullion from that and the Exchequer mill."[29]

In truth, the financial success of the local mines had as much to do with promotional "spin" as it did with any actual mining. Savvy entrepreneurs quickly grasped the common wisdom that the value of a mine increased with the reader's distance away from it.[30] Bulliona's Michigan Mine, for example, was funded largely by investors in that far-away state, while Monitor's Schenectady Mine was backed by an investor group from upstate New York. Chalmers' parade of ever-changing mining ventures similarly benefitted from their long-distance appeal to cash-rich capitalists an ocean away in London. Distant investors had little assurance that their cash would be spent as intended. All too frequently, it wasn't. One unusually candid newspaper item reported:

The affairs of the Active Co. at Monitor, after undergoing a searching investigation by Gen'l. James F. Hall, revealed the fact that of the thousands of dollars sent out from New York to their agent here, not one dollar had been expended for the benefit of the company's claims. The George Washington Company find themselves in a similar fix, regarding expenditures in the construction of their mill. True, they have a good mill, and in running order, but have the not pleasing knowledge of having to pay twice for its construction. Of the monies sent to Capt. Uznay, to pay for labor and materials . . . but a small portion of it has been applied to the object designated, but . . . has been used by Capt. Uznay to further his own individual interests.[31]

For mine promoters, of course, the nearby Comstock became Exhibit "A," demonstrating that silver mining could indeed generate get-rich-quick opportunities. As late as 1874, market prices for shares in Alpine's Buckeye, Franklin, and Globe mines could be found nestled companionably beside listings for shares of Virginia City's famously rich Chollar, Ophir, and Yellow Jacket mines on the San Francisco exchange.

Like Alpine's scattered ore pockets themselves, local companies' fortunes repeatedly waxed and waned. In 1871, for example, workmen at the Exchequer were "busy as bees" getting their quartz mill ready to run.[32] Three years later, the mine was in the hands of the Sheriff – under whose stewardship some $125 worth of candles managed to go missing.[33] A few months more, however, saw Chalmers re-taking control of the property: busily "un-watering" the tunnel, shoring up cave-ins, and urging his London compatriots to send him more money for the next round of taxes.[34] Hope, it seemed, sprang eternal.

Stock listings in papers like the San Francisco Morning Call included not only Comstock bonanzas like the Chollar but also Alpine mines including the Buckeye, Franklin, and Globe. (September 5, 1874).

Mining Technology

The earliest Alpine mine shafts were forged with only the most rudimentary of tools, and a miner's simple pick, hammer, and shovel made long and painful work of the process.

Young mining hopeful Addison Curtiss discovered for himself in 1864 just how painful that process could be. Having secured a contract to dig ten feet of shaft for the Pettibeau Company in Scandinavian Canyon, Curtiss confided ruefully to his journal on Day Two of the job: "Cut my thumb – bad."[35] Two days later he would add in disgust: "Nearly finished, and I ain't sorry – back lame."[36]

Luckily, about the same time as the Silver Mountain mines hit their heyday, mining technology began its own rapid evolution. Early miners had only a simple blasting powder at their disposal known as "black" powder – a variant of gunpowder, in which sodium nitrate was substituted for potassium nitrate. Then in 1866, Swedish chemist Alfred Nobel mixed volatile nitroglycerine with a stabilizing agent, kieselguhr. And *voilà*: the powerful explosive known as dynamite was born.[37] The local *Bulletin* gave a nod to this important innovation as early as 1867:

Dustman Collection

> *Nitro-Glycerine. – This powerful explosive compound, heretofore considered dangerous, is, we learn, being used with success, and with perfect safety, on the Central Pacific Railroad, the dangers apprehended in transportation having been overcome by mixing the three ingredients of which it is composed on the spot where needed. A Superintendent of one of our claims here left for Crystal Peak on Monday evening to witness its workings, preparatory to its introduction here in tunnel mining. Should it be found practicable, it will reduce the cost of rock tunnelling fully two-thirds in the saving of labor and powder.[38]*

Manufacturers were quick to respond to demand for the new form of mining powder. Though a patent was held officially by the Giant Powder Company, competitors like Vulcan and Hercules soon offered their own competing wares using different filler materials.[39] New mercury-fulminate "blasting caps" also were developed to detonate the charge.[40]

Alpine's local mines eventually embraced this new technology, although the changeover did not occur without resistance. Chalmers, ever the early adaptor, reported a "hard battle" to get his mining crews to use the new form of explosive. Still, he added confidently, "the agents . . . assure me that after a few days, men get accustomed to it, and prefer it to common powder."[41] While offering a significant increase in blasting force, the new explosives significantly increased hazards for the workers. Even the hardiest of miners could be overcome by the toxic fumes emitted by the blasts. Suspecting at first that his men were "shamming," Chalmers ventured into the Giant Powder fumes himself for a day and wound up with what he described as a "fearful headache."[42]

In letters home, Chalmers provided brief, sad descriptions of the new working conditions:

> *I have many Complaints from my men as to noxious fumes from the Powder I am using after a blast. . . .*

[T]he noxious fumes from the Powder had become so bad that after a blast it was <u>three</u> hours before the men could be got to go in: Some men who tried to go in an hour after[wards] were struck down as if paralyzed and run out on the stone Car almost lifeless.

I have pushed my men so that three and four at a time have been run out on the Cars senseless. . . .

There is scarcely a day passes without some of the miners being run out on the stone cars more dead than alive. On some again the fumes seem to have an effect similar to that produced by Nitrous Oxide or Laughing Gas. I have seen men under this influence have to be dragged out of the Tunnel by 3 miners, or forcibly held down on the Cars & in getting in the open air tear their strong Miners' blouses in ribbons & with apparently no effort, rip in pieces the empty Dynamite Cases at the tunnel mouth.[43]

As his tunnel grew longer and the air more foul, Chalmers attempted to improve the situation using an 8-inch Sturtevant blower.[44] He also experimented for a time with a "jet of steam introduced into [a] 6-inch air pipe" plus a 20-foot riser at the tunnel's mouth to help exhaust the noxious gasses from the tunnel.[45] But that, too, proved insufficient. Finally, after most of his men packed up and left in a protest over wages and conditions,[46] he turned to a 13-inch galvanized ventilating pipe, assembled in lengths at the tunnel's mouth[47] and connected to a large blower.[48] This new assembly provided reasonably effective ventilation but was anything but cheap; as Chalmers reported to London, the new contraption "ran away with" some $2,267.17, including shipping.[49]

Courtesy of Society of California Pioneers
(Detail of Lawrence & Houseworth Photo #707)
Gift of Florence V. Flinn

This early photo of Silver Mountain shows Silver Creek has been dammed for a mill pond, probably for a lumber mill on the south bank (out of sight, to the right). Note the pile of logs in center of photo. Water power was similarly used at some local quartz mills.

In addition to the latest new and improved explosives, mechanized rock drills were soon developed to bore the holes in which to place explosive charges, a huge improvement on tedious hand-drilling. Armed with an old-fashioned four-pound hammer and steel bit, a muscular miner could produce about a foot of hole per hour; an early machine drill could duplicate that result in just two minutes.[50] By the mid-1870s, Burleigh and other manufacturers were successfully marketing a variety of powerful air-driven mechanical drills.[51]

With freight running as high as $4 a ton,[52] proximity to a mill was a significant factor for any efficient mining operation, and a variety of local mills quickly sprang up to meet demand. Some of the earliest were simple arrastras to crush the ore. As early as 1864, Henry Van Horn constructed an elaborate pair of cast-iron arrastras "a short distance below Silver Mountain," powered by a mammoth 36-foot diameter water wheel at Silver Creek. Each arrastra's iron bed was nine feet across and sat atop its own brick furnace, ready to crush and roast a ton of ore every twelve hours.[53] An even larger arrastra began operating at Silver King about the same time, reportedly crushing two to three tons of ore per day from the nearby Excelsior Lode.[54]

The town of Silver Mountain soon boasted several of its own quartz mills, including the Washington Mill east of town and Whiteside's Star Mill at the foot of 8th Street.[55] At Markleeville, the water-driven Pioneer Mill was constructed in 1865 at a cost of $25,000. The Pioneer featured a "Rivot" furnace with a 35-foot chimney plus a 24-foot water wheel powering 10 stamps, and was optimistically estimated to have a capacity of 20 tons per day.[56] At nearby Monitor, both the Tarshish and the Globe mines erected their own mills about 1871.[57] Processing ore in these mills was not cheap: at the Tarshish Mill, for example, crushing alone cost $1.50 per ton without amalgamation;[58] chemical reduction at other mines added another $10 to $50 per ton.[59]

Alpine miners quickly realized that the traditional process of crushing and then chemically amalgamating the ore with quicksilver (mercury) was not sufficient to tame the "rebellious" local ore. Early experiments were made with the Freiberg process – a slow and somewhat costly amalgamating process using revolving wooden barrels. But even this tedious method proved unsuccessful with the highly sulphured local rock. The Washington Mill gave up and replaced its Freiberg barrels with Wheeler pans, and also switched from a dry to a wet crusher. "Freiberg notions, and Freiberg managers, are about played out in these diggings, having been found by sad experience to be unreliable and rather expensive," observed the *Bulletin* tartly in 1867.[60] Other roasting processes that were tried and discarded included the Pioneer Mill's Rivot furnace and a White's revolving furnace, adopted by the Tarshish for its supposed economy over a chloridizing furnace but quickly judged "a total failure."[61]

Some early almagamating pans were made of wood. A slightly later amalgamating set-up suggests metal construction (1878).

Chalmers touted the Stetefeldt furnace (below) as a superior method of de-sulphuring the rebellious Alpine ore, claiming "they will all have to come 'round to Stetefeldt."

Dustman collection.

For Alpine's refractory ore, the dual actions of roasting and chloridizing proved the only successful solution. Chalmers quickly became an advocate of the new gravity-fed Stetefeldt furnace in which ore mixed with salt was dropped through a heated 40-foot chimney, a process estimated to recover up to 85 to 95% of the ore's assay value.[62] Predicted Chalmers, "they will <u>all</u> have to come 'round to Stetefeldt" – despite an estimated $7,000 price tag for construction of the furnace plus a patentholder's royalty of $1 on every ton of ore processed using Stetefeldt's design.[63]

The Davidson Mill at Silver Creek – acquired by Chalmers in 1871 along with his "mansion," and quickly

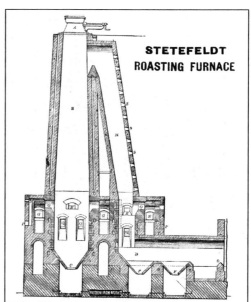

STETEFELDT ROASTING FURNACE

Alpine County Historical Society

renamed the Exchequer Mill – initially came with 8 stamps, a 40-horse power engine, four Hepburn pans and two Hendry concentrators.[64] Inside a separate "amalgamating room" were six wooden Freiberg barrels, each standing five feet tall and four in diameter, coupled with a round wooden agitator six and a half feet across.[65]

Such an array, of course, was hardly enough for Chalmers. He soon began lobbying his London backers for a Blake's Crusher as "a great improvement [which would] soon pay its cost,"[66] and a Stetefeldt furnace to chlorodize and roast the ore before amalgamation.[67] He also began improvements to the mill itself, including the addition of more stamps:

View of the Exchequer Mill about 1880, taken from the far side of the creek looking towards the back side of Chalmers' house and the Mill with its signature brick chimney. Note the team of oxen transporting wood, perhaps to keep the smelter running.

Courtesy of the Society of California Pioneers, San Francisco
Charles B. Turrill Collection

> *Your Mill should have (if you please by <u>degrees</u>) 22 Stamps added to it. Your present cam Shaft will hold now 4 stamps more and give you a 12 Stamp Battery; but it ought as ore product increases to be able to crush 30 tons a day to employ the furnace to its <u>full</u> [capacity].*[68]

It quickly became evident that the old Davidson mill – now re-christened the Exchequer – needed considerably more repair than Chalmers originally anticipated. "The whole of the foundations of the Mill Battery have been taken out and replaced," signed Chalmers in a letter not long after taking possession. "[T]he Cam Shaft Bearings [were] cut out for Babbit, – a new Bearing put in for the Centre one which was worn through, and the babbitting commenced to-day."[69] Roughly six months later he was writing again in disgust:

> *I have the honor to inform you, tho' with much regret, that after straining every nerve to carry out the letter of your telegraphed & written instructions to run the Mill & ship bullion, & overcoming many difficulties occasioned by the lateness of the Season and the state of the Mill from a long period of disuse, – I felt it to be my duty to shut down altogether on the 29th [of November], excepting the Barrels which are still amalgamating the ore . . . On Thursday the 23d at 8 A.M., the left hand Battery was knocked to pieces so far as running it was concerned. . . . On raising the [mortar blocks] the problem was solved – they were completely rotten at the <u>Core</u>, tho' good & sound <u>outside</u>.*[70]

Within the next six years, Chalmers managed to wangle funds from London to erect a brand new mill just up the road from his old Exchequer mill site. Featuring 70 *tons* of equipment including 20 stamps,[71] the elaborate new "I.X.L. Mill" was everything Chalmers could have hoped for. But its brand new stamps would never crush more than a few token loads of ore. Just a year after the new mill's completion in December, 1876, Judge Arnot and other creditors were advertising a sheriff's sale of not only the I.X.L. Mill but also the company's boarding house, the old Exchequer quartz mill, the Isabella claims in Scandinavian Canyon, and Chalmers' personal assets.[72] Although Chalmers would once again manage to stave off financial disaster for a few more years, the I.X.L. Mill's virtually-unused equipment was eventually dismantled and shipped off to a mine in Mono County.[73]

Inside the mines, the miners faced not only back-breaking labor but cold, wet working conditions. At the Monitor Consolidated G. & S.M. Co. in 1864, for example, water brought work to a sudden halt:

This 1876 photo titled "Exchequer Croppings" was probably taken to send back to England to show investors Chalmers's hard-working mining crew. The mysterious man in the hat (second from right) is far too portly for a miner; could this be Lewis Chalmers himself? Both this and the similar photo of the Exchequer Mill, below, were taken by pioneering photographer Eliza Withington.

> *This company were forced to suspend operations about ten days since, owing to a rush of water that rendered it almost impossible to blast. The water came in from overhead, under and in front.*[74]

Courtesy of Bienecke Library

Chalmers also vividly described the adversities faced by his crew at the Imperial Tunnel:

> *The flow of water is increasing, so is the stench: & the ground is getting very dangerous to work under. . . One of my men had his head severely cut by falling rock last week. . . [T]hey are all as wet as they can be when they get out . . . [The] men work in water to their ankles, and in a perpetual shower from above.*[75]

Similarly wet conditions prevailed in the Exchequer. At one point the mine became "so awfully wet" the men found themselves with "cold ice water" dripping on them from above for their entire shift.[76] Even the hard-nosed Chalmers was forced – grudgingly – to reduce his shifts from ten to eight hours a day.

Dustman Collection

Aside from being uncomfortable, work at the mines was also exceedingly dangerous. One miner installing shoring timbers was fatally injured at the I.X.L. mine when a portion of the tunnel wall collapsed, crushing his upper leg.[77] Another had the lower portion of his body buried in a cave-in at a Monitor mine;[78] a month after the accident, the local newspaper would carry the sad news of his death at the not-so-ripe old age of 36.[79] At the Imperial, a workman was "mashed to a jelly" when he fainted and tumbled down a 1,250-foot shaft,[80] and another was grievously hurt after falling down the winze at the Exchequer.[81] Three workers in the Imperial Tunnel at Bulliona were nearly asphyxiated when a wooden ventilation chimney caught fire – saved only when Chalmers, spotting the smoke, dashed across the creek and into the tunnel to pull them out.[82] A

Dustman collection.

Water, falling rock, and poor ventilation awaited miners entering the tunnel for their shift.

similar fire consumed the wooden building around the Mountain Mine's ventilating furnace, suggesting such conflagrations were not uncommon.[83]

Less-fatal injuries among workmen were similarly common. "Engineer Ward" at the Exchequer Mill lost the joint of one finger to an engine.[84] A portion of the new boiler room at the I.X.L. mill collapsed on top of three unlucky miners.[85] A teamster at the Exchequer suffered a broken jaw and ribs when a load of timbers shifted, pitching him down the ore dump.[86] And Supervisor Mercer fell off a scaffold at the Advance hoisting works and was forced to "retire" for a week to recover.[87]

Work at the roasting furnaces could be even more hazardous than inside the mines. Although describing a furnace elsewhere in California, William Brewer's narrative offers insight into conditions at the Alpine mills as well:

The work at the furnaces is much more unhealthy [than in the mines] and commands the higher wages. Sulphurous acids, arsenic, vapors of mercury, etc., make a horrible atmosphere, which tells fearfully on the health of the workmen, but the wages always command men and there is no want of hands. The ore is roasted in furnaces and the vapors are condensed in great brick chambers, or "condensers." These have to be cleaned every year by workmen going into them, and many have their health ruined forever by the three or four days' labor, and all are injured; but the wages, twenty dollars a day, always bring victims.[88]

Dejected miners occasionally committed suicide, victims of broken dreams and dreary working conditions. Charles Miller, for example, "formerly a well-known resident of this county," committed suicide in 1870, after moving on to the heart of the Comstock at Gold Hill, Nevada.[89]

Still, for many miners the hope of what lay ahead outweighed the certainty of a dismal present. Time and again reports would circulate of fresh strikes, promising lodes, and astonishing ore specimens. Rumors would surface anew of burgeoning commercial interest: the promised extension of a railroad to within three miles of Silver Mountain,[90] or the "contemplated" opening of a Wells Fargo office at Monitor.[91] As late as 1872, long after the initial blush was off the Alpine mines, rosy tales of the "richest ore ever seen in this county"[92] became the talk of the town.

Little wonder, then, that as one group of tired miners and merchants moved on, a fresh crop of restless spirits moved in. The life-blood of Silver Mountain, it seemed, was always circulating.

This rare gem of a photograph, looking north, shows an array of homes and fences as settlers began to sink roots in Silver Mountain City.

Courtesy of the California History Room, California State Library, Sacramento CA

Courtesy of Nevada Historical Society

Silver Mountain City, also looking north, circa 1864. The trail up Scandinavian Canyon is clearly visible and shows evidence of its frequent use. Also visible are the Fisk Hotel (far left), the Mammoth Hotel (just to the right of the pair of trees), and scattered cabins dotting the plain sloping towards the mountain. The Scandinavian Toll Road appears to taper towards the Fisk Hotel on First Street, rather than towards its later terminus at Third Street (toward the middle of the photo).

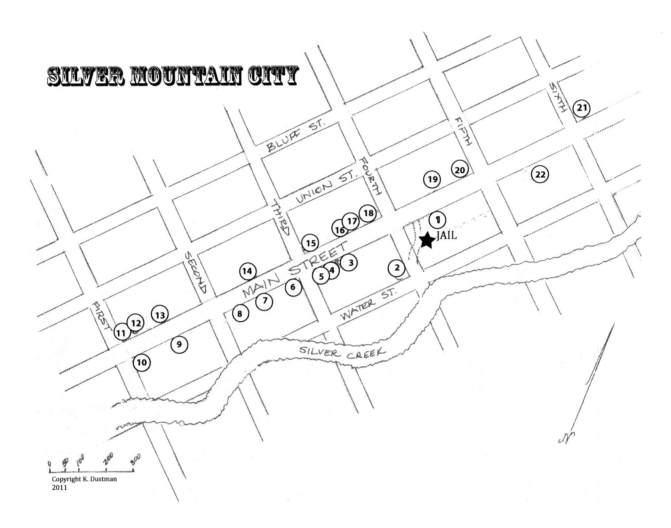

SILVER MOUNTAIN CITY

Copyright K. Dustman
2011

1. Jail
2. Peter Peterson's house
3. Ryan's Exchange (Courthouse)
4. Swinerton & Co.'s Pioneer Hardware
5. J. Davidson's Saloon
6. Gates' Drug Store
7. Betschmann's Stable
8. Jacob Struben's Shoe Shop
9. Mammoth Hotel
10. Legget (Balaclava G&SM Office)

11. Fiske's Hotel
12. Silver Mountain Bulletin
13. Reinstein & Harris' store
14. Gibson's Saloon
15. Pioneer Meat Market
16. Ford's Hotel
17. Errickson's Hotel
18. Ogden's Saloon
19. Brown's Hotel
20. Coursen's Grocery

21. Sauquet's Store
22. Brown & Kent's Hotel

Blocks are 160 x 300 feet each
Numbered streets are 50 ft. wide
Named streets are 60 ft. wide

Tip: Modern visitors may find it easiest to begin their tour at
Third Street, still visible as a dirt track intersecting Highway 4
(Main Street).

CHAPTER 7:
POLITE (AND IMPOLITE) SOCIETY

L ike any other town in any other time, Silver Mountain had its share of lawmen and law-breakers; its sellers of merchandise and its hawkers of dreams. And like any other town in any other time, the most fascinating stories whispered from ear to ear on dusty streets were, of course, about its *people*. Luckily for us, a few of those stories have survived through yellowed letters and microfilmed newspapers, allowing us to share in the gossip and – albeit second-hand – to learn a little more of what life was like in Silver Mountain.

Births, Deaths, Weddings & Accidents

In its earliest mining camp days, Silver Mountain's denizens were probably exclusively male. But any gender imbalance was predictably short. As early as 1863, the fairer sex already had put in an appearance. Visitor William Brewer describes the newly-minted town in August of that year as swarming with "hundreds of men," but also noted "[p]erhaps half a dozen women and children" leavening the mix.[1]

Close on the heels of the distaff side came romance. The first marriage in newly-formed Alpine county, uniting John Welsh and Louisa Gillan, was celebrated at "the half-way house, between Monitor and Markleeville" on September 6, 1864.[2] A little over two months later, C.B. Gregory – one of Silver Mountain's most eligible bachelors and soon-to-be Union Party candidate for Sheriff – also tied the knot with the former Mrs. A. Rutter.[3] *Bulletin* publisher W.O. Hayes succumbed to Cupid's arrows the followed year, marrying Mrs. E.L. Pearson at Silver Mountain in August, 1865.[4]

The stork was soon no stranger to early Silver Mountain as well. Alpine's first pioneer baby arrived at Silver Mountain on May 21, 1864, and was given the colorful name "Nevada Alpine Kent."[5] A virtual baby boom-let followed, with seven miniature additions to Alpine's population in the remaining months of 1864, including twins born to George Andrews and his wife.[6] Five of these newest of new citizens (including the twins) were delivered at Silver Mountain; two in Monitor; and one local birth was out-sourced to Genoa.[7] The following year witnessed a similar increase in the county's tiny tot population with another eight births, half of these Alpine newcomers greeting the world at Silver Mountain.

The grim reaper, too, put in his own not-infrequent appearance. As early as May, 1864, a "burying ground" had been set aside at Silver Mountain,[8] and by 1877 the town's plat reserved two full city blocks for

Sisters "Birdie" and Nancy Scott, daughters of Hiram and Agnes Scott, were born in 1866 and 1868 at Silver Mountain.

the cheerfully named "Sunny-Side Cemetery." Causes of death ran a morbid gamut. One tiny toddler fell into an irrigation ditch and drowned.[9] Robert Johnson, age 39, succumbed to "dropsy."[10] There were fatal accidents at the mines,[11] fatal accidents at the sawmills,[12] and fatal accidents during timber drives.[13] Travelers might meet their fate through a thousand hazards. Justice of the Peace John G. Slaven, who once enjoyed offices two doors north of the Silver Mountain court house, was rumored to have been "murdered by the Indians" while out prospecting somewhere to the South.[14] Those attempting any sort of long journey in winter might simply freeze to death.[15]

Some fatal ailments were purely self-inflicted. Paul Lambert, lauded by the newspaper as "a good man, a workman, strong, wiry, and active as ever entered Alpine and in the prime of life," fell victim to his whiskey bottle, succumbing to what his eulogizer sternly warned was "the fate of all who swallow the accursed stuff."[16] A similar affliction carried off "Poor Jake" Kip of Monitor, whose "last spree was too much for him" – despite a last-ditch "treatment" at the hot springs near Genoa.[17]

Perhaps the most gruesome exit recorded in the local press was that suffered by Peter Peterson, a veteran tippler with a home on Water Street near the Silver Mountain jail. The *Chronicle* recorded in horrific detail the mode of his passing:

> FOUND DEAD – A SAD END. – *About ten o'clock on Wednesday morning the dead body of Peter Peterson, an old and well-known resident of this town, was found lying in front of his cabin on Water street. An examination showed that the face had been terribly mutilated by hogs, one being near the body when it was discovered; one of his hands had also been mutilated. The hogs had eaten into his neck and cut the jugular, the head lying in a pool of blood. It is supposed that he had gone home intoxicated, and had fallen where found, the key of his cabin being found near him. He was probably stunned by the fall, or fell asleep, when he was attacked by a hog cutting the jugular vein and causing him to bleed to death. – The deceased was a good hearted man, but strong drink had been his greatest vice for some time past.*[18]

ACCIDENT. — Yesterday morning J. J. Rice was severely injured by his horse slipping from the grade, at the Devil's Elbow, Big Trees Road, and crushing him against the butt of a tree. He will be all right again in a few days.

GENOA HOT SPRINGS,

DAVID W. WALLEY, Proprietor.

Rheumatic and Scrofulous Affections Cured.

An Elegantly Furnished Hotel, with Thirty-nine Airy Rooms.

Table supplied with all Substantials and Delicacies.

MUD-BATHS,

And Twelve Furnished Bath-rooms, each with HOT, COLD, SHOWER and VAPOR BATHS of

MEDICINAL WATERS.

THE HOTEL AND SPRINGS ARE SITU-ated at the base of the Sierra Nevada Mountains, on the stage road, two miles south of Genoa, Douglas county, Nevada.
  An Experienced Physician is attached to the institution, with proper medicines necessary for invalids.   s7-tf

Walley's Hot Springs offered not only its 'medicinal waters' to cure rheumatism and other ailments but also the services of an 'experienced physician.'

Accidents, too, became a sad fact of life in the harsh working conditions of farms and mines. Exchequer foreman George Lowe managed to amputate his own toe while chopping wood,[19] while former Silver Mountainite Ole Lee severed his heel tendon with an ax in a similar accident, "doubtless permanently crippling him."[20] County Treasurer W.J. Johnston's baby had his clothes catch fire from an open hearth, and his mother's hands were "shockingly burnt" as she attempted to extinguish the flames.[21] H.W. Bagley hurtled out of his buggy near Centerville, injuring his head,[22] while another buggy accident left Markleeville resident W.A. Johnson suffering from broken ribs.[23] Least fortunate of all was Carson Valley resident Lute Olds, whose floundering horses drowned their driver as well as themselves while attempting to cross the high water of the East Walker River.[24]

Other life-threatening mishaps were anything but accidental. Markleeville's own Jacob Marklee was shot to death in May, 1863, in a property rights dispute. A gambler named Glascock suffered six stab wounds during a heated game of cards.[25] And a row between the co-proprietors of Markleeville's Empire Meat Market led one owner to bury a cleaver in his partner's shoulder, the victim retaliating by slashing his ex-partner's throat.[26] Suicide, too, was not unheard of. Monitor's Mrs. Bagley, tired of "everyone aggravat[ing] her so," drowned her troubles with a stiff shot of morphine laced with strychnine.[27] And a lovelorn suitor named Crippin took refuge in the solitary misery of one of Silver Mountain's empty buildings and shot himself.[28]

Courtesy of Alpine County Historical Society

Jacob Marklee, founder of Markleeville.

For women, the greatest and most predictable threat to life and health was childbirth. Lewis Chalmers' wife, Antoinette, was able to afford the services of both a midwife and a doctor at her confinement in 1881.[29] But the average Silver Mountain wife would count herself fortunate just to have a kindly female friend in attendance. Writing to Miss Nellie Barnum of Monitor, a married woman friend in Oakland warned pointedly of the dangers that lay ahead if Nellie should marry:

Courtesy of Alpine County Historical Society

George and Della Lukens, on their wedding day. George brought the Alpine Argus to Markleeville, and acted as its editor and District Attorney before moving east in 1884 to attend law school.

I presume you remember Mrs. Estey. . . . she was confined over two weeks ago, has a boy. She had a remarkably easy time [during the delivery], but the day following was taken with convulsions so that four men could not hold her in bed. Her tongue was bitten so that she could not get it in her mouth, it was so swollen. . . . I think I can never forget what a sight she was, and it fills me with horror when I think of what <u>women</u> have to endure. . . . [W]hen I spoke of what I had been through I meant simply the danger and agony of childbirth. . . . I tremble for those who, knowing nothing of such trials, venture out on the sea of matrimony.[30]

Once successfully introduced to this world, babies faced not only the usual host of childhood diseases but also epidemics of diphtheria and cholera. One typical issue of the local paper leavened the joyful news of a recent birth with sad announcements of two recent deaths, recording the separate passings of 30-year-old Mary Rebecca Powers and little Ella J. Calhoun, just one year of age.[31]

When couples promised to care for each other "in sickness and in health," they meant these terms quite literally. "Sickness" could assume a variety of deadly forms. Scarlet fever was "raging" in Carson City in 1870, for example, while smallpox was reported to have reached the East Fork area of the Carson Valley by late 1871.[32] Tuberculosis laid the hand of a lingering death on several Silver Mountain residents, including Lewis Chalmers' oldest son

The Reverend R.H. Ford

Ford's Hotel (more formally known as the "Silver Mountain Hotel" or "Alpine House") became a Silver Mountain landmark for more than a decade. Situated on the North side of Main Street between Third and Fourth Streets, the hotel building was leased by the energetic Reverend R.H. Ford in 1870.[46]

ALPINE HOTEL,

AND

STAGE HOUSE,

Main street, between 3d and 4th,
SILVER MOUNTAIN.
The undersigned respectfully solicits a share of the public patronage.
☞ POST OFFICE and OFFICE of the United States Mail Line of Stages are in this building

GEORGE H. DUNLAP,
s7-tf   Proprietor.

A Methodist minister and native of New Hampshire, Ford had been a Silver Mountain stalwart since 1864.[47] With wife Almira and at least one of his three children as helpers,[48] he managed to keep his hotel thriving through the ups and downs of the local economy by diversifying. His hotel soon included not only a restaurant and boarding house but also doubled as the stage stop and post office for Silver Mountain.[49] Even such luxuries as tickets to New York and Europe could be purchased at Ford's establishment.[50]

As a Justice of the Peace for the Silver Mountain township, Ford not only officiated at weddings and funerals[51] but also served on the occasional coroner's jury when necessary.[52]

Ford served multiple terms on the Board of Education and as Superintendent of Schools.[53] Like

Lewie,[33] Rev. R.H. Ford's oldest son Charles, and others.[34] A malady known as "delerious typhoid fever" carried off Mrs. S.G. Lewis's sister in Mariposa in 1864,[35] while that same year, typhoid fever "prevail[ed] to an alarming extent" in Antelope Valley and along the Walker River bottom.[36] Diphtheria killed two of Joseph Uncapher's children in 1877,[37] and the following year stole away both toddler sons of John E. Johns in Diamond Valley.[38]

Alpine Co. Historical Society

Little Nellie Grover died of diphtheria July 17, 1877, and was buried in the Markleeville cemetery with a simple wooden marker.

Townsfolk would turn out in force for both weddings and funerals. The good Reverend R.H. Ford must have preached a fine sermon – a task at which he received a great deal of practice. Among other occasions, Ford presided over the 1865 nuptials of William Chambers and Cornelia Arneson;[39] the wedding of E.A. Coursen to Hannah Blacklock in 1866;[40] the inquest for murdered teamster James M. Brown in 1870;[41] services for the ill-fated Peter Peterson in 1878;[42] and just few short weeks later, a pair of funerals for former county treasurer Thomas W. Legget and district attorney Thomas J. Orgon.[43]

When three miners were killed in a snow slide in Scandinavian Canyon, some three hundred mourners turned out for the funeral, with "deputations" from as far away as Silver King and Monitor. One of the deceased left a widow and four young children with "no means of support," and the *Monitor Gazette* rallied the community to her rescue, admonishing: "These must be our county's widow and orphans. Men of Alpine, see to it."[44] A benefit "gathering" was successfully organized, and kind-hearted local citizens opened their wallets to help the destitute widow:

> *Over one hundred dollars in coin were realized from the entertainment, which will twice bless the donors. Obligations resting against the homestead to an amount exceeding one hundred dollars were most generously cancelled by the law firm of Goff & Robinson of Markleeville, and the Messrs. Whitesides of Silver Mountain.*[45]

By and large, it seems, the community took its ups and downs in stride. Surviving newspaper accounts conjure up an image of a small but cohesive community that worked hard to survive together, and knew how to play well together, too.

Christmas was a particularly festive communal event. Committees were assembled months in advance to coordinate the local Christmas Tree Festival, and townsfolk turned out in force for the occasion. Trees would be trimmed with candles and oranges, dinner tables would groan under platters of "fine fat turkeys,"[60] and gifts would be distributed to even the smallest small-fry. At one such holiday gala, even a raging snowstorm described as "one of the most disagreeable days that mortal man ever passed in these rugged mountains" could not prevent the community from gathering at Gibson's Hall in Silver Mountain to celebrate Christmas together.[61] Weather permitting, a coach and "mud wagon" might ferry revellers up from Markleeville for the festivities to ensure that no friends missed the fun.[62]

For "good little boys and girls that mind their parents and uncles,"[63] there would be games of "blindman's bluff" and recitations of memorized poetry, and Santa Claus would distribute fruit and presents.[64] For the adults, "Professor Snow's Troupe" might be on hand to entertain with songs, dance routines and comic sketches, and there would be music and dancing until 3 a.m.[65] Plans for one especially elaborate holiday celebration promised "flying trapeze performances" and a dance contest between "two of the best dancers in the State," although whether this extravaganza actually took place remains unrecorded.[66]

Typical holiday gifts would include gloves, dresses, toys, books, and fruit. One year, local blacksmith J.J. Rice presented several pairs of "snow-shoes" (homemade skis) as gifts. The newspaper also praised Rice's "untiring exertions in preparing the room and tree."[67] Jewelry, too, might be exchanged among the wealthier citizens, with at least one creation boasting a uniquely Alpine flair: "splendid specimens of Morning Star ore in golden settings."[68]

FORD (Continued)

other local businessmen, he took a more-than-passing interest in the local mines, serving as a director of the Pennsylvania Gold & Silver Mining Co. and the Silver Creek Gold and Silver Mining Company.[54] But his wife, Almira, may have thought better of the notion of Silver Mountain winters;[55] on at least one occasion, Ford and his family left a manager in charge of their hotel in the fall to wait out the frigid winter months at Murphy's, returning again in spring.[56]

The Fords remained in Silver Mountain until 1882, when a fire destroyed their hotel building. R.H. and Almira moved in briefly with their daughter Anna and son-in-law Judge N.D. Arnot in Markleeville.[57] But with Silver Mountain now just a shadow of its former vigorous self, and the Fords themselves then in their 70s, the couple finally abandoned Alpine County entirely for the more felicitous climate of Ione. Almira passed away there in November, 1887 at the age of 76.[58] The hearty R.H. Ford finally followed her in death more than a decade later, on November 12, 1900, at the ripe old age of 90.[59] What memories he must have taken with him.

Townsfolk would be especially generous towards local businesses during the holidays. The wives of prominent citizens regaled the editors of the *Chronicle* one year with gifts of cake, wine, champagne, fruit, pastry and candy.[69]

Silver Mountain was not alone in its effusive Christmas cheer; surrounding communities hosted their own celebrations as well.[70] In Monitor, a Christmas Tree Festival at Cofflin's Hall brightened the holidays of 1870 with games of charades, songs, recitations, and "farces." Mrs. Larson, a Monitor local with a "well-earned reputation for getting up ball suppers," hosted a gala holiday event at the Oriental Hotel "reflect[ing] much credit on Mrs. Larson."[71] In 1872, not one but *two* communal Christmas Trees were decorated at Markleeville, while a separate tree graced Silver Mountain and yet another was found at Monitor.[72] Not to be outdone by its more metropolitan rivals, Woodfords hosted its own pair of holiday trees laden with fruit,

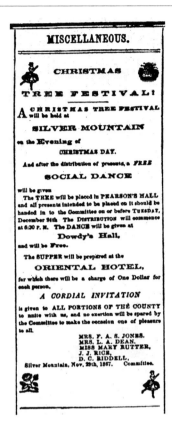

The annual "Christmas Tree Festival" took months to prepare, with many of the town's leading citizens helping with the arrangements.

and promised a programme of songs and speeches, followed by dinner and dancing at Orgon & Stalker's Hotel.[73]

Christmas wasn't the only event to be celebrated by the entire community. New Year's Day was similarly greeted with "fine suppers" at Ford's Hotel, Occidental Hall, the Fisk Hotel, and Woodford's Hall, followed by dancing to the music of Taylor's Genoa String Band "until the red, rosy morn put in an appearance," with a hearty breakfast to follow.[74]

Equally well-attended were lavish Fourth of July extravaganzas. In honor of America's birthday, mining work would be halted for most of the week[75] and local buildings were decked out in red, white, and blue.[76] When night settled, town streets would be ablaze with firecrackers. During one celebration the rockets and Roman candles of Virginia City could be seen by miners at the Exchequer.[77] In 1878, A.M. Grover hosted a "grand ball" and picnic at his Hot Springs for the Fourth, inviting everyone in the county to attend. Silver Mountain citizens later complained that their Fourth was "unusually quiet" because so many had left town for Grover's event.[78]

Thanksgiving, too, meant a gala celebration for the entire community. One day-long Thanksgiving party at Markleeville drew attendees from as far away as Monitor, Mogul and Silver Mountain with a chicken breakfast at Barnes' Hotel, followed by afternoon dinner at LaGrave's Union Hotel, dancing at the Armory Hall, and a midnight "lunch" back at the Union.[79] Not to be outdone, Silver Mountain would host "down-east" Thanksgiving turkey dinners at the local Alpine House and dancing at Ogden's Hall, inviting "delegations" from Bulliona and Monitor to attend.[80]

Music at such community gatherings was typically paid for by taking up a collection. And because out-of-towners were already paying hotel and stable bills to attend, local residents would often graciously foot the entire bill.[81]

With opportunities for entertainment scarce, no formal holiday was required for an event. One "grand ball" at Silver Mountain was gotten up on the excuse of celebrating the anniversary of California's admission to the Union.[82] Evening soirees might be advertised with "social dances" at the local Fisk Hotel.[83] For miners ensconced in their isolated boarding house in Scandinavian Canyon, entertainment might consist of a serenade by their own 13-member "glee club."[84] "Masquerade" parties were also popular, with faces carefully concealed during drawn-out affairs stretching from dinner through until midnight "when un-masking was in order" – as if anyone really found it difficult to recognize their costumed neighbor.[85]

Women & Minorities

For much of its early existence, Silver Mountain's population was predominantly male and largely white.[86] One visitor to Silver Mountain in 1867 "worked on [a] little wagon" for an African-American man named Jake,[87] although failing to mention Jake's last name. But the census of 1870 identified not a single Chinese or African-American resident in the entire settlement of Silver Mountain. The slightly more cosmopolitan Monitor had all of two Chinese residents, both male and employed as cooks. In the Woodfords/ Diamond Valley region, three residents of Chinese heritage and one "mulatto" were counted by the census-takers, while another three Chinese were living at Markleeville. Even a decade later when the total Chinese population of Alpine reached as high as 17, just one African-American resident was identified.

Such slim statistics may well understate both the numbers and the significance of minorities. Minority household workers may simply not have been reported by their employers and thus fell "below the radar" of the census-takers; or they may have been deliberately overlooked. But tantalizing hints sprinkled through brief newspaper articles and letters suggest that Chinese and other minorities had a small but enduring presence in both Silver Mountain and Monitor from the earliest days of those encampments.

Discriminatory attitudes were prevalent in the 1870s, especially towards Chinese who were viewed as unwanted competition for jobs and mining riches. In an effort to stem Chinese migration, a $100 per head tax was proposed in 1878.[88] At San Bernardino, one county clerk refused to naturalize applicants from China on the ground that they "couldn't take the oath in good English."[89] And when a properly naturalized Chinese gentleman finally cast his vote in San Francisco, the event was noteworthy enough to make the newspaper.[90] The alarm over Chinese labor spread like a contagion. A continent's-width away from the West coast, the *Kennebec (Maine) Reporter* advised its readers breathlessly:

> California is being overrun with Chinese Coolies. The last steamer from China brought over 1000 Chinese, and the entire steerage capacity of both lines is engaged for the next six months by the importers of coolies. A deputation is to be sent to Washington at once to have action taken by [C]ongress to prevent the State and the whole Pacific coast from being overrun by them.[93]

Anglo workers found it impossible to compete with the scanty wages paid to immigrants arriving under bondage contracts amounting to virtual slave labor. As early as 1870, a "mass meeting of working-men" in San Francisco fretted over the "wholesale importation" of Chinese bondsmen indentured at ten dollars a month for five years. A "large and attentive audience" unanimously adopted a series of resolutions including the following uncharitable sentiments:

> Resolved, That the Chinese are an alien race to us. Their God is not our God. Their customs, habits and ideas are opposed to ours. . . . Resolved, That the best interests of the whole country demand the prohibition of Chinese immigration to America.[94]

The year 1876 saw "Anti Coolie Clubs" being formed in San Francisco and elsewhere;[95] even the "working women of San Francisco" organized a female "Anti-Chinese League."[96] Unemployed laborers staged a march in the winter of 1879-80, demanding that employers discharge their Chinese workmen. The California State Constitution adopted in 1879 included vehemently anti-Chinese language:

> [The new state Constitution] forbids all corporations to employ any Chinese, debars them from the suffrage, forbids their employment on any public works, annuls all contracts for "coolie labour," directs the legislature to provide for the punishment of any company which shall import Chinese, to impose conditions on the residence of Chinese, and to cause their removal if they fail to observe these conditions.[97]

Taking matters into their own hands, some settlers determined to make life uncomfortable for the Chinese in their midst. In Grass Valley, all but one of the houses in the Chinese quarter were consumed by flames in a fire of suspicious origins. The next morning, a "body of armed men left Roseville . . . and proceeded up the Auburn road, warning all the Chinamen, numbering some sixty-seven, in seven camps, to leave before midnight under the penalty of death."[98]

Even the remote canyon community of Silver Mountain was tainted by the prevailing anti-Chinese sentiment. The usually mild-mannered *Chronicle* reported anxiously on the entry of the Chinese into the business of canning and drying fruit in California, observing that "unless checked they will yet engage in every calling followed by the whites."[99] And one blistering editorial concluded:

> *If we wish to put a stop to their immigration, the people of the State must resolve to discountenance their employment in any capacity; they must refuse to purchase articles of their manufacture; . . . starve them out, and in due time we will have a change for the better.*[100]

While Alpine's early Chinese residents remain largely invisible in much of its recorded history, Chinese names do crop up occasionally in letters and newspapers, often in snippets of tragedy and despair. As early as 1863, Silver Mountainites ejected a Chinese prostitute from the mining encampment, unceremoniously tossing her shanty in the river.[101] A "China wash-house" was one of the buildings identified as being lost in the great Monitor fire of 1872.[102] And a brief obituary in 1878 provided notice that "Ah Yet" had passed away in Markleeville.[103]

A few Chinese residents also achieved recognition for putting themselves on the wrong side of the law. An 1878 paper records the saga of two Chinamen embroiled in a "cutting affray" at Monitor, from which the loser suffered a "severe, but not serious" hatchet wound and the winner garnered nearly two months in the County jail and a $60 fine.[104] Another Monitor resident, Wah Kee, was brought up on charges involving the death of an Indian acquaintance from what may have been an unintentional overdose with opium-laced alcohol.[105]

The Chinese found the courts to be a one-sided institution, however. When three rowdy miners broke out the windows of Wing Lee's Silver Mountain wash house in 1877, a local jury returned a

---

Violence Against the "Heathen Chinee"

Chinese immigrants in California were subject to not only discrimination but occasional violence. One such episode erupted in Los Angeles in 1871, after two peace officers attempting to arrest a Chinese murder suspect were greeted by a hail of gunfire. The suspect's associates may have been acting more in self-defense than from any spirit of civil disobedience. As one sympathetic editor explained:

> *"The arrest of a Chinese in California is practically tantamount to his conviction. The race is excluded from the witness-stand and from the jury-box. It is not [surprising] that there is a very general unwillingness to be arrested on the part of the immigrants from the celestial kingdom."*[91]

Nevertheless, enraged by the brazen gunfire directed at officers of the law, an angry mob quickly formed, "composed mostly of native Californians and the dregs of society." This loosely-organized group surrounded the whole Chinese quarter, unceremoniously dispatched at least nineteen of its residents to the hereafter on suspicion they had been involved in the shooting, and then proceeded to set fire to the victims' houses. Meanwhile, an additional 500 well-armed citizens stood guard around the perimeter of the Chinese enclave, ostensibly to prevent escape by the original culprits.

Of the 19 dead Chinese victims of this vigilante "justice," only one would later be determined to have been linked to the shootings. The remaining 18 victims, the newspaper concluded, were apparently innocent, "the guilty ones having escaped before the mob assaulted their houses."[92]

verdict of "not guilty" – despite what was described as an "interesting trial, in which the dignity of the Court was sorely tried."[106]

If the Chinese were shunned by the fashionables of Main Street during the bright light of day, inside the seamier establishments was apparently another story. In 1873, Chalmers confided to his brother a tale about the mine foreman:

> I have been bothered with my men – Stuhr even, in whom we had so much confidence, took to playing poker with a Chinaman and drink. I had occasion to go to Silver Mountain on snow shoes about a fortnight ago – in a snow drifting day when he didn't expect me, and found him there in the middle of the day playing poker with a Chinaman and drinking. I had no alternative but get rid of him.[107]

Ultimately, despite steep walls of prejudice against the Chinese, their cheap labor proved hard to resist. Local lore suggests it was Chinese laborers who performed the back-breaking work of digging the town ditch to bring water to Markleeville.[108] Census records also show that by 1880, Chinese workers were a significant presence throughout the county as both cooks and household helpers doing "washing and ironing."

While courting Mrs. Laughton, Lewis Chalmers penned a short but telling letter promising to procure her "a China boy in Genoa" to help with the housework[109] – a promise he evidently fulfilled, as subsequent letters mention a houseboy named "Sing" who "does very well, and keeps the house clean."[110] The penny-pinching Chalmers employed Chinese laborers in his mining enterprises as well, including a Chinese laundryman to do wash at the boarding house and two Chinese helpers to assist the boarding house cook.[111] And as late as 1899, W.P. Merrill employed a Chinese cook in Woodfords.[112]

If there was a "Chinatown" district in Silver Mountain or a Chinese quarter in Monitor, these locations are long lost to history. But one tiny reminder of early Chinese immigrants remains preserved in a place-name; a small, level area dotted with cottonwoods near the turn-off to Monitor is still known to old-timers as "China Flat."

Native Americans, too, were treated with little respect and largely ignored in the pages of the local newspapers. But occasional columns hint at their customs and interaction with the early Alpine community. One account from 1863 includes this half-condescending, half-admiring description of the local Washoe:

> On the edge of [Markleeville] we saw a half-finished house, the owner of which was splitting a huge log to make shingles to roof it with, while the openings for doors and windows were festooned with carpets and rich curtains – while his wife [resplendant] with hoops and those indescribable little fixings that characterize the city lady, was busy outside cooking flap-jacks over a log fire, while looking on in stupid bewilderment stood a band of Indians. These Indians are a different set of beings from your regular California Digger. Their faces are not of that round, fat, stupid type, but their features are much more expressive. They come up much nearer to the Indians described by Fennimore Cooper than any I have seen on this portion of the continent. Nearly all the bucks have a good rifle and knife, and know how to use them too. They will hit a four bit piece at fifty paces.[113]

Another early account – similarly laden with the racial stereotypes and bias of the day, but one of the few descriptions to survive – reflects an encounter between Captain Jim, Chief of the Washoes, and a road superintendent for Carr & Company[114] endeavoring to open a new road to Silver Mountain inappropriately close to a sacred cave:

[Captain Jim] was dressed in the summer costume of the tribe, consisting of an old silk hat, which looked as if it had carried many 'a brick' when in possession of its original owner, a bow and a bunch of arrows in a fox skin slung across his shoulder. He was savagely painted on his face and breast with red and black. As the [road] superintendent approached, he was greeted with a grunt which would have done honor to an old sow and the remark: 'You build um road, Cap?' 'Yes Cap' was the reply. 'You jump um claim Cap,' was the reply; 'me want six dollars.' Cap found he was in a fix and commenced to argue with the Indian who replied, 'Pay, road; no pay, no road.' The pipe of peace was lit and after a long smoke between the two chiefs, the matter was satisfactorily arranged by the road Cap paying the Cap of the Washoes for the right of way, a large plug of tobacco.[115]

A photo of "Captain Jim," a Washoe chief, taken at Long Valley, California.

In a more satisfying retelling of this same tale, however, the pushy road superintendent not only was forced to remit the full $6 demanded but also lost his overcoat to the canny Captain Jim.[116]

A later (and probably fanciful) tale touted the discovery of a 20-foot-high "Indian Lookout . . . on the most elevated peak" of the Sierra, complete with remains of an old fire and kindling. On this site, the article confidently reported:

the wild savage raised his signal smoke to give notice of the approach of immigrant trains on the Big Tree road, telegraphed to him from other summits near the Carson Cañon.[117]

Many Silver Mountainites probably shared the common prejudices of the day about the Native Americans they encountered. Nevertheless, they respected the Indians' superior knowledge of the natural environment, believing that the Washoe could accurately predict the severity of a coming winter. When a Native American named Mr. Lo forecast a light winter,[118] for example, his opinion was significant enough to be reported by the local paper. Similarly, the *Chronicle* noted that Indians "remain camped near town, seemingly unconcerned in regard to the Winter"[119] as an indication of a gentle winter ahead.

What the Indians may have thought about their new neighbors the newspapers did not bother to ask. Even had their opinion been sought, the reserved and dignified Washoe were likely too polite to share their real views; but in traditional Washoe culture, the white settlers' airs of superiority would have been quietly frowned upon.[120] At least one early newspaper column also candidly acknowledged the adverse impacts of mining activities on traditional Indian hunting grounds, which must have been a source of sore resentment:

Our migratory prospectors have frightened the game from their usual haunts, and our saw and quartz mills have polluted the hitherto crystal streams, thereby driving the fish into the lakes that are inaccessible.[121]

Brief newspaper mentions show that Native Americans did interact occasionally with the strangers in their midst. One fall, after laying in a winter supply of acorns from over the mountains at "West Point," the Lo family was reported to be camped "on the outskirts of our town [Silver Mountain]," the women visiting local residences requesting "biscuit lah poo."[122] And when heavy snows prevented the stage from reaching Silver Mountain in 1877, the Lo family launched an impromptu business ferrying travelers' trunks down to Bulliona to catch the outbound stage for $2.50 per trunk.[123] Chalmers too apparently employed a number of Native Americans on his tunnels and mining projects, although offering them some of the least job security on his force; one letter directs his superintendent to "give the man I sent up last and Seaman and Wells and all the Indians their time tomorrow [lay them off]."[124]

The fall pine nut harvest was an important event for the Washoe, not only ensuring a stable food supply for the long and difficult winters but also offering an opportunity to socialize during the gathering process. The scale of these collective efforts was astonishing, with tribal members of all ages pitching in. Written coverage of such events is scanty, but a brief column from the *Genoa Courier* of 1893 describes that year's harvest as the largest "since 1872." This report noted that Markleeville residents James Stuart and William Thornburg and J.E. Wells of Diamond Valley were hauling wagonloads of this crucial food, an indication that local ranchers pitched in to help. A single team reportedly returned with an astonishing 1800 pounds of pine nuts, reflecting the massive scale of these efforts.

Dustman Collection.

A Washoe baby girl, in her traditional cradleboard.

The conclusion of the nut harvest was a time of great celebration. The Washoe held a "grand venison banquet" in Bear Valley in 1878, for example, after a successful acorn expedition to Calaveras. And the *Genoa Courier* of 1893 noted that "a grand pow-wow will take place at the wigwam at Woofer's" (presumably Woodford's) following the pine nut harvest, with Washoe dignitary Captain Pete Mayo to serve as orator.[125]

Fish were another abundant staple for Native Americans. Chalmers noted that the local Indians employed what he called a "very rude kind of spear" to catch local trout.[126] And the local Washoe may have traded pine nuts, obsidian, or baskets with nearby tribes for foodstuffs, or harvested other foods within the nearby mountain ranges. In 1876, for example, the *Chronicle* reported that a large group of Indians had gone over the mountains with a band of pack animals "after their Winter's supply of acorns," observing with amazement that "the squaws packed the heaviest loads."[127]

Relations between the native inhabitants and white settlers were not always harmonious. The local Washoe once inadvertently triggered local outrage by helping themselves to the cloth lining of Markleeville's Pioneer Mill building.[128] Indians were similarly blamed for burglarizing the Hammond & Musser Saloon and making off with a supply of wine and brandy.[129] And in the wake of a hostile confrontation between the Nevada cavalry and the Pi-Utes near Mud Lake, Nevada, Monitor residents organized a "committee of safety" to patrol the town perimeter and even sent out "skirmishers" to deter potential Indian incursions from Pine Nut Valley, although such fears would prove unfounded.[130]

Selling alcohol to Indians was considered a criminal offense in many parts of the West, and Alpine County was no exception. In 1889, the County Board of Supervisors directed the District Attorney to "use all lawful means to prevent the selling or giving of intoxicating liquors to Indians, and to spare no pains in

The Folger Brothers

Despite twelve years' difference in their ages, brothers Robert Macy Folger and Alexander C. Folger enjoyed a successful long-term partnership in the newspaper business. Both were born in New York (Robert in 1820 and Alex in 1832), into what may have been a family of Quakers.[140]

Catching the spirit of the times, Robert sailed west with the first rush of gold-seekers in 1849. After dabbling in a variety of unsuccessful business ventures in San Francisco and Sacramento, he moved to Markleeville in 1864. There he launched the *Alpine Chronicle*,[141] the first newspaper on the eastern slope of the Sierra, churning out a steady stream of weekly copies from his office on Montgomery Street "opposite the City Hall."[142]

A.C. Folger, courtesy Mono County Historical Society

Brother Alex apparently soon followed in his footsteps, and by 1866 had become the Markleeville postmaster.[143]

After the competing *Silver Mountain Bulletin* closed its doors in 1867, the *Chronicle* moved its operation to the new county seat of Silver Mountain, and Alex's name began appearing along with Robert's on the newspaper masthead.

For the next eleven years, the patient and unassuming Folger brothers would chronicle Silver Mountain life each week, earning a reputation for their staunch Union patriotism and dedication to "ethical journalism."[144] Physically, they were a Mutt-and-Jeff pair of opposites: "Bobby" a round, chunky figure known for man-handling the presses, and tall, lanky Alex, who brought a deft editing hand to the partnership.[145] Later observers would dub them the "long and the short of it."[146] Despite their physical differences, both were known for their "impeccable" manners and ultra-conservative dress, favoring "high, starched collars, frock coats, and striped trousers."[147]

searching out guilty parties; and to prosecute all guilty parties to the full extent of the law."[131]

Liquor evidently remained a thoroughly available commodity nonetheless. In 1875, the *Chronicle* reported that after an Indian had been "severely punished" for going on a "big drunk," he retaliated by shooting three cows.[132] Another news column reported a knife fight had broken out among Indians at Woodfords after "some scamp" sold them whiskey.[133] Such one-sided reporting was typical of the stereotypes of the day, and leaves readers to wonder how many intoxicated whites managed to escape similar editorial notice.

Perhaps the most racially-charged incident to hit the pages of local paper involved young James Stevens of Diamond Valley, who shot and killed a local Washoe man on the river about four miles below Markleeville.[134] Stevens suspected the Indian of stealing barley and swore that the Indian had shot at him first with an arrow, displaying "quite a wound" on his arm.[135] But other Indians asserted the victim was running away when Stevens pumped four pistol shots into him, and for several months tensions ran high. Rumors circulated that the Washoes and Piutes had joined forces and were plotting revenge against the whites at Woodfords,[136] and fears that an "Indian War" was brewing in Alpine County were picked up and reported as far away as Merced County.[137] Fortunately, local tensions eventually waned; it probably helped that young Stevens took the hint of his fellow citizens and moved away.[138] As late as 1878, however, fears of an Indian uprising were being stirred by rumors that the O.C. Wade family had been massacred on their journey to Oregon, and the local newspaper sternly admonished white citizens against selling either firearms or liquor to Indians.[139]

The *Chronicle* also offers a dusty window on the gender issues of the day. Social roles remained so tightly constrained during the 1860s and early '70s, for example, that even the length of a widow's veil was socially prescribed. Thus one intriguing news note reported that the "regulation widow's veil is now to be a yard and a half in length"[157] – a fashion norm

The brothers were unabashedly patriotic, given to lavish Fourth of July celebrations and known in later years for having the tallest flagpole around.[148] They also took a deep and abiding interest in local politics, although usually reserving their involvement to gentle but pointed remarks on their editorial pages. At one point, however, even the reserved R.M. went so far as to serve as secretary for the "Anti-Jail Meeting" protesting the contract for the expensive stone jail in 1867.[149]

Decrying what they felt was "wildcat" speculation in worthless mining stocks being promoted by other local papers,[150] the Folger brothers nonetheless dabbled themselves in local mining concerns. Alex served as Secretary/Treasurer of the Pennsylvania Gold & Silver Mining Company, for example, while brother R.M. owned stock and served as a director for the same company; similarly, Alex was Secretary for the Mountain Gold & Silver Mining Company, of which R.M. was a director.[151] R.M. served as the "attorney in fact" for the Globe Mine, filing for a mining patent in 1876.[152] And Alex (along with other Silver Mountain luminaries including Legget and McBeth) seems to have profited from a fast stock transaction in the fabled Buckeye No. One, acquiring the mine in early 1871 and re-selling it to Chalmers' London consortium just months later.[153]

R.M. briefly entertained political aspirations, running unsuccessfully for the California Assembly on the Union Party ticket. Quipped the competing *Bulletin* uncharitably: "His chances are four-fold greater in catching the Asiatic cholera than of receiving the nomination of that body."[154]

But as Silver Mountain's fortunes soured, even the stalwart Folgers began to waver. The final blow came in 1878, when the Board of Supervisors reneged on the *Chronicle*'s contract for printing legal notices.[155] Despite their long tenure as Silver Mountain boosters, the Folgers knew it was time to move on. By the end of that year, they had packed up their business – lock, stock and printing press – and moved to the new boomtown of Bodie. There, they launched the *Mono-Alpine Chronicle*, soon shortened to simply the *Bodie Chronicle*. Within a few years they moved again to the county seat of Bridgeport, eventually merging their new paper into the *Bridgeport Chronicle-Union*. By the time of his death in 1899, R.M. was recognized as "the oldest journalist on the Coast."[156] Brother Alex continued the family publishing business until his death about 1904.

For those whose imagination has been captured by Silver Mountain, the Folger brothers' legacy remains an unmatched treasure. In stories long and short, their aptly-named *Chronicle* leaves us a rich and enduring glimpse as the tale of Silver Mountain unfolded.

that even Silver Mountain widows were presumably anxious to emulate.

As wilder modes of dress began to emerge, the starched-shirt *Chronicle* tsk-tsked over the latest in women's attire, echoing admonishments that "[t]he tight waists, the low neck set dresses, and the high-heeled shoes are most flagrant abuses, and ought not to be longer tolerated. . . . The present fashion of leaving the neck and upper part of the chest bare, is fraught with evil consequences." Male finery like the stove-pipe hat, on the other hand, received a far more positive reception:

> *Absurd as the high, hard hat is, it does keep the head more comfortable [than low, soft hats], it does feel better, than any other form of head covering . . . . If they serve a good purpose in brushing cobwebs from the roofs of old garrets and stables, they also protect us from bad bumps, and keep our heads comfortable.*[158]

As the 1870s crept by, the pages of the local paper served as the backdrop for debates on such emotionally-charged topics as whether women should keep the dainty but precarious side-saddle, or venture boldly to "ride astride."[159] On this particular controversy, at least, the *Chronicle* editors took a distinctly *avant garde* view, commenting favorably on young ladies who recently had arrived in town on horseback, "like sensible

SIDE-SADDLE.

Dustman Collection.

girls, man-fashion at that!"[160] Other thought-provoking columns addressed such weighty matters as "Who Should Milk – Man or Woman?" – the editors gallantly concluding that the fairer sex should not be required to feed or milk cows.[161]

Aside from occasional mentions of women as the owners of hotels (generally of dubious distinction), the fairer sex was notably absent from most business endeavors at Silver Mountain. One happy exception was Reverend Ford's youngest daughter, Anna, who bent prevailing gender rules by working as a typesetter for the *Chronicle* editors – a far-from-mainstream occupation for a female of "not yet sweet 16" in 1872.[162] Another unusual

Dustman Collection.

Women's fashions like these "promenade costumes" from a ladies' magazine in 1876 were designed for anything but Silver Mountain's muddy roads. Although typically confined to riding side-saddle, some women were nevertheless adventurous horse-women, as the drawing to the right illustrates.

woman who briefly captured newspaper attention[163] was Eliza Withington, a widowed photographer who bundled her voluminous camera equipment over the mountains to Silver Mountain from Ione in the summer of 1876. Already suffering from throat cancer that would lead to her death just a few months later, Withington came to "take the waters" at the local hot spring and, while in town, captured some of the rare photographic views of Silver Mountain surviving today.

Divorce was extremely uncommon, although occasional Silver Mountain legal notices show it did occur. Louisa C. Brown sued Thomas Brown for divorce in 1872, for example, listing the grounds as "desertion."[164] Elizabeth Smith similarly commenced a divorce against husband J.B. Smith the same year, citing "cause[s] too numerous to mention."[165] Divorce law itself was considered an unseemly specialty for lawyers. One 1877 bill proposed that a separation known as "divorce from bed and board" be granted in cases of "extreme cruelty, habitual intemperance, desertion, neglect to provide and conviction of felony," but reserved "absolute" divorce only for cases of outright adultery.[166] The following year, to "suppress quackery in law," legislation was floated to create criminal penalties for those advertising "to procure a divorce with secrecy and dispatch."[167] Shortly thereafter, the Senate passed a bill making it a misdemeanor to "advertis[e] that divorces will be obtained in this state or out of it," the object of the legislation "being to reach divorce brokers and lawyers."[168]

With divorce so uncommon, the legal result of certain shenanigans could be downright humorous. One man who had "eloped with another man's wife" was arrested and sentenced to imprisonment at San Quentin. The criminal offense charged, however, was not adultery but rather larceny – for stealing the "wearing apparel" the woman had on.[169]

Women were still largely denied the right to vote. Although Wyoming granted suffrage rights to women in 1869, other states were hesitant about following suit. Traditionalists like Idaho's Rep. W.H. Van Slyke warned darkly that women's suffrage "would work an entire social revolution, disrupting the family tie and bringing on a conflict of sexes in the land."[170] Others, however, began to urge a more egalitarian view of the female partners who had slogged across the plains beside their menfolk. A few progressive thinkers argued that extending voting rights might be a way to encourage immigration by the fairer sex to outpost territories that remained heavily male-dominated. But opponents similarly pointed to migration as a reason to oppose female suffrage: "Nobody has gone to Washington territory because women are permitted to vote there," tartly admonished the *Idaho Statesman* newspaper.

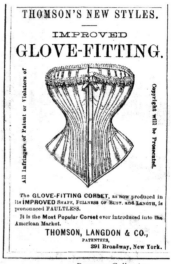

THOMSON'S NEW STYLES.

IMPROVED

GLOVE-FITTING.

The GLOVE-FITTING CORSET, as now produced in its IMPROVED SHAPE, FULLNESS OF BUST, and LENGTH, is pronounced FAULTLESS.

It is the Most Popular Corset ever introduced into the American Market.

THOMSON, LANGDON & CO.,
PATENTEES,
391 Broadway, New York.

Dustman Collection.

Women's fashions required constricting undergarments like this corset from 1870.

In California, the election laws provided three simple requirements: a voter had to be male; a citizen; and not an "idiot or insane."[171] Thus when nine "strong-minded women" applied to the county clerk at San Francisco to register to vote in 1871, the clerk merely "politely declined their application."[172] On the issue of women's suffrage, Silver Mountain appeared ahead of its time. As early as 1867, the *Bulletin* reprinted an enthusiastic pro-suffrage column:

> *When women vote, the death penalty will be abolished, except for rape; the inmates of those houses which are now the hotbeds of evil, will be sent to Houses of Correction, and there kept for life or years, doing light fancy work and domestic labor. All the legalized haunts of crime, which stand as rivals to virtuous homes, will at last have a struggle for life. Women will not work for half pay, and vice will not furnish her with the most profitable employment; and all parties will grow better and wiser, or the principle of self-government is founded in error.[173]*

The other great issue of the day championed by forward-thinking women was the temperance movement. In California, the evils of "social drinking" attracted early legislative attention to restrict if not halt its practice. One 1878 state Assembly bill, for example, proposed barring saloonkeepers "from receiving more than the price of one drink [from] any one at any one time, nor oftener than once in two hours."[174]

The temperance movement put in a brief but fleeting appearance at Silver Mountain. A meeting at the Silver Mountain School House was announced in 1876, "for the purpose of forming a temperance society."[175] The effort, however, was apparently short-lived; no further mention of the incipient temperance league survives. But the ill effects of strong drink certainly did not go unnoticed in Alpine County.

Woodfords in particular was noted for its hard-drinking excesses. The *Chronicle* printed one tart letter from a reader signed 'Rural' expressing his opinion that Woodfords was sorely "in need of a calaboose, or less Boca beer and fighting whisk[e]y."[176]

For a woman stepping off a horse, wagon, or stagecoach into the streets of Silver Mountain for the first time, the burgeoning metropolis must have seemed like a promising rainbow. But the dream would soon give way to the harsh realities of mining town life. Dirt-encrusted miner's clothes and hems dragging muddy streets would translate into endless hours at a washboard. More prosperous housewives might make do with countless trips to the Chinese laundryman down the street; for the wife of an unlucky miner, however, "blue Monday" earned its name each week in a miserable ordeal of boiling, scrubbing, rinsing and wringing out piles of filthy garments.[177]

Under the best of conditions, cooking required stoking a fire in a cast iron cookstove. At worst, it meant smoke-filled biscuits and smoke-filled clothes from hovering over an open hearth. And sub-zero winters brought months of chipping wood out of a frozen pile just to heat coffee for breakfast. Foodstuffs were readily available from vendors' wagons and Main Street shops, though they cost dearly. But the short, high-elevation growing season offered little alternative. Silver Mountain women depended on the root cellars beneath their cabins to keep produce fresh, and food storage was an art. Hand-dug and stone-lined, the root cellar had to be small and sturdy enough to support the house above, yet deep enough to maintain cool temperatures in summer. During winter months, staples like potatoes and onions might be packed in straw to prevent freezing. But even with such careful attention, humans were lucky to get them for dinner before mice and other rodents did.

The latest in washing innovations, circa 1870-72.

Spring brought a welcome change in both temperature and diet. By late summer, local gooseberries and elderberries would have found their way into homemade pies. Chickens furnished not only fresh eggs but the occasional Sunday dinner. The town's meat markets also assured a steady supply of fresh mutton, beef, and pork. In the fall, meat and fish would be salted or smoked to preserve it for the months ahead, while in the winter tinned oysters and canned fruit became necessities. Little wonder, then, that many households simply packed up and left town each October or November, returning the following spring.

As their men-folk searched for the fabled Silver Mountain lodes, the women too must have reached for their own version of heaven, coupling hard work with imagination to create a safe and comfortable life at home. They tended sick children and trimmed lucine lantern wicks; gossiped while hauling water from the town's public wells; and swept humble wooden floors. Their walls may have been rough-hewn, the chairs crudely homemade. But hand-stitched curtains would have fluttered at their windows, while wild lupine and penstemon brightened the dinner table.

Silver Mountain was a far cry from the high life at San Francisco or the frills and finery of Virginia City. But it was, for a time, home.

Dustman Collection.

CHAPTER 8:
TIPPING THE SCALES OF JUSTICE

Law and order was far more aspiration than actuality in early mining camps like Silver Mountain. As the *Silver Mountain Chronicle* reported, even the citizens of far-more-civilized Carson City found themselves battling violence, vandals, and vagrants:

> *Our neighbors of Carson City are trying the virtue of martial law, thus endeavoring to repress the acts of numerous incendiary characters in her midst who within the past few days have fired the town in several places. The measured tread of the patrol is heard day and night in her streets, and no one stirs within or without unless by permission of the military authorities. 'Al. Clayton' is said to have made a very inflammatory speech there on Monday night.*[1]

Law breakers were plentiful in Alpine County, too. An abundance of saloons kept strong drink flowing freely, a recipe for mayhem that did not keep even saloon-keepers mellow. Silver Mountain barkeeper Thomas Ogden, for example, found himself facing criminal charges after a scuffle with one George Cameron. The spat began with Ogden accusing Cameron of pilfering his watch and during the ensuing melee, Ogden bit Cameron savagely on the fingers. Ogden claimed self-defense, protesting that his bite was necessary "to save himself from having his eyes gouged out." The jury didn't buy the excuse, however, finding Ogden guilty of battery.[2]

The abundance of local firearms and firebrands did not deter at least one would-be burglar, who stole away in the night with George Lowe's gold watch and Colt revolver. Fortunately for Lowe, the culprit, Edward Casey, was soon 'nailed' by "the singularity of a track made by a boot nailed on the bottoms in a peculiar manner." Whether Casey ever stood trial on the charges is unclear; after posting $500 in gold coin for his bond, the accused swiftly "departed for the territory."[3]

Magistrates also tried the occasional cattle-rustler; when six hides bearing another man's brand showed up in the possession of butcher Louis Gullickson, both Gullickson and the seller were promptly arrested.[4] Other local crime involved what today would be called simple vagrancy or trespass. From time to time the newspaper would blaze with warnings of escaped convicts or other strangers abroad in Alpine County, poised to pilfer local homes and ranches.[5] One such visitor found "prowling about" was hauled before Judge Goff to be "examined" in chambers. Finding the intruder to be "more of a vagrant than an insane man," the judge sternly admonished that "unless he left the county immediately he would be arrested as a vagrant."[6] Reported the newspaper with evident satisfaction: the man "left immediately."

Murder Most Foul

While murders were rare, Alpine did occasionally find itself the scene of an outright killing. As early as 1863, Markleeville founder Jacob Marklee lost his life to the business end a pistol,[7] and the following year, businessman M. Peltier got his throat slit during a row with his business partner.[8] But because Alpine County was not officially in existence until August, 1864, its "first" real murder wasn't logged for another six years.

The victim bearing that dubious honor was teamster James M. Brown, fatally shot on the Big Trees Road in Hermit Valley on a quiet Saturday afternoon in September, 1870.[9] Brown, age 51, had been headed for Stockton with a 10-horse team to pick up a load of goods. His body was discovered lying a few hundred yards from his wagon, arms outstretched, with one hand resting in the wagon track.

Brown's body was removed to a nearby house for an inquest. Two different size slugs were dug out of the corpse, leading the coroner's jury to conclude that Brown had been shot with a pistol from the front and a rifle in the back. Harvey Cummings, the 13-year-old lad who found the body, claimed to have spotted a mysterious heavy-set man with "black whiskers" in the vicinity just before the killing. As for motive, the quick consensus was robbery: Brown had been known to carry "plenty of money," yet no cash was found with the body and his bedroll showed signs of being rifled.

Details of the murder and its investigation dominated the *Chronicle*'s pages for weeks.[10] Not to be outdone, a rival newspaper reported that a Monitor detective had been sent to investigate. Even California's Governor Haight posted a $300 reward.[11] Brown's son-in-law William Kent upped the ante, offering his own $700 reward for arrest of the killer. Almost a year later, the cold-blooded crime continued to generate news, or at least rumors. "It has been divulged that the murderer of J.M. Brown on the Big Trees Road last Fall, is a young Indian named 'Yellow Jacket,'" asserted the *Chronicle* the following June. "He should be hunted down and brought to trial."[12] Despite such leads, however, no suspect was ever arrested.

Just a month after Brown's killing, another "foul murder" hit local newspaper pages – this time, a death in nearby Douglas County.[13] Hiram Thornton, about 25, was found shot in the head "one half mile from the house of Mrs. Tim Smith on East Carson River." Authorities suspected Thornton had fallen victim to former business partners desiring to help themselves to the proceeds in his pockets from a recent cattle sale. Dispensing with such legal niceties as an extradition hearing, Sheriff McBeth swooped up suspect David Graham at Markleeville and nabbed Brigham Owens at a ranch between Markleeville and Woodfords, casually handing both over the state line to the Douglas County authorities. Owens, found with an incriminating $192 in his pockets, was promptly tagged as the primary suspect.

But perhaps the most sensational crime to stun the young county took place at Silver Mountain in 1872. Devilishly handsome thirty-nine year old Erik Errickson was a prominent man-about-town, operating his eponymous Errickson's Saloon next door to Ford's Alpine House Hotel. On the evening of December 17, 1872, Errickson was engaged in a game of cards inside his own saloon when he was shot through the front window, falling forward dead over his hand.

There was no question about who had committed the crime, or why. The shooter was Ernst Reusch, a jilted husband and the losing third of an ill-fated love triangle. A newcomer to town and originally a native of Denmark, Reusch had married young Emily Bergendahl just four months before the shooting.[14] But wedded bliss was not to be his fate. Reusch soon discovered that his bride had not relinquished her previous romantic ties with Errickson. As the local paper expressed it, Errickson not only stole away Reusch's wife but "forbid him the house, threatened his life, and continually abused him."[15]

Without a home of his own any longer, Reusch took rooms at Mrs. Brown's boarding house. Posting a brief, sad legal notice in the *Chronicle*, he declared himself no longer responsible for his wife's debts, "she having left my bed and board without just cause or provocation."[16]

Meanwhile, ignoring town scandal-mongers, the illicit couple continued to keep house together. To avoid prying eyes they hung a curtain over the front window, which only infuriated the jilted husband more. Finally, one cold December night Reusch loaded a borrowed shotgun with buckshot, toted it down Main Street, took deliberate aim at Errickson through the window, and pulled the trigger.[17] With equal *sang froid* Reusch entered the saloon to inspect his victim, then walked next door to the Alpine House and surrendered himself to Undersheriff Dunlap.

Courtesy Alpine County Historical Society

Handsome Erik Errickson had a twinkle in his blue eyes and an eye for the ladies.

Townsfolk were, on the whole, rather sympathetic to Reusch. As the newspaper put it, "[t]his result was not unexpected by our citizens, as the wife of Reusch had been living with Errickson for the past three months."[18] But community sympathy waned as the county's expense for the criminal proceedings mounted. A motion to change the venue of Reusch's case was granted, requiring that the matter be transferred to Mono County for trial – a financial liability that promised to exhaust Alpine's already-strained treasury.

And so an odd series of events began to unfold.

At 3 p.m. on April 17, 1874, Undersheriff James Davidson left Silver Mountain by wagon with the prisoner Reusch – an unusual time at best to commence such a journey.[19] The entourage also included an unusually large crowd to guard a single prisoner, with the four-horse wagon carrying a total of fifteen men.

The party stopped for dinner at Markleeville, a meal that would prove to be Reusch's last, then took to the road again around 8 p.m.. Night had long since fallen and with only a lantern to light the way, progress along the dirt road would have been slow. As the wagon approached the toll road bridge, a group of mysterious men suddenly materialized from the gloom. Undersheriff James Davidson later recounted at the inquest:

NEW TO-DAY.

NOTICE.

NOTICE IS HEREBY GIVEN THAT I will not be responsible for any debts contracted by my wife, Emily Reusch, she having left my bed and board without just cause or provocation.
ERNST REUSCH.
Silver Mountain, October 4th, 1872.

Reusch posted this sad notice in the Alpine Chronicle disclaiming responsibility for Emily's debts just two months after his wedding.

> *There we were stopped by several masked men who levelled their weapons on us, and demanded the prisoner, near 10 o'clock p.m.. They then took E. Reusch. I could not tell what the weapons were, the night was dark. After they demanded the prisoner I told them to hold on, gents, to give a man a fair trial, and that we were taking him out to where I thought he could get one.*
>
> *The spokesman of the party, I do not know who, said I will give him 10 minutes to make a confession. Just then another one of the party said[,] there he is in the middle. One of them reached for him from the ground . . . . Then Reusch got up and says, 'if I must go I will go.' Reusch then jumped down from the wagon, they then took hold of him and told us to drive on, which order we obeyed.*[20]

A rope was looped over a stanchion of the bridge and tied around Reusch's neck. But in their haste, the would-be hangmen apparently neglected to test the strength of their rope – or to measure the distance to the river. When Davidson's party returned to the scene hours later, they discovered a two-foot length of snapped-off rope still tied near the west end of the bridge. After a brief search, Reusch's body was located some 30 feet away downstream. Rumors remain to this day that Reusch survived the initial fall and had to be dispatched with a stone to the head – a result consistent with the inquest's finding that he was "bruised around the head."

Hangman's Bridge, where Reusch met his fate with a rope – and perhaps a well-aimed rock.

Courtesy Alpine County Historical Society

Joseph Mitchell, a woodchopper from Silver Mountain present during the incident, was closely questioned by Justice of the Peace J.C. Musser about an off-hand statement:

What did you mean by the remark made by you last night, in reference to the deceased ("that here he is, just as we left him")?

[Mitchell]:   Somebody said he looked natural, and I think I made the remark, here he is, just as natural as we left him, or something to that effect.[21]

The conclusion of the coroner's inquest was both brief and unsurprising: the cause of death was strangulation, "caused by parties unknown to this Jury."[22] The masked men were never captured or identified. The old wooden bridge has long since been replaced by a modern one made of concrete, but the site remains known even today as Hangman's Bridge.

Dustman Collection

J.W. Towle was the Alpine County Clerk who filed in the Inquest on the death of Reusch in April, 1874. Soon thereafter he moved to Bridgeport, where he was elected county clerk in 1875. This photo shows him running for reelection as incumbent Mono County Treasurer in 1914.

Sheriff Sagas

A resident of Pleasant Valley, James Krumm won the post of first Sheriff/Tax Collector in Alpine County's original 1864 election against competitor D.N. McBeth.[23] Krumm's tenure as an elected official, however, would also prove to be one of the county's shortest.

Krumm carried himself with aplomb, and was described as a "large, powerful, fine-looking gentleman." A stranger once exclaimed upon seeing him: "My God! If he is only a crumb, I would like to see the whole loaf!"[24] Almost immediately following the election, however, whiffs of scandal began to circulate. Inventory came up missing in a Markleeville drug store at which Krumm had placed a constable as "keeper,"[25] and within six weeks after the election, Krumm "defaulted" on his post. As the newspaper put it, "the people had lost confidence as to his honesty as a public officer; he was spending too much money, for a poor man."[26] Sheriff Krumm reportedly left Sacramento transporting a prisoner accused of stealing horses in Alpine, but made the return journey only as far as Strawberry Valley, and was never seen again.[27]

D.N. McBeth may have lost the first election but he soon succeeded to Krumm's post, serving as Alpine's Sheriff from about 1866 to 1871. Just twenty-four years old when he assumed the title of sheriff, "Mac" (as he was popularly known) was a pioneer resident of the pioneering mining county. As early as 1863 he had been linked with mining interests in the Monitor District,[28] and by 1864 owned a house and four lots in the boomtown of Monitor.[29]

By 1865 McBeth moved his abode to Silver Mountain, where local people-watchers evidently took great interest in his affairs. His heroic 36-hour journey on skis to marry Amanda Kittridge in Woodfords[30] provided romantic fodder for several issues of the local press, and even his fondness for horse racing made the news. (His steed was colorfully named "Chrome Yellow."[31]) Mac managed to make news occasionally in a less-happy way as well. Once it was reported that he had missed his footing and tumbled several hundred feet down a canyon, dislocating his shoulder. But luckily for the intrepid sheriff, companion Charles Fisk managed to "convey[ ] him on a hand-sled to the office of Dr. J.S. Adams, who replaced the shoulder. . . ."[32]

Mac's new family also became fair game for the local press. In one escapade, friends of his two-year-old daughter Nettie applied axle grease to the toddler's hair while playing "going to the ball," a pomade which the toddler promptly enhanced by rolling in the dusty street. The baby's mother, discovering to her horror that the grease resisted all efforts to wash it out called in a local doctor, who prescribed liberal applications of coal oil, after which the baby was thoroughly "soused . . . into a tub of warm water."[33]

Tragedy struck Mac's household in 1869, when infant son John died at not quite four months of age.[34] But following year, the newspaper carried the happy news that Sheriff McBeth "has a new deputy" – another son born at Silver Mountain.[35]

A restless spirit by nature, McBeth dabbled in a wide number of business ventures. He kept a hand in mining stocks, purchasing a part-interest in the "Sam Brannan" claim (a southerly extension of the Adolphus) in October, 1870, then re-selling his share to a British syndicate in February, 1871.[36] Even during his tenure as sheriff, McBeth brought a band of horses over the Big Trees Road to sell.[37] And the following year found him busy grading a lot in Monitor on which to construct a new hotel,[38] soon advertising himself as the proprietor of the "National Hotel."[39]

Perhaps as a result of his business aspirations, McBeth withdrew his candidacy for re-election as Sheriff in 1871.[40] The newspaper was less than kindly at first, chiding McBeth for having "removed from the County seat, and . . . fail[ing] to keep his office open, according to law."[41] A month later, however, the editors did an about-face, asserting that McBeth had "honestly and faithfully" performed his duties during his six years as sheriff.[42]

By the time of the Reusch inquest in 1874, McBeth listed his occupation simply as "Hotel Keeper."[43] But his fortunes apparently plummeted after his move to Monitor. He became embroiled in a number of lawsuits[44] and Chalmers described McBeth's financial circumstances as "embarrassed," noting that creditors were garnishing McBeth's assets.[45] By December, 1876, Wells Fargo was attempting to sell McBeth's interests in the Esmeralda Lode and several lots in Monitor to satisfy a judgment of $792.[46]

McBeth and his family joined the hordes moving to Bodie in 1878, even disassembling his hotel building and taking it with them.[47] At Bodie he tried his hand at mining again, working for the Standard Mine and garnering a broken arm for his trouble.[48] By 1880, McBeth was back in Monitor and, according to Chalmers, once again "hard up." Added Chalmers uncharitably: "money will make him say anything, I think."[49]

Mac surfaced again in the news of 1885 as he ventured to San Francisco for surgery to correct his old arm injury. He was accompanied on this journey by his now-17-year-old daughter Nettie, who planned to attend the University of the Pacific at San Jose.[50] San Francisco weather must have agreed with McBeth, as he was still residing there at the time of the 1900 census, along with wife Amanda, daughter Nettie (a spinster of 31), and 29-year-old son Frank.

Scams & Scandals

Early Alpine County saw scams enough of the stock-swindling variety. Mining riches were frequently overrated and seams likely at least occasionally salted. But local scams weren't limited strictly to mining shenanigans. The pages of the *Chronicle* carried frequent advertisements for financial opportunities such as a "grand gift concert in aid of the Mercantile Library Association of San Francisco" – essentially lotteries of the most dubious sort. Tickets for such enterprises could run a pricey $5 in gold coin for a purported chance of winning a top prize of $100,000, although a cautious modern reader might notice that such "gifts" were to be paid out only after payment of unspecified "expenses," with any balance to be applied to the "debt" of the Mercantile Library Association.

But such ads were enough to make readers – and editors – salivate. "Nearly all of the Mercantile Lottery tickets have been sold," one column noted gleefully. "It is rumored that another one will be gotten up soon after this one is drawn." The following week the editor added coyly: "We have a special agent in San Francisco to receive the $100,000 for us."[51]

But as the drawing date approached for the eagerly-awaited "gift concert," ticket holders found a further newspaper ad announcing that "the concert is postponed,"[52] and explaining: "Unexpected interferences have operated to make this delay necessary to accomplish the result of freeing the Library from debt. . . . This is positively the only postponement which will be made." And once the grand drawing finally was completed the *Chronicle* noted glumly: "Alpine invested about $1,500 in that enterprise," but mysteriously "not one dollar has been drawn on a ticket held in this county."[53]

The Library scheme wasn't the only boondoggle of its kind. Some 50,000 "season tickets" of $2.50 each "in aid of the Nevada School District, Nevada City, California" similarly were advertised, with a chance to win prizes ranging from $100 to $10,000.[54] And new variations on the theme began appearing almost weekly in Alpine's local paper. A group calling itself the "California Land Association of the City of Oakland" offered prizes ranging from a "grand hotel" or "elegant villa cottage" to "fine building lots" in San Francisco and Oakland.[55] Music and charity became popular themes for these offerings. A "Grand Gift Concert" was touted by the felicitously-named Sacramento Pioneer & Library Association. Likewise, a Fireman's Hall in Folsom offered its own Grand Gift Concert, while a dubious Calaveras County Relief Association hosted a Grand Music Festival proclaiming $250,000 in gold "gifts." The "Cosmopolitan Benevolent Society of Nevada City" was apparently so popular that it followed up its January, 1871 drawing with notice of a second drawing in June, urging readers to spring $2.50 a ticket for a chance at "all gold coin prizes." Another Grand Festival touting itself as a "Legal Enterprise!" was promoted by an Academy of Music ostensibly located in Omaha, Nebraska. Gushed the *Chronicle*: "delays are dangerous"![56]

But by February, 1871, even the positive-thinking editors of the *Chronicle* were permitting themselves a note of mild complaint. "Alpine county invested about $600 in the Nevada lottery scheme," they observed, "and up to this time we have not learned that it has drawn even a pair of ladies' drawers." Apparently recognizing that advertising revenue was a sure thing even when "gift concerts" were not, however, the editors

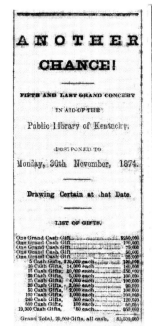

This ad for a Grand Concert purporting to benefit the "Public Library of Kentucky" promised millions in prizes – although advising that the drawing had been postponed.

The lovely "Cleoptra" necklace advertised in 1878 was likely another scam, promising an astronomical $10.00 a day for ladies "out of employment who wish to engage in a pleasant and good paying business."

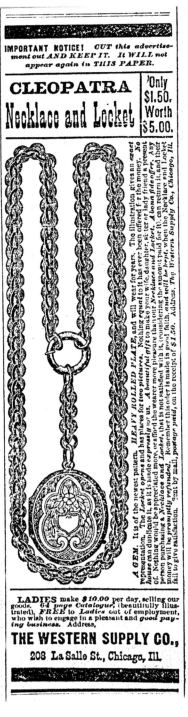

were quick to voice complete confidence in their latest advertiser, the "Sacramento Gift Enterprise," adding: "We are satisfied that everything will be conducted honorably."[57]

Yet another form of newspaper swindle were ads for "gold watches." Purchasers following directions to tender the sum of $3.50 by mail would receive in reply a request for yet another $1.50, but no watch (gold or otherwise) would ever manage to make its appearance.[58]

Scandals were plentiful in Alpine government, too, if somewhat less overt. Among Alpine's idiosyncrasies, one person often held multiple public offices at once, the concept of conflict of interest being lost on the office-holders. As one newspaper item observed:

> Probably there is no other county in the United States where county officials establish laws and precedents to suit themselves. The District Attorney appoints the County Judge [as] Deputy District Attorney, and the County Clerk appoints the County Treasurer [as] Deputy County Clerk. . . .[59]

Outright public scandals, too, erupted from time to time. One of the most costly to the County finances involved Thomas W. Legget, a Scotsman initially elected to the post of deputy treasurer in 1868[60] who moved up to county treasurer in 1870.[61] By 1873, Legget had managed to snag the plum post of County Recorder as well. Legget had been active in local mining ventures since 1863,[62] and proceeded to use his job as Recorder to his own advantage by simply refusing to record documents adverse to his own interests.[63]

Complaints were soon circulating that the county's accounting records were "not correct,"[64] and locals groused that the Treasurer himself had been "absent from the county."[65] Despite these allegations, Legget managed to win re-election as County Treasurer in September, 1875.[66]

THOMAS W. LEGGET,

NOTARY PUBLIC,

SILVER MOUNTAIN.

DEEDS, MORTGAGES, ETC., drawn.

☞ OFFICE.— *Treasurer's Office.*   d36-tf

Legget thought nothing of drawing up legal documents for private clients using his official Treasurer's Office in Silver Mountain – and even advertised his services in the local Chronicle, as shown in this 1873 ad.

When election time came around for the post of County Recorder two years later, R.H. Ford handily won the vote. But Legget (perhaps knowing all too well what the official documents would show) simply refused to turn over the official Recorder's books and records to Ford, making it impossible for a time for investors to obtain abstracts of mining titles.[67]

The Board of Supervisors conducted an investigation into the treasurer's accounts, suspending Legget from office "pending trial."[68] As had long been suspected, things were not quite on the up-and-up with the County's books. Chalmers, a fellow Scotsman, would later confess that to having routinely written checks to Legget that were never intended to be cashed, to help Legget balance his books: "he being short of cash on counting day."[69]

A criminal case was filed against Legget, claiming that he had embezzled some $4,392 from county funds.[70] Legget nevertheless managed to escape any actual punishment, albeit by the most extreme of measures: he passed away on January 15, 1878, after what was reportedly a brief illness.[71] But the furor over his records would continue for years to come.[72]

Legget was hardly unique among his fellow public servants. Calls to examine the Alpine supervisors' books had been voiced as early as 1866,[73] and tongues wagged that the "Devil himself couldn't make head or tail of the District Attorney's books, from 1864 to 1872."[74] As the Folger brothers frankly put it, "County affairs, with very few exceptions, have been slovenly conducted."[75] In one of their longest diatribes, they offered a litany of the County's more reprehensible political practices:

> [W]e doubt if there is another county in the State where the rights of the people have been more outraged and the laws governing officers treated as a nullity, and business slovenly performed than in Alpine County.
>
> The first Board of Supervisors, by the removal of one of its members to the county seat, within a month after his election, was able to hold sessions at a moment's notice and it was almost daily transacting business and plunging the county in debt; as there was only two of them they brooked no interference from outsiders, but would rid themselves of all such by one of them going out and staying so long that the other one went out to hunt him up; in a few minutes back came the first one and after waiting a short time would go out to ascertain where the second one was and so in turn they kept it going until the intruder was tired out. . . . The next Board, one of the two retiring, finding about $1,400 in the Hospital Fund conceived the brilliant idea of building a jail; one of them being a carpenter and another a blacksmith, and another official owning an old boiler, it was too good a thing to let slip, and, against the protest of the taxpayers and District Attorney, it was erected and the county involved in a further debt of $7,000. . . . The next Board lacked the backbone to resist the persistent appeals of the sheriff for an allowance of $30 per month for the jailor's fees – for an empty jail. . . .
>
> For six years, we had a District Attorney who was noted for making everybody pay taxes, except himself and [his] deputy. [76]

One letter to the newspaper signed simply "Taxpayer" decried the apparently common practice of selling one's elected office to the highest bidder:

> I undertake to say that such a state of affairs as has been exhibited in our county is entirely unknown in the annals of California. . . . [t]here have been officers going in and out of office every two years at least, and in some instance – by bargain and sale – oftener. . . .[77]

The high turnover in elected officials became something of a rallying cry for the high-minded editors of the *Chronicle*. As one September election approached, they urged residents to "vote for no man who has no permanent interests in the county" to avoid such insidious profiteering: "Let it be remembered," they admonished readers, "that within the past two years, three of our county officials sold their offices and took French-leave of their constitutents!"[78]

Procuring public office by "bargain and sale" apparently became so prevalent that even one local judge may have lent a hand in arranging one such transaction. Charged the outraged *Chronicle*:

> County Judge Goff acted as broker in the purchase of the Clerkship and not only sold the office for the present term, but the next also.[79]

It was not simply rough justice, but frontier justice: the best that money could buy.

Alpine's Pioneer Judges

Little remains recorded about Alpine's first county judge aside from his winsome name: Sextus Shearer. Born in Massachusetts in 1802, Shearer owned mining interests in Alpine County as early as 1864, and he was selected as the local county judge that same year, when the county was formed.

As a county judge, Shearer would have heard all criminal cases "short of murder and treason"; civil disputes involving more than $500 in value; and a wide assortment of other cases including bankruptcies, landlord-tenant disputes, probate matters, and naturalization cases. County judges also acted as a court of appeals for decisions of the local justices of the peace. But oddly enough there was "no appeal from the County Court in civil cases – in that respect [the judge] is a little autocrat," as one later judge would observe.[80]

Shearer's most lasting legacy was a ruling issued not from the bench at all but rather from the bully pulpit of the local newspaper pages. In a letter to the editor dated August 22, 1864, Shearer shared his persuasive view that the operative date on which Alpine County had been officially "formed" was not August 1, as some citizens apparently believed, but rather August 11, 1864, the date when the County officers had been elected.[81]

Shearer's term as county judge proved extremely short. Stiff competition quickly emerged for his post, and during the election season of 1865 at least seven candidates crowded the field.[82] In the elbowing that followed, Shearer found himself elbowed out, with newcomer Henry Eno making off with the prize.

Shearer, it seems, lost faith in Alpine County as quickly as it lost faith in him. He apparently retained his Alpine mining interests for a time, continuing to serve as president of the Mountain Gold & Silver Mining Company through 1866.[83] But by August, 1867, Shearer had moved to Oakland, where he served as a "Police Justice."[84] By that December, he was listed among the delinquent shareholders in the Mountain Company, owing $200 in unpaid assessments on his 50 shares.[85]

Dustman Collection

Sextus Shearer's son (Sextus Shearer, Jr.), in 1865. The junior Shearer was born October 14, 1865 in Buffalo, New York, and attended Yale University, where he befriended classmate and poet Edward Roland Sill. Traveling with Sill, he left New York in 1861 for San Francisco, where he worked in a law office (perhaps his father's). Shearer, Jr. returned to New England in 1866, briefly attending Divinity School at Cambridge, Massachusetts, but returned to California for health reasons in 1868, and died of tuberculosis on March 5, 1869 at San Diego. An obituary praised his "rare talents, kindness of heart, and devotion to high purposes."

Shearer continued to serve as a Justice of the Peace in Oakland well into his seventies, with an 1880-81 city directory listing his offices at 476 - 8th Street and a residence on Filbert Street. Still feisty despite his advanced years, Shearer sued the City of Oakland over a salary dispute, a tiff that ended in a California Supreme Court ruling in his favor in 1885. Shearer passed away in March, 1888 at the age of 86, and is buried at Oakland's Mountain View Cemetery.

Shearer's successor to the post of Alpine County judge, Henry Eno, was a reluctant lawyer. "I don't like my profession, never did," he once confessed, "and won't practice when I can do anything else as profitable. It comes in play . . . as a [last] resort."[86] Left to his own devices Eno would have much preferred the life of a simple farmer, but deemed himself "too poor" to become a successful one.[87]

Born in New York State and already on the grey-haired side of 50 by the time the Forty-Niners began their rush to California, Eno eyed the mining boom through a purely practical lens: as a golden opportunity for political office or at least abundant legal work litigating land titles. "I may be the lawyer, I may be an office holder, or I may be the merchant," he wrote as he contemplated the move, "and if worse comes to worse I may be obliged to work for a living."[88]

By October, 1851, Eno and wife Elizabeth had settled into a little canvas-covered home in the boomtown of Mokelumne Hill.[89] Eno ran for and won a Calaveras County judgeship in 1852, then entered – and lost – the political race for Lieutenant Governor in 1853.[90] He tried his hand at business, serving as president of the Mokolumne Canal Company, a large-scale scheme he hoped would bring water to the town to work the rich gravels – and not incidentally rich profits for himself.[91]

Then, sometime after 1857, both Eno's wife Elizabeth and their daughter "little Carrie" succumbed to an unknown illness. Eno lost himself in an alcohol-fueled haze, eventually winding up in a hospital in Sacramento County in 1865.[92]

But Eno's motto was *nil desperandum*: never despair.[93] Having befriended publisher Robert Folger, Eno followed Folger to Markleeville in the spring of 1865, intending to eke out a living as an editor for the tiny mining newspaper. And by June, he had set his sights on running for Alpine County judge.[94]

Eno submitted his name for the post at the July 3, 1865 Union Party convention, but was passed over for the party's nomination. Refusing to accept defeat, Eno spun the rebuff to his benefit, contending that "[t]here was such a bargaining and selling of votes, such a trading of offices, that I would not submit to [the convention's] decision."[95] Eno proceeded to take his case directly to the public, holding a "mass meeting" to endorse his candidacy, and eventually won the judgeship.

Eno was similarly a renegade as a judge, refusing to bow to such fundamental legal concepts as precedent. "I make it a rule to decide all cases according to my ideas of right and wrong," he wrote, "and not according to the ideas of any of our Supreme Judges – for whom I don't have much respect. I make the law bend to equity, not equity bend to [the] law."[96]

Nearly 68 years old by the time of his election as judge in Alpine County, Eno confessed in letters home that the twelve-mile walk from Markleeville to the county seat of Silver Mountain "tires me, and to come back the same day to save the expense of staying over night fatigues me." But he refused to openly acknowledge either his age or limitations, noting: "They all believe I am about sixty, and I don't deny it. To be old in such a new country is a great sin, and I am trying to be considered one of the righteous."[97]

Perhaps to save himself the lengthy walk, Eno moved his quarters from Markleeville to the new county seat of Silver Mountain shortly after his election. There he led a frugal existence, sharing rooms with a mining superintendent. In his letters, he describes his strict economy:

> *You will ask how I live? Well I board myself, rent a house, cook for myself. Buy no clothes, wear my old ones, and all I have would not bring a dollar and a half at a paper mill. . . washing 25 cents per shirt and $4 per week pays my board. . . . I make it a rule to get out of bed when I wake up, let it be what time of night or morning it is, make my fire, wash, bake some corn bread or biscuit from graham flour, each costing here more than superfine flour. . . . Cook some potatoes – my corn bread, beef or bacon with good butter costing only 75 cents per lb. and some dried apples cooked, with a good cup of tea (no coffee) makes me a first rate breakfast. Once in a while a grouse [bought] of an Indian for fifty cents and occasionally some speckled trout costing only the fun of catching them makes the variety.*[98]

The most significant legal issue Eno addressed while on the bench involved the county's right to impose a tax on logs being floated down the Carson River – a tax which the State Legislature itself had authorized and the impoverished County was intent on collecting, but which Eno was equally adamant imposed an unconstitutional burden on interstate commerce.

The State Legislature expressly authorized such a toll on cordwood about 1865,[99] an invitation that the Alpine County's supervisors avidly took up. The toll was a hefty $1.00 fee for every 1,000 feet of "saw

logs" or 75 cents per cord for any other wood, with the tax collector himself permitted to retain ten percent as his salary.[100] Woodcutters also were required to pay for a county "license" before cutting any timber destined for dispatch down the Carson River.[101]

Wood drives provided an important source of income – for both woodchoppers and the county.

Timber was big business in Alpine County. During a single wood drive, some six million board-feet of logs might make their way along Alpine rivers to Empire, Nevada, with up to six separate wood drives occurring per year.[102] Thus for the revenue-starved new county, the cordwood tax represented an important source of income: more than $4,500 in wood taxes in 1866 alone.[103]

Not surprisingly, lumbermen vociferously opposed the tax. A flurry of lawsuits were filed in the Spring of 1866 attacking the constitutionality of the wood bill.[104] Judge Eno issued injunction after injunction restraining the Alpine tax collector from collecting the tax, holding that the levy was unconstitutional because the wood was being floated from California into Nevada and thus represented a form of interstate commerce.[105] The Folger brothers, too, repeatedly editorialized against the tax, pointing out that "everybody receives a portion of the woodchopper's dollar" and underscoring the potential liability to the county if the "Carson Wood Bill" were found invalid.[106] District Court Judge Theron Reed, however, took the opposite view, repeatedly dissolving Eno's injunctions and ruling for the tax-starved County – on at least one occasion, without even bothering with a hearing.[107]

In the end, Judge Eno's legal view of the matter would be vindicated. With "no less than eight suits pending," the California Supreme Court issued a decision "adverse to the County," striking down the tax in 1867. "Even as we stand at our case setting this [issue], the rushing waters in front of our office are laden with the treasures of our Alpine forests . . . and no toll has been collected," crowed the *Chronicle*.[108] The cost of the decision to the County proved enormous – and not just in future lost revenues. The county treasury was also forced to cough up restitution and damages for its previously-collected illegal taxes.[109]

On an issue more near and dear to his own wallet, however, Eno was less successful. Nominally paid $1,800 per year as county judge, Eno's effective salary was considerably less because his pay was issued in "county scrip" worth as little as 50 cents on the dollar.[110] An irate Eno brought suit to compel the county to remit his judicial salary in gold. District Judge Theron Reed and the California Supreme Court ruled against Eno, with the court of public opinion also solidly against him on purely practical grounds. As the *Chronicle* pointed out, to pay both the Judge and the District Attorney alone in gold "would take from the Treasury of the County at least two thirds of all her available revenue, thus leaving a mere trifle to apply on the other warrants."[111]

Theron Y. Reed

In 1866, California formed a new Sixteenth Judicial District, which in practical terms meant that Alpine, Inyo, Kern, and Mono Counties got their own District Court to handle larger cases. The first judge appointed to ride this new circuit was a former State Assemblyman named "Colonel" Lee, garnering his appointment through what some in Alpine grumbled was "collusion."[124] When Lee was killed in a buggy accident just a few months later, his successor would be a figure already well known in Alpine County: the up-and-coming young lawyer Theron Y. Reed.[125]

Reed was born about 1832[126] near the home of Abraham Lincoln in Springfield, Illinois, and reportedly had been acquainted with Lincoln in his youth. In 1854, Reed left home to enter the "preparatory department" of Illinois College, joining a literary fraternity known as the Phi Alpha Society. The Society's motto was 'Onward and Upward,' a sentiment that stamped its mark on much of Reed's later life.[127]

Reed moved to California about 1860 and soon was drawn to the boomtowns of Silver Mountain and Markleeville, taking an active interest in the local mines. As early as July, 1863, Reed's signature as a notary can be found on a document involving a town lot at Silver Mountain – amid the boomingest boom days of that raw mining settlement.[128] In the months that followed he also notarized articles of incorporation for four separate mining companies,[129] suggesting that he had likely opened a law practice at Silver Mountain.[130] It was Reed who drew up the official

map of the early Alpine mining districts. And when Markleeville's pioneer citizen Jacob Marklee perished of a gunshot wound, court-filed accountings show that Marklee's estate owed $170.00 to Reed not only in attorneys' fees but also for a plat of the town of Markleeville.[131]

Just how a small town lawyer was able to secure such a prominent judicial appointment is unclear, but Reed evidently had powerful supporters in Silver Mountain and likely Sacramento as well. Only 34 years old when appointed in 1866 to the post of District Court judge, Reed enjoyed a salary of $4,000 a year – more than twice the stipend that Henry Eno received as a "little petty County Judge."[132]

The District Court convened at Silver Mountain just twice a year,[133] but the job of a traveling judge serving multiple counties required Reed to spend much of his time in exhausting travel over primitive roads. As the *Inyo Register* would later note, "[h]is journeys to this part of the bailiwick were arduous, involving some hundreds of miles of staging by the time he visited all his county seats."[134] Weather and road conditions could result in unexpected delays. After one Spring session at Silver Mountain, for example, Reed found himself "snow bound at Silver Mountain for several weeks," and reportedly delighted to finally make it back to "the metropolis" of Markleeville.[135]

Required to reside somewhere within the four-county district, Reed chose as his permanent home the toastier climate near Bakersfield.[136] In 1879, Reed threw his hat in the ring for a Kern County judgeship, only to be defeated by a coalition of prominent landowners offended by his property and water rights rulings.[137]

Even from such a distance, however, he retained an avid interest in the Alpine mines. In 1879, for example, a rumor circulated that Monitor's famous Tarshish mine would soon re-open, with Reed named among the luminaries who would serve as directors for the new mining company.[138]

Young though he was, Reed did not enjoy robust health. As early as 1867, after remarking on the judge's recent arrival by stage at Markleeville the local paper added: "We regret to learn that his health is not good."[139] Five years later, the newspaper similarly commented on the Judge's "poor health" and his wife's sickness, noting that they had been obliged to stop at Walley's, which would delay the District Court calendar.[140]

But whatever his health constraints, Reed was feisty on the bench. He earned himself the nickname "Shotgun Reed" for toting a double-barrelled shotgun to court during a particularly contentious court proceeding in Independence to deter any "abuse and disputing" in his courtroom. "Gentlemen," he is said to have remarked after cocking the gun, "there will be order in this court today."[141]

In one of the earliest cases to come before his bench at Silver Mountain, Reed presided over the prominent murder trial of *People v. Harris*.[142] Other hotly disputed legal issues that came before him included the highly contentious (and repetitious) wood tax cases, in which County Judge Eno regularly issued injunctions to prevent collection of the tax, and Judge Reed just as regularly dissolved Eno's injunctions.[143] Reed also managed to earn Judge Eno's wrath by ruling against the county judge's petition to be paid his salary in gold, rather than in County warrants.[144]

In Kern County, too, Reed did not hesitate to issue rulings that gave great offense to powerful land-owners and county officials. In one case, for example, he had the fortitude to find that the land on which a $30,000 courthouse and school had been erected actually belonged, not to Kern County, but to an individual named W.J. Yoakum.[145]

By 1878, Reed's solid performance on the bench had earned him widespread respect in his district. The *Chronicle*'s editors opined that Reed "has given general satisfaction in Alpine, his decisions being just," and quoted the *Carson Tribune*'s verdict that Reed was "a pleasant companion, a fine lawyer, and as independent as a prince."[146] His handling of land issues in Bodie in particular drew warm accolades from the press:

The general tenor of these decisions is that a title to property does not depend entirely upon a man's ability to stand by it with a double-barreled shot gun, prepared to blow off the head of the first intruder. If a person takes a fancy for a piece of property, he must first take the trouble to find out if some other person does not own it, before taking possession.[147]

But in 1880, Reed found himself suddenly out of a job. The California voters approved a new Constitution abolishing the state's 23 District Courts, replacing them instead with a new system of Superior Courts.[148] Just 48 years old, Reed took the opportunity to indulge his wanderlust. He offered up his "fine residence" in Kern County for sale, complete with furniture, and announced his intention to move to San Francisco.[149] There for the next sixteen years Reed made his home (with a brief interlude in Amador County), later moving to Yreka in Siskiyou County, near the Oregon border, about 1896. Now in his sixties, Reed devoted himself to the mining passion he had enjoyed since his earliest California days, operating a small assay office until his death in 1909.[150]

In October, 1867, Eno assembled a Grand Jury to examine the circumstances surrounding the first sheriff's "absconding" and to take a thorough look at the Supervisors' account books.[112] But Eno's pursuit of propriety earned him powerful political enemies, including the county's treasurer and the district attorney.[113] The same Grand Jury that Eno had empanelled began to poke its investigative nose into allegations that Eno himself had cast his vote improperly at Bear Valley, rather than from his legal residence, and went on to roundly chastise him for his actions enjoining the wood tax collections and attempting to force payment of his own salary in gold.[114]

The Grand Jury report concluded by calling for Eno's resignation, and even former supporter and publishing friend Robert Folger took sides against him.[115] The Monitor newspaper, however, saw the charges for what they were, calling them "unfounded and originating from petty spite."[116] In the end, no criminal indictment was issued[117] and Eno continued to sit as county judge.

For the now nearly 70-year-old Eno, judicial life was filled with continuing rigors and few rewards. His duties, for example, required that he travel with the county clerk to Woodfords and points in between to register voters, leading Eno to complain bitterly: "What a dignified situation a County Judge occupies when he has to walk 50 miles on Official business because he is too confounded poor to hire a horse."[118]

Still eager to pursue the latest mining excitements, Eno made a brief expedition to the mines at White Pine, Nevada in June, 1869, living in a "brush-covered tent" and returning just in time to hold his October-term court in Silver Mountain.[119] Discovering that the State legislature had just voted to cut his meager salary from $1,800 to just $1,000 a year, the disgusted Eno declined to run for re-election again, bidding *adieu* to Alpine County for good in November, 1869.[120]

Still driven by a spirit of adventure despite his advancing years, the 72-year-old Eno made a prospecting trip to Death Valley in the Spring of 1870. But by August, poor health and financial reverses forced him to seek funds from family to help him return East.[121] He would while away the next dozen years on a nephew's farm in New York State before passing away at the age of 84.[122] During those quiet years, Eno's thoughts must have returned again and again to Alpine County. As he had written some thirty years earlier, "The best country, you know, is always west of where we are."[123]

Tipping The Scales of Justice: Judge Goff

The not-exactly-honorable Charles P. Goff mixed frontier justice with a dash of the wild, wild West. A Markleeville property owner as early as 1864,[151] Goff was one of the first lawyers to open a practice in newly-formed county. Following Judge Eno's departure in 1870, Goff won the election for County judge.[152]

But Goff was hardly content to simply warm the bench of the County court. Winking at such legal niceties as conflict of interest, Goff boasted a variety of official titles by 1871, including notary public; Commissioner of the U.S. Circuit Court; probate judge for Silver Mountain; Deputy District Attorney; Internal Revenue collector; Commissioner of Deeds for the State of Nevada; school trustee; and "General Machinist of the County."[153]

At the same time he was wearing the black robe in California, Goff maintained an active law practice on the side in neighboring Nevada. An air of judicial entitlement came with him, it seems. Goff once took the liberty of stripping off his coat in Genoa's District Court, prompting Nevada Judge Harris to order that Goff be removed from the courtroom unless he resumed appropriately sedate attire. Anything but contrite, Goff reciprocated by ordering that any Nevada lawyer caught coatless in *his* Alpine courtroom thereafter would be not only thrown out of court but imprisoned.[154]

Goff's confrontational attitude displayed itself in other encounters as well. As one of his earliest acts as presiding judge, Goff refused to accept a legislative cut in his judicial pay, filing suit against County Auditor Barber to demand his original $1800 per year salary.[155] Goff also managed to incur local displeasure by maintaining not only his personal residence but also his official judge's chambers in Markleeville, rather than at the county seat of Silver Mountain.[156]

CHAS. P. GOFF,

COMMISSIONER OF THE UNITED STATES
CIRCUIT COURT FOR THE DISTRICT
OF CALIFORNIA.

PETITIONS in BANKRUPTCY received and
verified and all other business appertaining to
the duties of said office promptly attended to.

**COMMISSIONER of DEEDS FOR THE
STATE of NEVADA.**

SILVER MOUNTAIN.

Alpine county, California.

Will practice in the Supreme and District
Courts of California; and all the Courts of the
State of Nevada.   a23-tf

*Goff was one of Markleeville's earliest
lawyers. See ad (above, right) from 1864.*

*By 1873, Goff unabashedly wore multiple hats,
touting not only his active legal practice in both
California and Nevada but also his services as
a bankruptcy court Commissioner – all while
presiding as Alpine's County judge.*

Residing in Markleeville meant that in bad weather, Goff had difficulty meeting his judicial obligations at Silver Mountain. But for some causes, he was willing to undergo almost any hardship. In 1872, he trekked the twelve miles on foot to Silver Mountain in a "driving snow storm" to represent Mrs. Louisa C. Brown in her divorce suit.[157] Perhaps as a result of that snowstorm epiphany, Goff finally sold his Markleeville home, setting up a new office on Silver Mountain's Main Street between Second and Third Streets.[158] Before long he also branched out into another line of business, purchasing the former Swinerton hardware store between Third and Fourth Streets and fitting it up as the "Occidental Saloon," replete with a pair of billiard tables.[159]

C. P. GOFF,
Attorney and Counselor at Law,
NOTARY PUBLIC,
MAIN STREET, (next door to Webster House) MARKLEEVILLE.
All business intrusted to his care will be promptly
attended to.
June 4 1864. 1 tf

By the time the 1873 judicial election rolled around, Goff found himself rather unpopular and he was handily defeated by the local district attorney, S.W. Griffith.[160] But it seems Goff didn't depart the bench quietly. A petition had to be gotten up the following May by a group of concerned citizens, demanding that he vacate the Judge's chambers.[161]

By 1874, Goff's relationship with his former client Mrs. Brown (now going by her previous name, Mrs. Britton) had clearly transcended the purely professional. Gossip-mongers speculated the couple would soon be wed in Genoa.[162] Ugly rumours also circulated that Mrs. Britton's young ward (legally placed in her care by none other than Goff) had been forced into prostitution in Mrs. Britton's saloon.[163] Neither Goff nor Britton found themselves welcome in polite Silver Mountain society.

The pair soon left town, owing money to just about everyone.[164] Grand jury indictments swiftly followed. In June, 1874, Goff was charged with embezzling a client's money and accepting pay-offs from an opposing party to delay litigation.[165] And the following year, Goff was held to answer in San Francisco on charges of extortion.[166]

Goff somehow managed to continue practicing law, maintaining offices for his firm "Goff & Piuto" at 625 Merchant Street in San Francisco. Goff's final day on earth at the tender age of 70 included a drunken brawl during which he was pushed through a window of his San Francisco firm. Despite the circumstances, the coroner's inquest ruled that Goff died of natural causes, delicately citing "nervous apoplexy."[167]

N.D. Arnot, Jr.

In 1876, Nathaniel Dubois Arnot, Sr., owner of the Vulcan Iron Works in San Francisco, contracted to build a 20-stamp mill and boarding house for I.X.L. employees near Lewis Chalmers' house, about a half-mile below Silver Mountain.[168] His son, N.D. Arnot, Jr., may have arrived in Silver Mountain to supervise construction for his father – or could have been sent there to try to heal his broken heart. The junior Arnot had graduated from the College of California at Berkeley in 1869, and attended law school at Albany, N.Y. On April 19, 1871, he married the former Eugenie Holbrook at San Francisco. But poor Eugenie would die in 1875, leaving the junior Arnot a widower, with a young son, Raymond.[169]

Whatever the reason behind his move to Silver Moutain, by 1877 the junior Arnot had opened a legal office in the tiny

Dustman Collection

This rare view showing expansion of the Exchequer Mill in 1876 features Judge Arnot (standing, with hands in pockets), who had invested in the project, with a stout gentleman on a horse (likely Chalmers himself), overseeing operations. The landmark brick chimney remains visible even today beside Highway 4. Note the light-colored dressed stonework at the bottom – identical to blocks used in the original Silver Mountain jail.

The photo above is an election card for Judge Arnot in 1914, when he ran as incumbent for the post of Superior Court Judge in El Dorado County.

Courtesy Huntington Library

mountain town.[170] And by October that same year, the mid-30s lawyer would wed 21-year-old Anna Melissa Ford, daughter of prominent hotel-keeper R.H. Ford.[171] Together they would eventually have a total of nine children, their first-born – Mary Eugenie – entering the world on August 11, 1878, at Silver Mountain.[172]

Arnot successfully won the post of Alpine Superior Court Judge in the September, 1879 election. By that time, Silver Mountain had lost its position as the county seat, and Arnot moved with his family to the new seat of government at Markleeville. Their Main Street residence once stood on the site formerly known as "Brown's Cafe," today called the Toll Station.[173]

Mining magnate Lewis Chalmers once boasted that he "got [Arnot] elected judge, or rather helped him in."[174] But the relationship between Arnot and Chalmers was complicated and the two were often at odds. Tellingly, Chalmers also noted: "Arnot professes to be my ardent admirer (for fighting him, I suppose)."[175]

By May, 1877, the Arnot family held judgments totalling $14,659.61 against the Isabella, Exchequer, and I.X.L. mines, and Chalmers personally.[176] Property subject to their attachment included not only the I.X.L. quartz mill and boarding house, but also Chalmers' own house and blacksmith shop.[177] And the Arnots were not the only creditors hounding Chalmers for payment. A.S. Hallidie, patent-holder for a "wire tramway," also held a $2,303.75 judgment against the Exchequer and I.X.L. properties (again including Chalmers' house).[178] And another creditor, C.B. Gregory, had similarly levied against the Exchequer properties for his own $2,530.93 judgment.[179]

Sheriff's sales attempting to collect some six separate judgments were repeatedly advertised – and repeatedly postponed. Finally, in August, 1878, the Arnots secured title to the properties through foreclosure, in the name of Amanda Arnot (the wife of N.D. Arnot, Sr.) – who promptly sold them back to Chalmers.[180] Chalmers would later claim that the Isabella property "was redeemed by Mr. Arnot (for me), but not with Exchequer money,"[181] and that the property "was sold to Arnot, bought from him by one Dunn (my friend) and reconveyed by him to [Exchequer Debenture] Trustees for Debenture holders."[182]

Meanwhile, now-Judge N.D. Arnot, Jr. was energetically defending Chalmers in a variety of mining-related lawsuits. In at least one case, Arnot succeeded in getting the plaintiff's costs of suit recalculated, "resulting in great reductions" in Chalmers' obligation.[183] Acting apparently in his own behalf, however, the junior Arnot also "relocated" a variety of mining claims in which Chalmers held an interest, including the Adolphus, Pine Tree, Badger Hill, and Jessie claims, much to Chalmers' dismay. Chalmers instructed his secretary George W. Jones to visit Arnot to "review" the relocation records, but Arnot kept giving Jones the slip, sneaking out the back door whenever Jones attempted to catch Arnot at home. "Arnot Jr. is leading I.X.L. and Ex[cheque]r a merry dance," grumbled Chalmers, adding in another letter: "[I]rrespective altogether of the legality or illegality of his election, his conduct in this matter would appear to me to disqualify him for the office."[184] Chalmers determined to file suit against Arnot, if necessary. Eventually, however, he was able to wangle a quitclaim from Arnot of those "relocated" mining interests.[185]

By the time Chalmers left Alpine for good about 1885, any cozy relationship with the Arnots seems to have soured. Chalmers' declining fortunes may finally have left him unable to pay his swelling debts. Or perhaps despite using the Arnots to engineer end-runs around other mining creditors, Chalmers was unable to evade the spider-web of the Arnots' claims himself.

In 1900, Judge Arnot foreclosed yet another judgment against Chalmers' properties. By this time, Arnot must have lost hope that any money would be forthcoming from England to redeem the mining interests. Nevertheless, in what appears to have been a last act of kindness, Arnot re-conveyed the lot containing Chalmers' old house and its two fenced gardens to Antoinette for $105 – reserving to himself the right to remove the "18-stamp quartz mill, engine, boilers, pans and settlers, agitators, rock breaker, lathes, pans, furnaces, bricks, chimneys, buildings and all other machinery and property."[186]

Perhaps to leave Markleeville winters behind, Arnot served as a visiting judge in Placerville during the winters of 1892 and 1894.[187] Despite his legal duties, he continued to invest in mining ventures as far away as Green Creek Canyon in Mono County, lending his name to the "Par Value and Arnot Mining and Milling Company" in February, 1899.[188] Arnot returned to preside as Superior Court Judge in Alpine County through the turn of the century, officiating for example at the historic marriage of Charles Barrett and Clara Mayo in 1902, which joined two prominent early Alpine families.[189]

But Arnot had apparently acquired a taste for more temperate climes. In October, 1904, Arnot moved for good with his family to Placerville,[190] and that November won election as a Superior Court judge for El Dorado County.

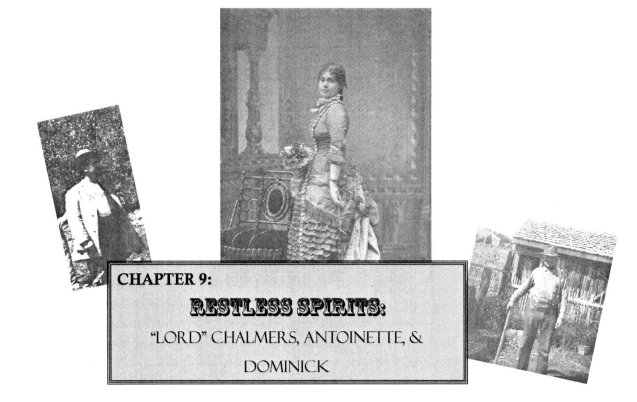

CHAPTER 9:

RESTLESS SPIRITS:

"LORD" CHALMERS, ANTOINETTE, &

DOMINICK

A Cloud of Misfortune

The single most influential man in Silver Mountain – and for that matter, in all of early Alpine County – was Lewis Chalmers. A lawyer by training, with a dash of the con artist by disposition, Chalmers managed to acquire a taste for living the high life with other people's money long before reaching American soil.

Chalmers was born March 9, 1825, to a well-to-do Scottish family whose members had long been prominent in their home town of Fraserburgh. As Lewis would later proudly note, "My father, grandfather, and self were Bailies (chief magistrates) of Fraserburgh, Aberdeenshire for many years, [serving as] factors for Lord Saltoun and others."[1] As a young man, Lewis received his degree from Marischal College of Aberdeen, where he won prizes in Greek and Latin. Contemporaries would later recall that Lewis "always moved in the best society, [displaying] the manners and address of one who has done so."[2]

When Chalmers' father (also named Lewis Chalmers) died in 1850, the young Lewis succeeded to his father's wide-ranging business interests.[3] Among other posts, the now 25-year-old found himself serving as agent for the Scottish Provincial Assurance Co.; agent for the Bank of Scotland; and Factor and Commissioner for the Right Honorable Lord Saltoun. As time went by, Chalmers would assume a variety of civic roles in his hometown, becoming chairman of not only the Town Council but also the Parochial Board and the Police Commissioners.[4] He similarly served as chairman of the Fraserburgh Harbour Board, overseeing contruction of a new North Pier in 1850.[5] And it was said that Chalmers was instrumental in helping to bring "railway communication to his native town" just months before his eventual departure.[6]

But of all his various titles, Chalmers' most important role was as Chief Magistrate of Fraserburgh, a judicial post he held for some seventeen years and in which he won wide acclaim. He quickly proved himself a gifted speaker, leading one contemporary to wax poetic over the "persuasive powers with which he is so eminently endowed, to soothe opposition and win respect;"[7] another called him "one of the best at any ceremonial or demonstration."[8] Observers praised his "gentlemanly manners" and "courteous manner and amiable disposition" on the bench, adding that "we never hear of him ejecting the widow or unfortunate, but in many cases assisting them with his own personal means."[9]

Shortly after assuming his father's duties, Chalmers married Elizabeth Ann Cameron.[10] Their first child, a boy named Lewis to carry on the family tradition, brightened their household on November 30, 1851. But within weeks of this happy event, Elizabeth passed away from "inflammation . . . after her confinement."[11]

Chalmers ventured down the aisle again two years later, taking 19-year-old Ellen Miller MacEwen as his second wife.[12] Over the next decade Ellen would bestow six more children upon Lewis before she, too, passed away, from tuberculosis.[13] Chalmers' burgeoning family now included two more boys: Alick (or Alexander), born April 28, 1854,[14] and Willie, born September 23, 1856;[15] daughter Laura, born December 3, 1857;[16] Jessica Louise (also known as "Detit"), born March 3, 1860;[17] and twins Ellen Mary (Elleny for short) and Johnny, born July 21, 1861.[18]

At roughly the same time as Ellen's death in 1863, Chalmers' prosperous world began to unravel. According to one version, Chalmers had been "victimised by a brother-in-law to the extent of above £5,000"[19] – a grand sum for the time. Other sources suggest that a financial scandal had erupted concerning his management (or mismanagement) of Lord Saltoun's estate, and the Lord's consequent displeasure with Chalmers' high-flying lifestyle. As one Fraserburgh historian explained:

> [W]hen Lord Saltoun was away for a time, Lewis built 'Witch Hill' house _without permission_ and when Lord Saltoun returned and found this, he was very angry and dismissed Lewis immediately. So it was not finances that caused him to leave[,] but the loss of his job and his respect in the town.[20]

Humiliated both personally and financially, Chalmers resigned his many appointments and left Fraserburgh about May, 1864, "enveloped in a cloud of misfortune."[21] Despite his financial woes, however, Chalmers retained a number of influential friends and connections, and it was perhaps through these acquaintances that he eventually found his way to London. There Chalmers resurfaced in 1866, studying assaying with the firm of Johnson, Matthey & Co.[22]

Whether Chalmers intended at the outset to launch a fresh career as a mining engineer is unclear, but the recent magnificent discoveries of silver on the Comstock Lode likely added spark to his studies. It would not be long before the glittering promise of the American mines an ocean away would offer him a chance at a brand new start.

George Dey, courtesy of Fraserburgh Heritage Society

Witch Hill House in Fraserburgh, Scotland, circa 1950.

Michigan Tunnel Days

By the late 1860s, English investors had become scandalously famous for their deep pockets and unblinking infusions of capital into a variety of speculative mining enterprises "across the pond." The lucrative practice of mining the pockets of these gullible investors had become so widespread that European newspapers were sternly warning their readers against investing in American mines.[23] Qualifications for the title of mine superintendent for such speculative enterprises were similarly well-recognized. As one tongue-in-cheek article observed, typical credentials for the post included:

> *A fast horse, a fast buggy, and another fast horse; a heavy gold watch with a heavy gold chain, and a fine diamond pin; must have at least three fast women, a taste for liquors, and some knowledge of poker.*[24]

Chalmers brought no real-world mining experience with him whatsoever to London. But thanks to his brief study of the art of assaying, his well-honed gift of gab, and likely the requisite gold watch, he managed to secure an appointment in 1867 to become mining superintendent and "Temporary Secretary" for a wildly speculative American venture known as the Michigan Tunnel Company.

The Michigan Tunnel's assets included more than a dozen supposed silver lodes striping a hill called Mount America near Monitor, California. In the hands of its new British owners, the blandly-named "Michigan" was alluringly retitled "The Imperial Silver Quarries Company, Limited." This new venture managed to attract a high-profile list of directors, touted by Chalmers to be "men of the highest standing and social position in London."[25] For his duties as superintendent Chalmers was promised a salary of £1,000 Sterling per year[26] – money he desperately needed to repay his debts and to support his large family.

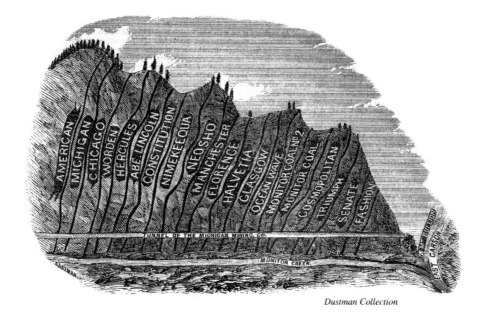

Dustman Collection

Unbeknownst to Chalmers, the original owners of the Michigan Tunnel project were some of the most notorious sharps of Alpine County. Location papers for the Michigan Company had been filed during the go-go days of 1863 by mining speculators Frank Jones and his brother "Captain" James Jones, while the post of secretary was held by Monitor ne'er-do-well O.F. Thornton. Several years before the British investment firm snapped up the property, F.A.S. Jones had candidly written to his brother: "As to the Michigan Tunnel, I think that it is a complete failure."[27]

The now 42-year-old Chalmers must have had high hopes indeed for his new life as he set sail from Liverpool on September 11, 1867, to assume his new post. But upon Chalmers' arrival some two months later at the rough-and-tumble mining camp of Bulliona, he would quickly discover that things were not quite as rosy as they had appeared back in London. The Imperial's investors had successfully purchased the *stock* of the old Michigan Tunnel company, all right; but the company's assets had been tied up by creditors' attachments a year earlier.[28] Despite his title as "superintendent," Chalmers found himself unable even to take physical possession of the tunnel property upon his arrival, with one Jones brother claiming he had not received proof that the $5,000 purchase price had reached his brother.[29]

But if Chalmers was anything, he was tenacious. Alternately threatening legal action against the lienholders[30] and cajoling the sellers,[31] he finally succeeded in taking official possession of the tunnel property in February.[32] Just weeks later, he was able to proudly report to London that the first fifty feet of the tunnel project had been successfully run.[33]

The primitive mining camps of Monitor and Bulliona were a far cry from the genteel society of London or Fraserburgh. But Chalmers set about making his new life in the California mountains as comfortable as he could. Co-opting his tunnel crew to serve as carpenters, he had a small two-story house built for himself at Bulliona, acquired a housekeeper, and laid in a supply of wine glasses, decanters, ivory-handled knives, and similar necessities.[34] He also broke ground for a new blacksmith shop beside the tunnel opening, and made sure that his house plans included a separate office and assay room.[35] By the end of May, 1868, Chalmers was able to report that the Imperial Tunnel had now reached 150 feet in length, thanks to three pair of miners working around the clock plus a seventh hand kept busy sharpening tools, laying track, and adding supporting timbers.[36]

Chalmers quickly earned himself a reputation as "the hardest, meanest man ever came in to the camp."[37] At four in the morning he could be found standing at the window of his shanty in his night dress, "watching my night shift that they don't leave before their time."[38] Even on Christmas Day, when the ordinary laborers were permitted the day off, his foreman was expected to remain hard at work "laying track &tc. &tc."[39] Alpiners took to calling the hard-driving Scotsman "Lord" Chalmers for his imperious demeanor and extravagant tastes.

Chalmers could display an equally demanding side in his correspondence to London. "[O]n receipt, it will be necessary that a supply of the needful be telegraphed," he penned politely but sternly in November, 1868.[40] As infusions of "the needful" began to arrive somewhat irregularly, he chided more pointedly: "[L]ast remittance was not to hand till after Pay day." And by the following March, Chalmers was openly growling about his financial predicament: "I was obliged to discharge two men the other day, since which [time] my foreman has had all his hogs poisoned but one, and all manner of threats are made against myself."[41]

On July 1, 1869, a year and a half into the Imperial Tunnel project, the crew finally struck traces of sulphurets at the 980-foot mark, a sign Chalmers relayed excitedly as confirmation that the "Triumph" lode must now be near.[42] Inch by inch and painful foot by foot, the tunnel kept going. But as each successive lode in the expected chain of silver lodes failed to materialize, the Imperial's finances began a downward death spiral. Finally, in February, 1870, Chalmers received the long-dreaded order from London to "stop work."[43] Chalmers promptly lodged his own creditor's claim against the Imperial's assets for $5,600 in unpaid manager's fees – an effort, he assured his former employers, to preserve whatever equity the Imperial might have left.[44]

It had been more than two years since Chalmers first set boot on Alpine soil, and his hard-driven crew had managed to pick, shovel, and blast their way an astonishing 1,406 feet into the side of Mount

"Hall's Hair Renewer" was one of the many patent remedies advertised in the local Chronicle newspaper. Chalmers purchased not just one but two bottles in 1868, commenting in his letters "there is something in the [Alpine] climate prejudicial to luxuriant hair."

America. But the grandly-named Imperial Gold & Silver Company had failed to unearth any trace of its dozen supposed silver lodes.[45]

Exchequer Days

The Imperial Tunnel's demise may have shocked its shareholders but it came as no surprise to the canny Chalmers. Months before receiving the official order to halt work, he had begun scouting for a new lily pad to land on. This took the shape of a fresh mining venture known as The Exchequer Gold and Silver Mining Company, launched in the fall of 1869 by the same cadre of London investment brokers that had floated the spectacularly unsuccessful Imperial. Rather than gambling again on unproven mines near Monitor, this time the Exchequer proposed to develop a group of better-known silver claims in Scandinavian Canyon, above the town of Silver Mountain.

Chalmers successfully wangled an appointment for his younger brother, "Captain" John Chalmers, in this new venture. As luck would have it, John arrived on-scene in February, 1870 to assume his duties as manager of newly-floated Exchequer just as the ill-fated Imperial was shutting down.[46] By early April, the two brothers had managed to mine and mill enough Exchequer ore to dispatch a miniature brick of .901 fine silver to London, touting it as a "first" shipment of bullion from the new set of silver claims.[47]

Lewis and John were riding high – literally, having acquired "a pair of spirited horses to facilitate their transit between the different points of their charge."[48] Investors poured in to the new Exchequer, and Chalmers wasted no time finding ways to expend their money. A "large and commodious" boarding house was quickly thrown up at the Exchequer mine "for the comfortable housing of their miners."[49] Always a fan of the latest in mining technology, Chalmers began agitating for an expensive new "Leschot" power drill.[50] Perhaps most important of all, Lewis was finally able to afford to send to London for his eldest son, Lewie, to come out to join him.[51] Poor Lewie, like his step-mother, suffered from lung-wasting "consumption," and it was his father's fervent hope that Alpine's dry mountain air would work its gentle magic on Lewie's lungs.

With John now running the day-to-day operations of the mine, Lewis turned his attention to scouting for new mining properties to acquire. Before long the local newspaper would report that "[a]nother claim near Silver Mountain has been sold to an English company, and negotiations are pending for the sale of three other claims to London Companies."[52]

Courtesy of Huntington Library

The Exchequer Mine near the top of Scandinavian Canyon included hoisting works and a boarding house. Note the steepness of the climb for the wagons, and the flume bringing water on the left. Timbers beside the open door were likely destined for shoring in the mine below.

Chalmers' keen eye may have been drawn to Daniel Davidson's "very valuable property" on Silver Creek as early as 1868.[53] The Davidson compound included an aging quartz mill and a lumber mill, with a stretch of good timber land thrown in for good measure and – perhaps best of all, from Chalmers' perspective – a rundown but serviceable residence. Chalmers repeatedly pressed his financiers in London to acquire the mill property, touting the cash-saving possibilities of having a quartz mill in close proximity to their mine. But Davidson, a smart businessman, was not all that eager at first to sell and held out for cold, hard cash – a commodity not as eagerly parted with by the London consortium.

Finally, in September, 1870, Chalmers managed to talk Davidson into parting with the mill for a combination of stock and cash.[54] Happily abandoning his two-story shanty at Bulliona, Chalmers tucked into the far more comfortable quarters at Davidson's old house, renaming the property the 'Exchequer Mill'

Courtesy of Alpine County Historical Society

in a nod to his English backers. He shared this new abode with brother John and a 29-year-old housekeeper from Ireland named Annie Kelly.[55]

Davidson's Mill on Silver Creek included a sawmill facility, abundant water close at hand, and a valuable timber ranch.

Never one to be content with the status quo, Chalmers quickly embarked on extensive renovations to both the house and the millworks. After a tour of the improvements in November, 1870, the local *Chronicle* editor gushed:

> [A] two-story building has been erected, and now nearly completed, in which the Manager has a spacious office and chemical room on the second floor – the first, or basement, story, being intended for the weighing, retorting and assaying departments. . . . The amalgamating is carried on in six massive, wooden barrels with the Freiberg process. The machinery is propelled by an engine [steam] of sufficient capacity to run the quartz and saw mills at the same time. . . . The sawmill can cut 20,000 feet of lumber per diem.[56]

By the following July, however, things were no longer going quite so swimmingly with Exchequer's finances. Having seen no further evidence of riches beyond that first teasing bar of silver, the investors were growing restless. None other than the *London Times* was again warning English capitalists against California mining investments, "in consequence of the number, daily increasing, of valueless and even counterfeited mining shares which have for some years past flooded the European markets."[57]

As the spigot of funds from London slowed to a trickle, Chalmers' missives home grew more and more desperate. "Bank is overdrawn – men not paid, debt daily increasing," he wrote urgently.[58] "Day after day I have been looking for a telegram, or [for] rich ore. . . I owe the men [back wages] . . . where's the £600 promised?"[59]

To add to his woes, the old Davidson mill began demanding significant repairs. A cam shaft pulley thought to have been "thoroughly repaired some time ago" suddenly "flew to pieces."[60] Hard on the heels of time-consuming repairs in June, even more serious troubles emerged just a few months later:

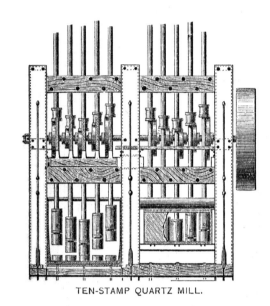

TEN-STAMP QUARTZ MILL.

Dustman Collection

> *The Stamps had not run half a day when I observed leakage of ore under the Battery. Caulking was resorted to without effect. Four different times I had to stop for days on end, to have the mortars pulled to pieces, new bolts made, keys placed under the nuts, & slots cut in the bolts under the nuts, & wedges inserted to prevent them from slipping, new blankets with tar placed under the mortars and all screwed down again – tight, only to work loose again after a day's running.*[61]

The problem, it turned out, was a major one. Lifting the floor, Chalmers discovered that the mill's mortar blocks were "completely rotten at the core."[62]

Despite this setback, Chalmers managed to eke out enough ore by December, 1871 to generate another small, crude bar of bullion worth $305.77, which he hastily shipped off to London via the Wells Fargo agency in Monitor.[63] The sight of a fresh silver bar may have helped soothe the ruffled feathers of the impatient London investors. But it did nothing to solve Chalmers' own immediate financial distress.

Chalmers fired his mine superintendent and, owing money to his cook, reluctantly concluded to let her go, as well. Soon, even food for the mine oxen was becoming scarce.[64] The once-proud Scot stewed over the indignities to which he was now reduced:

> *I owe [money to] Davidson and Mrs. Hanson [my housekeeper], my butcher, &tc., and have to sell my furniture, bedding and transit instrument to pay them. We can now scarcely get credit for a pound of meat. . . . We are all going about in mended rags, the worst-dressed men in Alpine County – a disgrace to the Company. We live <u>worse</u> than any of the Miners.*[65]

Privately, he confided to a friend back in London that the Exchequer "I believe to be a dead horse now."[66] But still he soldiered on. On January 24, 1872, Chalmers departed for London, determined to lend his own copious powers of persuasion to the Board's efforts to raise fresh capital.[67]

Tragedy struck the little house by Silver Creek while Chalmers was away. On May 11, 1872, just days before what would have been his twenty-first birthday, young Lewie quietly passed away – the victim of the tuberculosis he had brought with him from England.[68] The newspaper tendered its condolences, describing Lewie as "a young man with whom it was a pleasure to be acquainted," and observing that "his death will be deeply regretted by those who have known him intimately."[69] One local miner joked uncharitably in his own correspondence that "It would not be such a loss if it was Captain John."[70] Returning from abroad the following month, Chalmers mourned the loss of his eldest son deeply. "The House looks very dull without poor Lewis," he confided to a friend. "I can't turn without being reminded of him."[71]

Despite this sad news upon his return, Chalmers had once again been successful in his fundraising efforts in London, returning with "lots of money and some very rich presents," according to his enthusiastic housekeeper.[72] But John, who had kept the mines running in Chalmers' absence, concluded he had had enough of mining life. "John never liked the business," Chalmers confided to a correspondent, borrowing funds to send his brother home via Panama steamer that fall.[73]

Dustman Collection

The I.X.L. Hoisting Works building was finished in November, 1872. By early 1873, Chalmers was able to report that the engine shaft was 110 feet deep, and a "pigeon's egg"-sized lump of "pure ruby-silver" had been exhibited in London. "[A]n expert cannot distinguish some of this ore from Yellow Jacket ore on the Comstock Lode," he boasted. Note how the I.X.L. building was identical to the hoisting works facility at the Exchequer (photo on page 100).

Fresh infusions of investor capital following Chalmers' return to Alpine County[74] permitted him to successfully re-engineer the old Davidson Mill into a 20-ton facility[75] and to erect hoisting works at the I.X.L. Mine.[76] The I.X.L.'s new hoisting works were shipped in from New York, and a 30-by-50-foot building to enclose the machinery was finished in November, 1872, a duplicate of the hoisting works facility at the Exchequer.

The following years brought a rollercoaster of mining ups and downs. Exchequer claimed to have "struck its lode" in August, 1873, yielding tantalizing specimens that would assay up to $2,000 a ton.[77] But demonetization of silver that same year fueled a nationwide financial panic and, more importantly for Chalmers, dropped the bottom out of the silver market.[78] By mid-October, Chalmers was $5,000 overdrawn at his bank.[79] And as if to add insult to the recent injury inflicted on the silver market, Alpine County voters withdrew the title of county seat from the struggling town of Silver Mountain in 1875, bestowing that crown instead upon the far more accessible Markleeville.[80]

By 1876, however, a fresh mining boom was again in progress, with renewed activity at the mines in both Scandinavian Canyon and Monitor. Even mining properties near Fredericksburg that had been "abandoned 10 years ago" began to get a second glance. Suddenly, Silver Mountain was teeming with activity. Additional workmen were being hired by the Exchequer and I.X.L. "as fast as working space can be had," and "The stage, now a days, arrives loaded down with passengers," trumpeted the newspaper gleefully.[81]

Chalmers eagerly jumped aboard this fresh tide of mining interest. With another mill site slightly farther up Silver Creek already tucked in his portfolio, Chalmers drew up plans for a new 20-stamp mill to be dedicated solely to processing I.X.L. ore, signing a contract that called for the new mill to be completed by Christmas Day, 1876.[82]

About this same time Chalmers also acquired a new housekeeper:[83] pretty Antoinette Laughton. A young widow some 30 years Chalmers' junior, "Nettie" brought fresh life and liveliness to the old Davidson house. Raised in Shaw's Flat, California, Nettie's early life had been a tragic one. Her father, a French blacksmith named Bavia Depuy,[84] had passed away when Nettie was about twelve years old.

Courtesy of Huntington Library

Chalmers' "mansion" at Silver Creek as it looked in 1876, about the time Antoinette Laughton first arrived. Chalmers himself likely commissioned these stereoviews, taken by photographer Eliza Withington.

Courtesy of Huntington Library

The following year, Nettie's mother Catharine too passed away, leaving Antoinette an orphan at the age of thirteen. Six years later, young Antoinette would follow her mother's lead by marrying a man more than twice her age, wedding 42-year-old L.H. Laughton in San Francisco.[85] But Laughton, too, soon passed on, leaving Antoinette a young widow at just 22 with a son not quite a year old.

Exactly how Antoinette came to arrive at Chalmers' mining compound on Silver Creek remains a mystery. She may have been a friend of Chalmers' previous housekeeper, Annie Kelly.[86] Or perhaps Chalmers had boarded with a member of the Laughton family on one of his many trips to San Francisco.[87]

If young Nettie's presence brightened the old Davidson house by Silver Creek, it was a sorely needed diversion. By January, 1878, the Exchequer Company was again deep in debt, and Chalmers was forced to make yet another pilgrimage to London in an attempt to raise funds.[88] A sale of the "English mines" was advertised in the local papers for February; postponed until March; then postponed once again.[89] All of the company's personal property,

Dustman Collection

The headstone for Nettie's parents, Bavia and Catharine Depuy, in Shaw's Flat Cemetery, states that the stone was erected in September, 1879 – long after their deaths in 1865 and 1866, and probably with Chalmers's money.

however, was successfully auctioned off, as newspaper put it: "to good advantage – to the purchasers."[90] By June, the *Chronicle* was predicting that the mines would soon "pass out of the hands of the English owners and into those of San Francisco capitalists."[91]

A half-step away from financial ruin yet again, Chalmers turned once more to what he did best: concocting a fresh and even more ambitious investment scheme.

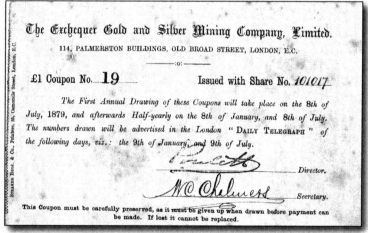

An 1879 dividend coupon for The Exchequer Gold and Silver Mining Co., with the signature of W.C. Chalmers (Lewis's son "Willie") as Secretary. The dividend coupon also features a stamped endorsement by the Right Honorable Earl Poulett of Buckingham Gate, one of the wealthy British investors who not only sank their own funds into Chalmers' projects but also helped to induce their affluent friends to purchase shares.

By the time this dividend drawing took place, the Exchequer was deep in debt.

Dustman Collection

The Great Isabella Tunnel

The year 1879 marked a dozen years since Chalmers' arrival in Alpine. In that short span he had already left a trail of investor tears with his first two high-flying – and spectacularly unsuccessful – mining schemes. The once-hopeful town of Silver Mountain, too, had seen better days. From a bustling community of more than a thousand souls during its initial explosive boom the settlement had now become, as Chalmers put it, "almost defunct."[92]

But Chalmers clung tight to his belief that a treasure trove of ore lay buried beneath Scandinavian Canyon. The legendary I.X.L. and Buckeye claims, two of Alpine's earliest silver strikes, had been discovered there. And Chalmers had never forgotten the fabulous specimens of ruby silver ore in a "beautifully defined ledge," seen with his own eyes.[93] As early as 1870, he had enthusiastically reported to London:

> [N]othing better could be wished than is to be seen in the upper tunnel on the Buckeye ledge. . . . Selected specimens of the best ore assay as high as $2,000 per ton, and all the ore contains more or less gold.[94]

Little wonder, then, that as the Exchequer's fortunes began to wane, Chalmers' thoughts turned to new ways to reach the company's yet-untapped lodes. His solution required an ever-grander scheme, of course. And an amazing project it would prove to be: the Isabella Tunnel.[95]

In Chalmers' creative vision, the Isabella was to be a "second Sutro," driving 7,000 feet horizontally from the base of the mountain to intersect the rich lodes he was confident lay waiting beneath Scandinavian Canyon.[96] And according to his confident predictions, the first rich lode – the "Balaclava" – could be reached in a mere ten months,[97] at an optimistic 200 feet of progress per month.[98]

Dustman Collection

Beinecke Library

This portly gentleman shows up in a number of stereoviews taken in 1876, and clearly is not a working man. Could this be Chalmers?

It was music to British investors' ears, and the tempo was marked by fresh influxes of capital. The Company's checking account with Bank of California soon swelled with a deposit of £2000 (nearly $10,000) in October, 1878, followed quickly with a remittance of £500 ($2,412) in November; another £500 on December 16th; and £500 more the following week.[99] Yet another large deposit of £1500 ($7,000) would follow in January, 1879.[100]

By November, 1878, start-up preparations for the Isabella Tunnel were well under way. Shovels were set to flying leveling a building site beside the tunnel opening; track lumber was purchased; and shingles were ordered for a host of new buildings.[101] A boarding house was thrown up for the convenience of the Isabella tunnel workers, and given the lateness of the season, winter supplies were hastily laid in.[102]

Under the direction of H.C. Ginn, a crew of carpenters began to throw a heavy-timbered bridge over Silver Creek to facilitate the delivery of supplies and machinery at the tunnel mouth and permit convenient disposal of waste rock on the far side of the creek.[103] None other than Deputy U.S. Surveyor L.L. Hawkins was engaged for a formal survey to make certain the tunnel would be properly angled into the mountainside, and two stone monuments were erected as benchmarks to guide its future progress.[104]

Especially when it came to such scientific details, Chalmers could not sit idly by. Paying frequent trips to the site to oversee his new brainchild, he checked and re-checked the technical details, interrogating the professional surveyor when unable to confirm the surveyor's readings himself:

> Having borrowed Griffith's Gurley Transit, I set it very carefully over the Centre of the plug, which Thomson turned [towards] the initial Monument at Tunnel mouth. I then made the correction for variation with the Vernice 16° E. & sighted back to the second monument on the side of the Road until the cross hairs cut the centre of the pipe at its

junction with the Stone, & the reading invariably is S. 69° 25" E in place of S 72° E, or a difference of 2° 75". An initial error like this would land me in a nice mess at 7,000 feet. Is your direction correct, N. 72° W Var. 16° E, or, this being correct, are your monuments correctly set? Either you are wrong or the Instrument, and I am afraid to run the Tunnel further until the course is put beyond a doubt and this I look to you to do.[105]

Chalmers also busied himself with ordering equipment from San Francisco for his new project, another task he clearly enjoyed. Orders were sent for a brace of twelve-inch National compressors along with two No. 2 air-driven National machine drills, supporting columns and associated valves, hose couplings, and sharpening dies – all for the astronomical sum of $3,850.[106] Also on Chalmers' acquisition list: a pair of large steam boilers, which now had to be hauled up the mountain somehow before winter set in.[107]

Chalmers advertised for workers, offering extremely low wages of just $2.50 a day for "graders" – a full dollar of which would be retained by the company for board.[108] An "A-1 machinist" could expect $3.50 to $4.00 for a 12-hour workday from the parsimonious Scotsman to run the compressors, while a blacksmith – expected not only to sharpen drills but also "shoe a horse occasionally" – would get just $3.00.[109] Workmen were required to bunk at the new boarding house to be closer to their duties, and married men were sternly advised to find alternate housing for their wives. As Chalmers informed his foreman:

> *At present I have no accommodations for Ladies and in fact rather object to them at the Works. But I can get you a small house 1-1/2 miles off for your wife, if you must have her with you – you would have to be at the Works.*[110]

Shrugging off any criticism of the paltry pay, Chalmers wrote his compatriots in London: "So long as I am in funds with which to pay off a growler, it does not matter to me whether they like it or not."[111]

A foreman by the name of J. H. Bugbee was procured from San Francisco and promised a salary of $150 a month. The miserly Chalmers, however, knocked off a dollar a day for his board until the heavy machinery actually arrived.[112] "You will require to bring [your own] bed and blankets," Chalmers wrote Bugbee tartly, adding, "I have always used candles. Bring a Miner's Lamp with you [if you want one]."[113]

Long bars of octagon drill steel for making drill bits;[114] assorted pole and drifting picks; nearly a ton of dynamite and ten thousand feet of fuse; 20 boxes packed

Courtesy of Calaveras County Historical Society

The Isabella Boarding House kept workers conveniently close to their duties at the tunnel project - and away from the saloons of Silver Mountain.

with caps and another 20 of candles – all were ordered up from San Francisco.[115] The Isabella Tunnel's state-of-the-art facility soon boasted not only drills, boilers, and compressors, but also a 40 x 32 foot building with separate engine and boiler rooms. The brace of boilers was handsomely outfitted with an 8 foot x 40 inch air receiver, capable of withstanding 200 pounds of pressure per square inch.[116] Nearby stood a large new blacksmith's shop and separate carpenter's shop.[117] Also on hand were a No. 4 Knowles steam pump, a No. 1 Blake pump,[118] and six mining cars capable of hauling 1,600 pounds of ore apiece.[119]

By December 30, 1878, the wooden bridge over Silver Creek was nearing completion.[120] But other details for the tunnel operation were not falling together quite as swiftly. Lumber for the building housing the compressors and to use as planking on the bridge proved impossible to obtain. Chalmers finally managed to solve that dilemma by purchasing and demolishing an existing building in Silver Mountain, and hauling the lumber to his site.[121]

It would also prove more difficult than Chalmers expected to procure "an A-1, sober bricklayer" to build the brick foundation for the pair of new compressors.[122] It didn't help that Chalmers was offering such paltry wages. He reluctantly upped the ante, promising $4 a day to entice a "good, steady Brick Layer,"[123] and sweetening the deal by offering to pay the fare both to and from Carson.[124]

Dustman Collection

Mules provided the motive power for the ore carts at the Isabella Tunnel.

Despite a precautionary letter from Chalmers to the road-master advising him of the imminent arrival of heavy equipment and warning that the bridges and roadway from Bulliona to the tunnel site would require repair to ensure the equipment's passage,[125] Chalmers soon found his new compressors had become mired at Markleeville, a dozen miles away, "[o]wing to the state of the Roads."[126] He was obliged to send all hands from his tunnel to assist the teamsters – notwithstanding the $1,000 in freight he had already paid.[127]

Like the compressors, the new boilers, too, were delayed in arriving by deep snow.[128] Chalmers chafed:

Alpine County Historical Society

A rare postage cancel from Silver Mountain in 1874, featuring the name of the Exchequer Gold & Silver Mining Co. In 1879, after Silver Mountain City was largely abandoned, Chalmers managed to get postal service transferred to his Silver Creek compound, with his bookkeeper Mr. Thomson serving as the postmaster.

[W]e have had the heaviest fall of snow of the Season – in many places 5 and 6 feet deep. . . It is very annoying when we are so anxious to get our drills under way. It has also prevented our finishing our second Compressor foundation. Masons won't work in freezing weather – lime does not set well in frost. . . You may have some idea of the storm when I tell you that it took me nearly an hour to get from the Exchequer Mill to the Tunnel on snow shoes [skis] on Saturday – snow in places where it had drifted, 6 feet deep, blowing a hurricane – and to get into the Tunnel I had to crawl over 6 feet of snow, the rock from the face being thrown back until the storm abated sufficiently to permit its being run out.[129]

Other start-up woes would prove similarly frustrating. Once the new compressors had finally been manhandled into place, workmen discovered that the hoses necessary to run them had not been sent and a mounting template proved to have been drawn incorrectly.[130] One of the cylinder heads turned out to be "honeycombed" by imperfect casting, and the vendor was not anxious to rectify the mistake. After a flurry of caustic correspondence from Chalmers, a replacement part was finally sent – only to turn out to have been made for the wrong end of the cylinder. And the new drills came with columns too short for the tunnel.[131] Equipment issues would prove hardly the least of Chalmers's troubles; before long, labor woes too raised their ugly head:

> *The Teamster who engaged to bring shingles, after delivering one load, got alarmed and refused to bring more – the roof being only three-fourths shingled. Two of my men struck work permanently, on account of the excessive cold and wet. The others threatened, but when the two got their pay, concluded (they said) to go to work.[132]*

Chalmers' magnificent dream of a tunnel was off to a nightmare of a start. But in his letters back to London he remained determinedly up-beat: "Hitherto I have toiled in vain – I am, however, not discouraged – 'cast down' it may be, but not destroyed. I hope yet to make even my enemies admit that patience and perseverence have their own reward."[133] And a few days later he reported encouragingly: "The Tarshish Mine in Monitor has been again started with a full force, and I hear The Advance will follow suit. In this district, there is some talk of resuming operations in The Mountain Tunnel."[134]

The comparison with Sutro's famous tunnel was not entirely hyperbole. As Chalmers was quick to point out, the Sutro's 10' x 8' cavity was only slightly larger than the Isabella's roomy 9' x 8' dimensions.[135] Such a size allowed the Isabella to accommodate a double pair of inch-and-a-quarter iron rails laid side by side, permitting mules to pull cars both in and out simultaneously. The floor of the Isabella tunnel sloped upward a gentle three inches per 100 feet,[136] ensuring that gravity would drain excess water down a channel in the floor to the tunnel mouth.

Chalmers' acquisition of a pair of expensive air-driven National mining drills was true to form; he might scrimp on laborers' salaries, but when it came to equipment nothing but the best would do. Drills powered by compressed air had only been used since about 1870, when Burleigh introduced his pioneering

Ever an early adaptor, Chalmers employed new air-powered drills in his Isabella Tunnel.

Dustman Collection

design in Colorado.[137] These bulky early contraptions were a "slugger" variety, using a piston to drive a steel drill rod some 200 to 600 strokes a minute. Their advantage over old-fashioned hand-drilling was huge; a hand-hammered drill could make progress of about one foot per hour, while the same one foot could be produced in about two minutes using a good machine drill.[138] But these early drills were extremely heavy (one early Burleigh weighed in at a bulky 372 pounds),[139] and required the support of a vertical mounting column to hold the drill and resist its powerful recoil.

By the end of March 1879, Foreman Bugbee was expressing hope that the new National air drills could be deployed within a week. Cautioning that "[w]e cannot expect to get the <u>full</u> benefit" until the men had been thoroughly trained to use the new equipment, Chalmers added his own note of optimism: "After that I hope, even with only 2 drills, to make <u>well on to</u> 300 feet per month."[140] With each mechanically-aided drill hole averaging 6 feet deep, Chalmers soon could report that an amazing ten feet of tunnel was being made every 24 hours.[141]

Nitroglycerine-based blasting powder too was a relatively new innovation,[142] and Chalmers supplied his workmen with not one but two different brands: Giant Powder, procured from the San Francisco-based Bandmann & Nielson Company, and a competing explosive product called Vulcan Powder.

Dustman Collection

The Isabella's brick-lined powder magazine was located away from the tunnel mouth for safety.

With some 26 to 40 holes being detonated in 24 hours and consuming 100 pounds of powder per day, blasting powder became an expensive commodity;[143] for a nine-month supply of powder alone, Chalmers estimated the cost to be $13,500.[144] Little wonder, then, that both powder manufacturers dispatched sales agents to pay personal calls at Chalmers' site, each hoping to convince him to use their product exclusively.[145] Chalmers shamelessly played the two suppliers off against each other, complaining to each about their quality, wangling samples of Bandmann's Giant Powder to "put quietly into a Vulcan box" to test which was "the better powder,"[146] and requesting special "arrangements" like cash discounts or deliveries in advance, to be paid for only when used.

Although far more stable than earlier explosive products, these newer blasting powders were still entitled to due respect. In January, 1879, for example, an explosion at the San Francisco powder works of the Giant Powder company took the lives of four men.[147] In a rare but practical nod to safety, Chalmers had a brick-lined powder magazine dug into the hillside a short walk away from the tunnel mouth.

For all his lavish expenditures on equipment and supplies, Chalmers was relentlessly penny-pinching when it came to his hired hands. He lambasted foreman Bugbee: "You use altogether too much powder. . . . This is simply ridiculous, apart from being extravagantly wasteful." Like an instructor lecturing a young schoolboy, Chalmers directed him to "use only half a case at a blast, tamp with water, carefully greasing your primer cap . . . until I give different instructions."[148] Before long, disgruntled at the lack of progress in the tunnel and having discovered that "a good deal of whiskey was consumed about the works at night," Chalmers fired Bugbee outright and replaced him with a new foreman he called "one of Sutro's best men," Robert Andrews. So much for penny-pinching; in order to persuade Andrews to come, Chalmers was forced to offer him an astronomical $8 per day.[149]

What was life like inside the Isabella Tunnel? A description of the great Hoosac Tunnel in Massachusetts offers a glimpse what visitors would have experienced upon entering the Isabella for the first time:

> *[The] ride into the tunnel is far from being a cheerful one. The fitful glare of the lamps upon the walls of the dripping cavern, – the frightful noises that echo from the low roof, and the ghoul-like voices of the miners coming out of the gloom ahead, are not what would be called enlivening. . . . The roof of the tunnel for the rest of the journey is very low, and the scenery does not on the whole improve as we go forward. Through the smoke before us spectral lights are seen flitting about, and a frightful din in the region of the lights grows louder as we approach.*[150]

For the miners it was cold, wet, dirty work, conducted in near-darkness. With only flickering candles for illumination, they would drill a pattern of holes in the face rock, scooping out the dust from each hole with a long-handled spoon. Next came inserting and tamping the explosive charges, and finally detonating the blast – all a mere prelude for the grueling toil of shoveling the heavy waste rock into cars before starting all over again.

At the outset Chalmers pushed his crew seven days a week. Having received his Board of Directors' surprising but humane order that "no work shall be done on Sunday," Chalmers grumbled: "I need scarcely say that [the Directors'] wishes shall be attended to. Of course, the discontinuance of Sunday work will take 52 days off my Tunnel work and reduce my annual run by 52 feet . . . ."[151]

As the tunnel grew longer, the air at the face grew more and more foul, and vapors from explosions took longer to dissipate. But blowers were expensive. Chalmers experimented with a number of contraptions including rigging a steam jet into a 20-foot standpipe at the mouth of the tunnel, which apparently did little to improve the situation.[152] In January, 1880, with the Isabella now over 1,600 feet in length, Chalmers was still employing only a meager three-inch air pipe powered by a 7-1/2 inch Sturtevant blower.[153] It was only after most of his men finally quit on account of the "sickness caused by fumes" that he broke down and beat a hasty trip over the mountains to San Francisco to buy new ventilation equipment, including a Baker blower and 2,000 feet of 13-inch air pipe.[154] About this same time five drillmen, both shift bosses and his engineer also "struck for wages."[155] Chalmers demanded that his bookkeeper, foreman, and carpenter fill the vacant posts in the tunnel,[156] and soldiered on.

The financial collapse of the Exchequer Company in 1879 had left Chalmers personally deeply in debt, though still ensconced comfortably enough in the pretty house beside the company's mill. The defunct company not only owed Chalmers £4000 (roughly $19,000) in unpaid salary[157] but also had left him to fend off a flock of irate creditors eager to attach his furniture.[158]

By March, 1880, critics within his own firm in London were also nipping at his heels. Chalmers was forced to pen a nine-page letter in his own defense, justifying his mining methodology and management strategy.[159] Short on funds, he began to be short with his suppliers as well, complaining *inter alia* upon receiving their bills: "[T]he last pipe was poor quality of iron, very brittle;"[160] "You have charged too much for solder and $1 too much for the gauge & the hose is very dear;"[161] and "[Y]our last 2 barrels [of] lard oil arrived ½ a Barrel short from leakage."[162]

Progress at the tunnel, too, was proving less than could be desired. With the workmen now slaving away in rock Chalmers described as "adamantine," as much as 80 pounds of Giant Powder was required for a single 16-hole blast.[163] Chalmers had his foreman write a letter confirming that the rock was "harder than anything we ever met in Sutro."[164] No longer the fluff of dreams and fairy tales, the Isabella was spiraling into a horror story.

His recent ventilation improvements had allowed Chalmers to push his crew faster, and by April, he was suddenly able to report lightning-like progress of 300 feet in the tunnel a month.[165] But with no remittance from London since late March, his accounts were now more than $3,400 in the red.[166] "Funds are now exhausted. Am I to continue driving[?]" he demanded pointedly of his London overseers in early May.[167]

A few token remittances trickled in: £500 here, £200 there.[168] But even without funds to meet a scheduled payday, Chalmers was dropping hints about the benefits of a new "Diamond Drill" for future core prospecting, adding, as if to shame the directors into the purchase: "[I]ndeed a Tunnel such as ours should not be without one. Sutro has half a dozen."[169]

Other new-fangled inventions too caught his eye. Chalmers wrote off to San Francisco, eager for "particulars" about an electric motor and electric lights to illuminate his tunnel.[170] In letters to the London syndicate, he agitated for a locomotive to haul rock debris out of the tunnel, observing with perfect practicality that engines, unlike mules, "don't get sick; snow don't scare them; [and] they don't eat their heads off if idle for a day."[171] Having heard of a remarkable new invention known as a telephone, he enquired about the cost of installing a "complete Telephone Rig" – contemplating one system to connect his tunnel to the engine room, and possibly a second one later from the tunnel to his house a mile and a quarter away.[172] And perhaps sensing trouble in the wind for the grand Isabella Tunnel, he also put plans in motion to acquire a new mining property known as the Morning Star Mine, in Monitor District.[173]

In a sudden burst of largesse, the London syndicate wired £1000 in July and another £1500 in August to keep the tunnel going; Chalmers promptly asked for £500 more.[174] His September report boasted an astonishing 328 feet of progress, a feat that had required the drilling of 8,460 feet of two-inch blast holes, and removal of 2,798 <u>tons</u> of rock "so tough that we had to charge and blast our centre cut holes twice."[175]

That was the good news. The bad news was that the anticipated Balaclava Ledge had finally been reached, only to find the lode "broken up by later formations" – in other words, barren of silver.[176] The only thing the miners had successfully struck was water, which now was "literally gushing from face and sides" of the tunnel.[177]

Chalmers was granted his much-wished-for Diamond Drill that October,[178] and by December a finer operation could not be imagined. Twelve mules were neatly housed in a comfortable stable, complete with grain and hay loft. The tunnel's rolling stock included 13 new ore cars. The brick-lined powder magazine – large enough to hold 50,000 pounds of powder – had been neatly finished inside with Portland cement, and a tramway constructed to ferry the powder to a thawing house where steam from the boilers could gently warm the frozen powder. An on-site tinsmith to fabricate ventilation pipe was ensconced in his own tin shop close to the tunnel mouth. The engine room was outfitted with a new engine; lathe; blower; circular saw; and drilling machine. And so much rock had been extracted from the tunnel already that the wooden trestle over the creek had been extended by 800 feet to reach fresh dumping ground.[179]

The Isabella tunnel now stretched nearly a mile deep into the mountainside: over 4,400 feet.[180] And that was as far as it would ever go.

With Kindest Love

Letters suggest that the relationship between Lewis and his housekeeper Antoinette quickly evolved beyond the purely professional. As early as 1878, his handwritten notes to her were signed "with kindest love,"[181] and blazed with jealousy as he urged her not to "throw herself away" on other potential suitors.[182]

Their living arrangement was certainly well-chaperoned. According to the census conducted in June, 1880, Lewis, Antoinette, and her five-year-old son Henry shared the roof of the old Davidson house with

Chalmers's former housekeeper from Bulliona, Mary Hanson and her husband John, as well as his mining engineer and right-hand man, George W. Jones. That same census also discloses the presence of a miner named Domenico Bari at a boarding house just two doors away, destined to play a starring role in Antoinette's future.

Perhaps in part to quiet gossips in nearby Silver Mountain, Chalmers officially took Antoinette as his bride on November 30, 1880, exchanging their vows at the beautiful Grace Church Cathedral in San Francisco.

Courtesy of Alpine County Historical Society

But the Isabella's finances were again in trouble – this time, big trouble. Just a week after his wedding, Chalmers admonished his backers in London: "I am without a remittance to pay the men for November, the last I had being the £600 on 4th November. . . . The Taxes are, as I wrote, delinquent on the last Monday of this month . . ."[183]

Matters quickly went from bad to worse. On December 15, Chalmers dispatched an urgent telegram: "Miners mutinous. Cable immediately Six Thousand [for] 45 days' pay and taxes."[184] The following day, he dropped a note to his meat supplier that spoke volumes about his circumstances: "Send no more beef, and kindly give me 3 or 4 weeks grace for what I owe you," he wrote, adding "Would you like any of the last beef back[?]"[185]

Two days later, Chalmers wrote London pointedly:

> *[T]he men are on a drunk and threatening attachments, personal violence and all manner of things, unless paid: and no money to pay with. . . . [I]n a few days the Sheriff will be in possession. . . . [I] dare not attempt to leave till all is paid. It got rumoured about that I was about to go away, and the sleigh carrying the mail was stopped to take me out by force. . . . There will be trouble here unless you pay up – of more kinds than one.[186]*

Pretty Antoinette Laughton married Chalmers at Grace Church Cathedral in San Francisco in 1880, wearing a dress whose color was described as "ashes of roses."

The Christmas holiday was a doleful affair. Sitting down with his pen on Christmas Eve, Chalmers reiterated to one of his London backers: "Men unpaid, are threatening everything."[187] And shortly before New Year's Day he cabled tersely: "Suits commenced."[188]

But by mid-January, 1881, money had begun flowing again from London and there was talk that work in the Isabella Tunnel would soon resume. And by mid-February, Chalmers was able to pay off the delinquent taxes. Furious at his latest close call, Chalmers swore he would never be so misused again. "I was <u>trapped</u> this time," he wrote angrily, "but won't be caught again."[189]

An air of domestic peace settled over the Exchequer Mill home. In his letters home, Chalmers affectionately addressed Nettie as "My own wee wifie."[190] That Spring he ordered packets of everything from radishes to cabbage, tulip bulbs to hollyhocks for his new bride.[191] Lady Chalmers soon announced happy news of her own: a baby would arrive that September to bless the newly-wedded couple.[192]

The new Mrs. Chalmers apparently no longer did housework. By April, Chalmers was on the lookout for household help, specifying "a middle aged, strong Scotch or German steady woman, unmarried or widow,

Dustman collection

In his leisure moments, Chalmers made furniture and fancied himself an amateur "wood-turner."

widow preferred, no Irish or American."[193] Meanwhile, for himself he was ordering a new buggy harness with silver-plated buckles, a case of 100 expensive Colorado cigars, and a length of black walnut lumber for a "top finish" around the bathtub.[194]

Although the taxes had been paid, the Isabella Tunnel's finances were still not completely caught up. Now eyeing new mining ventures in Colorado, Chalmers admitted he needed "a little time tidying up the balance" still owed by the tunnel project to Vulcan.[195] Deflecting criticism from London that the Isabella tunnel should have been "an <u>immediate</u>" success, Chalmers snipped: "I am tired preaching to an unappretiative audience, like a jury I once saw in Alpine – every one dead asleep."[196]

The Isabella, however, was far closer to dead than asleep. The tunnel work, suspended at just over 4,400 feet,[197] never really resumed.

But the resourceful Chalmers had fresh mining irons in the fire. By January, 1882, he was able to knock out another silver brick from ore at his latest venture, the newly-acquired Morning Star mine. Here, too, labor woes dogged him. His millmen becoming troublesome, Chalmers sought replacements who would be not only "sober, competent, and reliable" but also thoroughly "non-union" men.[198] Then on top of his business troubles, a personal one was added; a letter from Bavaria brought the sad tidings that Chalmers' eldest daughter Laura had passed away in March, 1882.[199]

Courtesy of Fritz Thornburg

Dominick Bari resided with Antoinette as a "boarder" after Chalmers left Alpine for good about 1886.

The years ticked slowly by. Chalmers made yet another pilgrimage to London in 1884 seeking funds; the following year, his family grew one baby larger as Antoinette gave birth to a daughter, Louisa.

And here the voluminous Chalmers record begin to get spotty. The last known copybook of Chalmers' letters concludes with an entry dated January, 1884. Exactly what transpired next is unclear. Did Chalmers have a falling out with Antoinette? Did the handsome Dominick play a role in Chalmers' departure? Whatever the underlying reasons, Chalmers apparently took leave of Alpine County about 1885 or 1886, for what would prove to be the last time. Dominick Bari, perhaps just a helpful boarder and perhaps something more, moved into the old homestead to assist Nettie with household duties.

In 1888, tragedy struck the old house by Silver Creek yet again when Lewis' and Nettie's young son drowned in the river. We may never know exactly how the drowning happened, but local legend has it that the little seven-year-old was pushed into the water by his half-brother, Henry.

Chalmers kept up a polite correspondence from a distance with Nettie and Dominick from London, hinting at plans to return someday to Alpine. In one letter in 1891, he thanked Bari "for all the kindness and good offices you have shown my family during my enforced absence," describing himself as "much distressed" that he was "as yet, unable to send you the money you so generously advanced to my poor wife."[200] And as always, Chalmers seemed to have fresh mining schemes up his sleeve. Alluding to an impending visit by potential mine purchasers, he instructs Bari to "show them the IXL, Isabelle, Exchequer and Stella Mines" – while warning him to keep the potential sale secret from prying Alpiners for the time being. But another fresh mining adventure was not to be.

Did Chalmers give up on Antoinette as well as on Alpine? Tantalizing entries from the British census disclose that by 1891, Chalmers was residing in Hackney, England, in the home of a 62-year-old French widow named Constance de Ridder, and that a decade later he still lived with Constance and her children, at a new address.[201]

In January, 1904, nearing his 80th birthday, Chalmers passed away of a "heart complaint" after what was reported to have been "only two or three days' illness."[202] The Reno newspaper remembered Chalmers with an obituary observing that he "altogether blew in about $1,500,000 in mills, furnaces and tunnels" in Alpine County, concluding tartly: "He was a generous, high-minded English gentleman, but knew nothing of mining."[203]

Courtesy of Alpine County Historical Society

Antoinette Laughton and her oldest son, Henry Laughton, circa 1910 – just a few years before her death.

Long considered odd by the local townsfolk, Antoinette grew even odder as the years went by. Stories circulated that she would answer the door with a vial of acid in her hand and a revolver tucked in her apron.[204] As late as 1910, the census shows that Bari was still living in the old house beside Silver Creek with the once-fair Antoinette.

A sudden and unexplained disappearance of daughter Louisa about June, 1913 proved to be the last straw for poor Nettie. That November, after signing a deed to sell off the old house,[205] Nettie moved to a rented room in Oakland and searched unsuccessfully for her missing daughter. Three days after Christmas, Nettie could take no more. She switched on the gas jets in her apartment, stuffed cloth and paper around the door and window, lay down on the bed, and let the fumes wash away her troubles.[206]

Antoinette's ashes were buried in the family plot near Silver Creek,[207] beside the body of her little boy who had drowned in the creek and that of Chalmers' oldest son, Lewis. The casket of Henry Laughton would later be added to the tiny family graveyard.

With Antoinette gone and the old homestead sold, Dominick moved to Markleeville and in 1914, the year following Antoinette's death, he too passed away. Blessed with a kind face and hard-working hands, Dominick was also blessed, it seems, with staunch friends; a fine black granite headstone marks his grave near the edge of the old Markleeville cemetery.

Dustman Collection

The grave of Dominick Bari at the Markleeville Cemetery. Above right, the Chalmers Graveyard, where Nettie's ashes are buried.

CHAPTER 10:
TRADE & TAXES

The local mines may have attracted the lion's share of investor attention and all of the glory, but they were hardly the only drivers of Alpine's early economy. Other local sources of profit and wages included "timber-slaying" with its associated sawmills; cattle and hay ranching; and an ever-shifting array of small shops purveying everything from meat to medicine. Hard-working proprietors in all of these industries did not operate in a vacuum, of course; just as today, the tax man quietly served as a much unloved business partner.

Ranching, Agriculture & Rustic Gardens

Alpine's luxurious meadows were quickly discovered by sheepmen, becoming a rich temporary home each summer for flocks herded up from the Carson Valley and as far away as San Joaquin, Stanislaus, and Calaveras counties to forage.[1] As early as August 1868, the *Chronicle* records 60,000 head of sheep "grazing in the mountains adjacent to the Big Trees Road between [Silver Mountain] and Murphy's."[2] Three years later, a spring influx of 70,000 sheep flowed into Alpine's pastures over the Big Trees and Amador Roads (Carson Pass) by early June.[3] And by mid-summer that same year, an astonishing 131,000 head of sheep had traipsed into

Courtesy of Alpine County Historical Society

Thousands upon thousands of sheep were herded to Alpine summer pastures as early as the 1860s. Here, sheep dot the lush grasslands in Hope Valley.

Alpine County by way of Blood's House in Bear Valley.[4] Similar mass incursions were reported in 1878 with 102,500 woolly critters reported to be grazing Alpine's green pastures.[5] As the *Chronicle* editors sighed, "Our 'hills' are pretty well filled with sheep now, but we presume there are thousands yet to come."[6]

Later commentators would tactfully observe that migratory sheep grazing was widely "resented" by locals, noting that the sheep stripped vegetation from hills and meadows while contributing little to Alpine merchants.[7] But local sentiment likely had deeper and more personal roots. The dust, noise, dung, and general inconvenience of these passing flocks were a seasonal nuisance intruding upon the otherwise peaceful daily life of Silver Mountain townsfolk. On a single day in May, 1871, for example, some 2,200 sheep meandered down Silver Mountain's Main Street and right through the center of town, "bound for the Humboldt."[8]

Herds of cattle and horses from the Carson Valley took similar advantage of the lush Alpine summer pasturage and, like the sheep, could sometimes make themselves disruptive guests. In 1878, the *Chronicle* vigorously cheered a legislative proposal for a new "animal trespass law," complaining that Alpine farmers "are yearly run down by cattle and horses from Carson Valley, straying or driven into Alpine for grazing," and expressing fond hope that the new legislation would rid them of this "continual annoyance during the Summer months."[9]

Cattle, like sheep, were often herded along the roads of the county to summer pastures or markets elsewhere. As early as 1859, William Dennis brought 300 head of "half-breed and American" cattle to his range in Silver Valley,[10] while in 1864 some 400 cattle reportedly trouped through Monitor on their way to "Walker's river."[11] Smaller numbers of animals were imported to provide meat for the local populace as well. Locals J. Christie and J. Davidson arrived at Silver Mountain with a "band of beef cattle from the other side of the mountains" in 1868,[12] perhaps destined for Kirby's slaughter house on Silver Creek,[13] the "Empire Meat Market" in Markleeville,[14] or the establishment of "French & Gulickson, Practical Butchers" in Monitor.[15]

While Alpine's frigid winters hardly offered the most hospitable climate for year-round ranches, at least a few herds were raised locally for meat and milk. One Capt. W.M. Smith of Fredericksburg launched a goat-ranching enterprise in 1869 with 150 sturdy specimens, and just three years later was able to boast a herd numbering 1,400.[16] Wealthy stockmen hundreds of miles away sometimes partnered with locals to their mutual profit. In 1871, Daniel Davidson contracted with Barnard D. Sloan of Contra Costa County to tend Sloan's 2,015 ewes for a period of two years, in exchange for half of the "increase" in the herd and the wool profits.[17]

A handful of dairy farms sprouted in the early 1860s in the lush meadows of Hope Valley, and by 1867 there was talk that "the whole extent of the valley will [soon] be brought into requisition for this purpose."[18] A single dairy could churn out between 350 and 400 pounds of butter a week, much of it destined for the booming Comstock markets of Gold Hill and Virginia City.[19] Successful dairying clans in the Hope Valley area by 1869 included the Barton, Nott, Scott, and Stevens families, collectively tending herds numbering 700 cows.[20] Hope Valley was noted not only for its dairies but for its strong-minded politics as well; one cheeky local *Chronicle* article dubbed it a "hot bed of Republicanism, trout, and good butter."[21]

At the junction of Alpine, Amador, and El Dorado counties, another small dairy operation was tended by Zacharius S. Kirkwood. Kirkwood had thrown up his original log cabin about 1864 and as one of the few way-stations on the Amador-Carson road, his felicitously-placed homestead soon evolved into a multi-purpose hotel, stage station, and post office. As late as 1895, one traveler wryly reported that the establishment still provided "good rough accommodation, if one is fortunate enough to escape quarters in the corral."[22]

Local ranchers found they could turn an additional profit from their acreage by boarding animals or raising feed crops. The famous Snowshoe Thompson offered pasturage for horses at his Diamond Valley ranch for $1.50 per month, and once boarded Chalmers' mine oxen for a winter – reaping a tart letter afterwards for his trouble from the prickly Scotsman grumbling that the animals "are not nearly in as good condition as they were in when I sent them to you."[23] Thompson also raised commercial feed crops, harvesting 1,600 bushels of oats and barley in the fall of 1871, and "more hay than any other farmer in the county."[24] A ton of that hay might sell for as much as $30 at Silver Mountain, with prices dipping to between $20 and $22 at the ranches.[25]

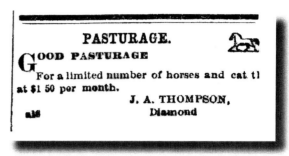

"Snowshoe" Thompson advertised pasturage at his Diamond Valley ranch at just $1.50 per month in February, 1873.

Dairy and ranching businesses faced some unusual challenges in the emerging wilderness. With so many forms of livestock dotting the Alpine landscape, the local bear population found it too convenient a dinner to ignore. Thus, news reports from the summer of 1871 indicated that, of the multitude of sheep which had crossed via the Big Trees Road that season, "[b]ears have killed a large number," while John McColloch was forced to dispatch a 500-pound bear at his dairy ranch about seven miles from Silver Mountain, "the Bruin family being a little too numerous in his neighborhood."[26]

Not all agriculture was conducted strictly for profit. Despite the bitter winters and short growing season, at least a few Alpine families tended gardens for home consumption. Chalmers ordered up a variety of seeds and roots by mail, suggesting that he and Nettie attempted to grow everything from asparagus to verbenas in the garden at their Silver Creek home.[27] "Fine currants" were raised nearby in J.B. Thompson's garden by the Exchequer Mill,[28] while the Woodford House hotel was well known for its "extensive" fruit and vegetable garden.[29]

If the kitchen garden should fail, local wildlife was abundant – free for the catching, and occasionally even profitable. Chalmers wrote home almost breathlessly upon his arrival in Alpine County of the profusion of local wildlife: grouse, hares, "sage hen" (quail), fox, coyote (which he deemed a "species of wolf"), and the occasional grizzly bear.[30] In letters to his children he described "beautiful lizards, rich green [in] color" and "butterflies . . . beyond anything you can fancy."[31] Henry Eno similarly described the local hare and grouse as "rather plent[iful]" in the vicinity of Silver Mountain, and those staples plus local venison no doubt graced many a miner's dinner table. One successful Monitor marksman returned after only a few hours on the Silver King Road with 27 pounds of "mountain grouse," suggesting a hearty appetite or a ready market.[32] For those with a knack for trapping, the fur trade offered yet another opportunity; a "white weasel" pelt might net the fortunate hunter a day's wages at $5, while a single silver fox skin commanded an astronomical $40 to $70.[33]

But if there was one free-for-the-foraging commodity most likely to be found on Silver Mountain tables, it was probably what Eno called "speckled trout" – the native Lahontan, which he describes as "abundant."[34] "Trouting" became a "favorite pastime" for early Silver Mountain citizens.[35] Chalmers, too, reported on the "good trout (large) fishing," observing "they don't rise to fly" but adding that the locals were successful using bait.[36]

The disruptive twin forces of wood drives and mining dams soon "demoralized" the local trout, much to the consternation of Alpine citizens.[37] Efforts were launched to require that "fish ladders" be constructed

Dustman Collection

FISH NOTICE.

NOTICE IS HEREBY GIVEN TO ALL parties interested, either as owners, agents or managers, in dams built upon the rivers and creeks in Alpine county, to forthwith erect or cause to be erected proper FISH LADDERS at said dams. If ladders are not erected at said dams on or before the 25th day of July, A. D., 1876, the penalties of the law will be strictly enforced against all offenders.

THOS. J. ORGON,
je24-4w   District Attorney.

Fish ladders were required to be constructed around all dams within the County, as this 1876 newspaper notice advised.

around dams,[38] but such regulatory attempts proved less than successful. The *Chronicle* editors fairly shouted their displeasure over one Monitor company's failure to construct a fish ladder at its dam, admonishing the District Attorney to pay heed: "[W]e want our streams well stocked with trout next season – which has not been the case since the d--- dam has been in existence."[39]

Even when owners did take the trouble to build a fish ladder, however, it often suffered in either design or execution. At the Advance Dam below Bulliona, for example, the fish ladder was found to be "not working to the satisfaction of the trout that desire to visit Silver Mountain," as the *Chronicle* lamented in 1878.[40]

Fish nevertheless continued to flourish in bodies of water more removed from the wood drives and mining enterprises. In 1876, trout were so prolific at Silver Lake that one non-ecologically-minded fishing party proudly hauled in over 1,400 of the finny creatures in just half a day.[41] And a proud "excursionist" on the nearby Walker River made news by snagging a 23-inch specimen.[42]

Timber

The timber business rivalled the mines as a source of local employment, forming a parallel mainstay for the local economy. Alpine's old-growth forests made bountiful fodder for the voracious Comstock Lode, winding up as shoring timbers for their ever-expanding mines, framing lumber for Virginia City houses, fuel for the legions of steam engines that pumped its water and drove its stamp mills, and firewood in Comstock woodstoves.

Local Silver Mountain residents, too, required extensive wood supplies for heating and cooking. As many as 17 cords of wood might be turned to smoke to keep a single building warm for the winter.[43] One *Chronicle* news item mentioned that a "wooding up" party was hauling firewood into Markleeville after a heavy storm, using handsleds "propelled by from two-boy to four-man power" and cheerfully reporting on the "exciting sport" when a wood sled escaped and went "kiting down hill, leaving the poor fellows in attendance nothing to do but follow on and gather up the fragments."[44]

The commercial wood business required year-round preparation for a few brief weeks of springtime production. Woodsmen would walk the length of the streams in September, carefully removing dead trees and other obstructions that might interfere with a future drive.[45] Over the winter, crews would fell trees and split them into cordwood,[46] stacking vast piles along the riverbanks.[47]

Opportunity to float the logs downstream came in a brief window each spring, as snow run-offs raised water levels to peak carrying capacity. Logs or cordwood would be pitched into the river and corralled with a boom, then cut loose to churn their way down the raging torrents. On narrow upper creeks a wooden dam might be built to impound the logs as the water rose, designed with a "key" that could be blown out to topple the entire dam and release the precious cargo down-river.[48]

At interim staging areas, a portion of the logs might be converted into finished lumber at local mills. Timber from the Silver King area, for example, was floated down the East Carson River to Centerville, a

Logs being restrained by a boom at roughly the location of today's Power Dam Road, prior to entering the Carson Valley.

Courtesy of Alpine County Historical Society

town primarily known for its two sawmills.[49] The aptly-named settlement of Splinterville above Monitor similarly converted a portion of the floated logs into lumber before forwarding the finished product farther downstream.[50]

In the Carson Valley, vast clusters of cordwood would again be corralled, awaiting high water to ferry the harvest on to Empire. Drive crews accompanied the logs on their watery journey to break up jams if they occurred, followed by a chuck boat carrying food and supplies for the workmen.[51] Once safely at Empire, the soggy timbers were hauled out of the river and loaded onto V&T railroad cars to be ferried up the mountain to Virginia City. For drive hands, the entire trip from forest to flatcar could take as long as 21 days.[52]

The scale of these wood drives was mind-boggling. As early as 1864, some 50,000 cords of wood were stacked and waiting on the riverbanks for the following year's drive; the following year, six million board-feet of Alpine timber floated downriver during a single drive.[53] Two years later, a similar spring drive ferried another 6 million feet of "saw logs" on their watery journey. And as many as six separate wood drives might be conducted per season.[54]

Vigorous crews of "wood-slayers" would be hired and assembled into camps each fall to fell as many trees as possible for the coming year's wood drive. Brief news notes over the years identify woodchopper camps in such widely disparate

Vigorous crews of "wood-slayers" would be assembled each fall."

parts of the county as Markleeville;[55] Silver King; Pleasant Valley Creek;[56] Noble Canyon;[57] Centerville;[58] and Silver Mountain.[59]

Although used extensively elsewhere, wooden flumes were few in Alpine County; instead, most timber was probably hauled by wagon or dragged by teams to the riverbanks, and propelled on to its destination by the raw confines of the river itself. Nonetheless, at least a few wooden flumes were either built or proposed. In 1865, a survey party scouted a route for a proposed timber flume that would span the 34½ miles from Woodfords to Empire, a grandiose project that never materialized.[60] In 1872, a V-flume was proposed "to be erected, extending from the head of [Carson] Canyon to just below Woodfords" to facilitate clearing Carson Canyon of its heavy timber.[61] That same year, the Spratt Brothers successfully completed a three-mile V-flume "from their camp, three miles

Logging in winter. "They slay timber for the good of mankind," wrote the Folgers.

southeast of Markleeville, into the Middle Fork" of the Carson River near town.[62] Dr. James Caples proposed a flume project in 1873 to convey logs through Diamond Valley, Long Valley, and Dutch Valley to Nevada.[63] As late as 1878, at least one company owned a flume associated with its sawmill on Pocket Mill Creek, and circa 1884, William M. Thornburg reportedly constructed a sawmill in Thornburg Canyon, west of Markleeville, to produce "flume lumber."[64]

While lumber drives generated handsome profits for their operators and seasonal employment for a multitude of hired hands, logging operations were not universally applauded. One

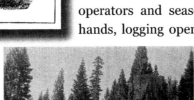

An 8-foot tall stump left by the pioneer "timber slayers" near Indian Creek shows the size of the old-growth trees once standing in Alpine County.

Courtesy Alpine County Historical Society

Sacramento Bee article decried the "vandalism" being wreaked on the pine forests of the Eastern Sierra. An early column in the *Monitor Gazette* advised local citizens to start filing timber claims "as the only mode by which they can save to themselves fuel in time of need," observing that "unless some check is placed upon what we consider an illegiti-

mate if not an illegal drain upon [Alpine's] wood and timber resources, she will be stripped bare of them by the time her mills are in operation."[65] The utilitarian Folger brothers staunchly defended the loggers, editorializing that "[T]hey slay timber for the good of mankind," and adding reassuringly: "[T]here are trees enough to meet all demands for generations upon generations to come."[66] The press in Carson Valley, however, expressed the concerns of valley ranchers:

A few more years and the beautiful pine forests that surround Lake Tahoe and cover the eastern slope of the Sierras . . . will have been laid low by the woodsman's ax. . . . This done, the Carson Valley will be left a barren waste for the remainder of the summer and fall. . . . [T]he wood business promises to inflict upon our farming interests irreparable injury.[67]

Loggers and sheep ranchers sometimes clashed – one valuing trees, the other open grazing space. Whether deliberately or unintentionally, shepherds occasionally set fires that savaged valuable timber stands.[68] Alpine property owners with land adjacent to the creeks also despised the loggers. Buildings abutting streambeds were sometimes swept away during wood drives, and toll road owners regularly found their expensive bridges carried away by the logs careening downstream.[69] Wood jams and retaining booms also caused occasional flood damage to adjacent lands.[70]

By the spring of 1871 the Alpine wood business was thriving, with anticipated prices of $60,000 for every 15,000 cords successfully delivered to Empire – a third higher than the previous year's figures.[71] The

following season, with the price of wood expected to be "as high [in Silver Mountain] as it is in Virginia City today," people were "going crazy" filing claims on timber locations.[72] Speculation in wood properties ran rampant,[73] and competing claimants sometimes clashed.[74] Agents from companies as far away as Virginia City and Carson were reported to be in town, scouting for timber ranches to acquire.[75]

During the following spring and summer, Alpine forests produced an estimated 20,000 and 25,000 cords, a harvest worth more than $75,000.[76] But even that was nothing compared to the projected yield from the *next* seasonal drive, when an anticipated 100,000 cords would be floated down the Carson River. By the fall of 1872, wood companies were desperately trying to hire 400 more woodcutters for the next four months.[77] Woodchoppers were arriving in Silver Mountain "as fast as they can be procured," with room for "a great many more" and "good wages" promised of $3 per cord.[78]

For the "wood slayers" it was hard and dangerous work. Over the span of just six months, one woodsman from Temple's wood camp in Stowell's Canyon was killed when a rolling log crushed his skull, and another drowned in the Carson River while breaking up a jam.[79] Woodchoppers also had little economic security for their labor. Until 1878, they were not even allowed a laborers' lien on the logs if a timber company should fail to pay their wages.[80]

For the "wood slayers," the timber business was hard and dangerous work. Frank Young (above), age 34, drowned in the Carson River during a wood drive "above Sturgeon's Camp" in June, 1878. His body was finally located almost two months later below the falls, where it had been partly covered by sand.

But while the work was challenging, it was also immensely profitable – at least for the operators. Chalmers reported that the price of cordwood at Empire "don't go below $6" a cord, speculating that at those figures he would be able to produce $20,000 worth of wood in a single season from his company's timber ranch, if competition from the nearby Truckee forests didn't restrain the price.[81]

By 1873, however, overproduction began to take its toll. The price of wood that year plummeted to a mere $3 a cord, delivered.[82] The logging industry nevertheless experienced periodic bursts of activity for several years. In 1876, for example, woodcutters were reportedly "raiding through this town [Silver Mountain], slaying every available tree" – including some venerable specimens that formerly had graced the town cemetery.[83] But by 1878, the *Chronicle* was lamenting: "The stagnation of the wood business on the Comstock has killed the chopping in this county for this year."[84] And by about 1880, logging profits had declined so far that woodsmen Boer and Flanders simply abandoned 2,600 cords of already-cut wood near Dixon Creek.[85]

Sawmills

Hacking raw logs from the forest was one thing; converting them to usable finished lumber was another. A surprising number of small sawmill operations sprang up throughout the new county to meet the growing demand, churning out neatly-sawn boards for local buildings and sturdy square timbers for the mines.[86]

The county's first sawmill – launched a full decade before Alpine's boundaries were drawn – is said to have begun operation near Woodfords about 1853-54. But exactly *which* of two early sawmills could claim the honor is unclear: Orville Wade operated one early mill at Woodfords, while another small water-powered sawmill was erected by William and John Carey near Fredericksburg Canyon, and later moved to Woodfords.[87]

Courtesy of Society of California Pioneers, San Francisco
(Detail of Lawrence & Houseworth #707)
Gift of Florence V. Flinn

The creek at Silver Mountain was evidently dammed to provide water power, as this picture includes a portion of the millpond. The logs on the bank may have been destined for Robinson's Saw Mill on the east side of Silver Creek (out of sight to the right).

As early as 1863, Silver Mountain was able to boast two lumber mills of its own. These reportedly were working "both night and day," and still "could not meet the demand" from the booming settlement.[88] These may have been the Buist & Pearson mill, a "whipsaw" operation able to produce up to 600 feet per day;[89] and Robinson's Saw Mill on the east side of Silver Creek. Another source mentions yet a third mill near Silver Mountain, still under construction as of May, 1864 but anticipated to be able to turn out some 30,000 board feet every 24 hours, once completed.[90]

Several additional sawmill operations were either being constructed or already running full tilt by 1864. A water-powered sawmill in Forest Dale Valley on the road to Summit City was apparently so new even the assessment records described it as "unfinished."[91] And names of other sawmill operations or potential future mill sites at Silver Mountain are sprinkled through various records, including "Sander's [*sic*] millsite, near Eighth and Main streets, and adjoining the cemetery," and "Sanders & Jacob's millsite" at Murphy's Canyon Creek, "on the southwest side of Silver Mountain";[92] a mill site owned by "Smith, Turner and Thompson & Co." northeast of the grave-yard;[93] a one-acre mill site on the east side of Silver Mountain just north of "Mammouth Cañon," owned by James White;[94] and the possibly related "Dake & White's Mill."[95] Chalmers later expressed interest in purchasing "Gilman & Weed's saw mill" near Silver Mountain, both for its engine and its timber and water privileges.[96]

Sawmills were blossoming elsewhere in the county, too. A pair of 60- and 64-inch circular saw blades were toted in from Mount Gregory in El Dorado County in July, 1864, installed in a roomy 27 x 70-foot building east of the town of Centerville, and hooked up to a 40-horsepower steam engine to become Richardson's Sawmill.[97] Close by Richardson's on the East Carson River an enterprise known as Harrell's Saw Mill was launched.[98] Ira Luther improved his squatter's ranch near Hope Valley with a small, water-driven sawmill.[99] And in 1866, Cathey & Hash were operating a specialized "shingle mill" at Stevens' Ranch in Hope Valley.[100]

The Cohn or "Diamond" Sawmill near Woodfords was operated from the late 1880s until about 1900 by Isadore Cohn, milling lumber from logs like these. Note the solid wooden wheels on the cart.

Courtesy of Alpine County Historical Society

Markleeville had its own share of local sawmill operations, with two separate facilities in operation as early as February, 1864, and a third still under construction.[101] From about 1866 to 1868, the "Pocket Saw Mill Company" operated a 600-acre timber ranch approximately three miles northwest of Markleeville on the "Cary's Mills" road which included a steam sawmill on Indian Creek.[102] Other early Markleeville lumber mill operations included the Hungerford Sawmill on Markleeville Creek;[103] the "Curtz & Griffith," a steam sawmill northwest of Markleeville;[104] and the Bemis Mill, a steam-driven circular sawmill about a mile from the Curtz-Griffith – whose equipment was later moved to Mrs. Hawkins' ranch and purchased by Isadore Cohn to become the "Diamond Mill."[105] In later years, William Koenig ran a steam-powered sawmill near Pleasant Valley.[106]

Near Monitor, sawmills included the Buena Vista mill managed by Thomas McAllister[107] and, between Monitor and Silver King, the Minnesota Sawmill.[108] Mill site "locations" near Bulliona – though apparently never developed – included the Hanson and Lecony Mill Sites.[109] Close by the junction of the Carson's East Fork with Silver King Creek, the tiny sawmill town of Splinterville emerged "for the convenience of the lumbering industry."[110] This was likely the home of Paul Curts (or Curtz's) 34 x 80-foot mill known as the "Silver King Mills and Lumbering Company," a facility equipped with a water-driven, 60-inch circular saw capable of milling 8,000 to 12,000 board-feet per day.[111]

All told, by 1871 some thirteen sawmills were operating in Alpine County[112] – with more on the way. In late 1872, Elliot & Co. were laying plans for a new sawmill in Carson Canyon[113] while pioneer settler Fred Frevert's water-powered sawmill in the lower end of Fredericksburg Canyon was employing 20 men in 1876.[114] About the same time, entrepreneurs Soddar and Scott had their own sawmill in operation in Woodfords Canyon.[115] But by 1880, declining demand from the Comstock generated a parallel decline in the market for timber, and just two Alpine sawmills remained in active operation.[116]

Davidson's Mill

Daniel Davidson's sawmill beside Silver Creek was a prominent enough landmark to be recorded on Theron Reed's 1864 map of the Silver Mountain Mining District,[117] and was mentioned in Davidson's homestead claim of July 5, 1865.[118]

Once Chalmers took over the Davidson mill property in 1870, he wasted no time in improving the facility. Soon it featured a pair of circular saws driven by a new 60-horsepower turbine engine.[119] One

saw featured an enormous 60-inch Spaulding blade equipped with just ten cutting teeth.[120] Over the years, Chalmers continued to upgrade the mill's equipment, purchasing a "Huntington shingle machine" from the Vulcan Iron Works in September, 1876.[121] The following month a planing, molding, and tongue-and-groove machine too was on its way.[122]

The sawmill would prove to be a synergistic acquisition for the Exchequer mine. As Chalmers emphasized to his financial backers, the sawmill "supplies the mine with timber, the teams returning with ore [and] the slabs supply the furnaces."[123] By the end of 1872, the old Davidson mill had churned out 370,000 feet of lumber for the mine's timbering and for associated buildings.[124] The following year, the mill furnished not only all of the lumber needed for the mining operation but also generated $1800 from outside lumber sales.[125] And when the county seat was moved to Markleeville in 1876, it was the Davidson sawmill that sold the County some 7,000 feet of lumber for a new wooden jail building to house the old iron cells.[126]

Today, lumber that was milled over a century ago at the old Davidson Mill is still visible at the Alpine County Museum, forming the walls of the historic jail building and lining the interior of the blacksmith exhibit.

Courtesy of Alpine County Historical Society

Timber was an important early resource for Alpine County. This photo shows the Hellwinkle Sawmill in Hope Valley about 1900. With no building surrounding it, the sawmill was a "portable" affair, which could be moved as necessary to be closer to its work.

Shops

Shopkeepers came and shopkeepers went as the fortunes of Silver Mountain waxed and waned, providing an ever-shifting panorama of businesses lining the town's commercial district. Depending on the year, a stroll down Main Street might offer visitors a chance to salivate over the gold jewelry offered by W.W Harris[127] or more pragmatically, a good pair of duck overalls at George J. Harris's "stand."[128] Miners too poor to pay $7 for a new pair of boots could have the holes in their old ones mended at Struben's shoe shop.[129]

Shopkeepers made the most of their shelves and many took a "variety store" approach, presenting customers with an incredible array of household and mining goods. From saloons to simple dry goods stores, many merchants included a brilliant assortment of alcoholic beverages among their wares. Patterson's Exchange, for example, carried an astonishingly diverse selection of intoxicants: brandies, wines, ale, porter, cidar, and lager, all hauled in over difficult-at-best dirt roads but somehow arriving miraculously unbroken.[130] Merchant Louis Wichelhausen indulged those with a taste for fine cigars and tobacco as well as San Francisco and Virginia City newspapers to peruse while smoking them, and packed his aisles with an eclectic array of other goods as well: law books, guitar and violin strings, lamps, willoware china, and candy.[131] "Blind Tom" Johnson had only a small fruit stand in the summer of 1867, selling grapes and other fruit to hungry workmen,[132] but managed to host his own Main Street "variety store" a few years later.[133]

A profusion of dry good merchants also quickly blossomed along Main Street, selling clothing, mining supplies, pots and pans, and other essentials. As early as September, 1863, I.S. Powers was already in the process of throwing up his store on Silver Mountain's Main Street – an establishment then trumpeted as one of the finest stores in town.[134] But competition was not long in arriving. W.R. Swinerton soon opened his narrow Pioneer Hardware Store with $2,000 worth of "groceries and hardware" on a half-lot near Third Street.[135] And Frenchman John Sauquet's dry goods store gracing the northeast corner of Main and 6th as early 1865 would prove to be one of the longest-lasting businesses in town, hanging on to become one of the few remaining landmarks emblazoned on the 1877 town plat.[136]

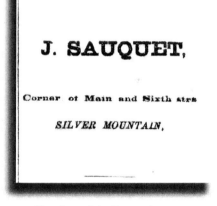

Frenchman John Sauquet's dry goods store at the corner of Sixth Street and Main was one of the longest-lasting businesses in Silver Mountain.

Surprisingly, even fresh grapes could be purchased in the tiny mountain town, in season.

Businessmen from as far away as the Bay area smelled opportunity in Alpine's early mining rush. San Francisco storekeeper Solomon Wangenheim swooped in to launch a branch location in Markleeville in 1864, stocking everything from powder and fuses for the mines to farm implements for the ranches, along with groceries, clothing,  stoves for housewives, and – for good measure – revolvers.[137] S. Reinstein, another San Francisco merchant, took over the stock of Harris's Silver Mountain dry goods store in December of 1866,[138] and as late as 1871 still had an agent at Monitor.[139] In summer months, traveling vendors brought grapes, apples, apricots, plums, peaches and nectarines to town by wagon "almost every day" from the other side of the mountain.[140] And Silver Mountain's Main Street always boasted at least one, and in its earliest days, *two* meat markets.[141]

Early Silver Mountain resident Henry Eno grumbled at the high cost of goods in 1866:

> *Living is of course high here, $10 a week, because we are high up and a long ways from the low lands of California, from which we draw all our supplies. . . . Flour is $16 per hund[red pounds],* *beef 16 cents per pound, eggs 75 cents per dozen, bacon and pork 40 cents per pound.*[142]

Mine owners like Chalmers complained bitterly about "the exorbitant prices charged here for everything in the shape of mining necessaries," sometimes joining with others to order in bulk from Sacramento, as "teamsters will not load under 7000 pounds."[143] Yet even the penny-pinching Chalmers purchased a wide range of supplies from local businesses, ranging from soda and cream of tartar for his boarding house to kegs of powder, resin soap, and pick handles.[144]

A wide variety of other small shops and businesses flourished during the brief intervals when Silver Mountain's mines were alive with miners and excitement. The smell of fresh-baked bread wafted down Main Street from the Pioneer bakery[145] while a "French Restaurant" and similar eateries provided meals for travelers, often as an adjunct to the local hotels.[146] Livery stables tended to weary horses,[147] and blacksmiths hammered out wagon parts and horseshoes. Hopeful claim owners could pay to have their most promising specimens assayed by the local assayer,[148] while would-be land purchasers might consult "Owens & Fine, Real Estate & General Agents" at the corner of Main and 4th Streets.[149] Dr. J.S. Adams welcomed patients at his office between 5th and 6th Streets, and cheerfully promised to "respond promptly to calls from all parts of Alpine."[150] "Doctor" D.V. Gates touted one-stop-shopping at his "drug, medicine and general variety store" at the corner of Main and Third.[151] And for those beyond a physician's healing powers, A.D.L. Payne later advertised "coffins made to order on short notice" at his combination carpentry/undertaking business a block to the west.[152]

But as local mines hit "the doldrums," many early merchants folded up shop as quickly as they had arrived.[153] Sauquet managed to hang on a decade longer than most,[154] but Wangenheim and Gates[155] likely moved on to greener pastures about the same time as Reinstein, who sold off his Silver Mountain inventory in 1870.[156]

For the hardy denizens who remained, barter and self-help would replace gold as the currency of the day. O.S. Adams,

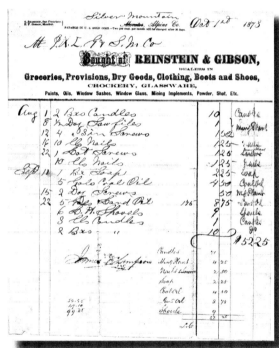

Courtesy of Alpine County Historical Society

Reinstein & Gibson's letterhead, showing a Silver Mountain outlet in 1873. The careful handwritten reconciliation at the bottom is Lewis Chalmers', confirming the total with his initials "L.C."

HARRISON CHILD,
Wheelwright and Blacksmith,
COR. MAIN AND SECOND STREETS,
SILVER MOUNTAIN.

Wheelwrighting, general blacksmithing, and horseshoeing promptly attended to and neatly executed.
[d6-tf]

for example, had his pants mended by "Sutherland the Tailor" and appears to have reciprocated by cleaning a clock for Sutherland in return.[157] And rather than part with his hard-earned coin for the services of a barber, Adams made do in rough pioneer fashion, recording in his diary: "cut Maxwell's hair, and Maxwell cut my hair."[158]

Taxes

> *"Among the many curses heaped upon this county*
> *heavy taxation is not the least."*
> *-- The Folger brothers, 1878*[159]

Taxes and fees were slapped on just about every kind of article or activity. There was a broker's license; a merchandise-seller's license; a theater license; a peddler's license;[160] a billiard table license[161]; and even a dog tax.[162] Would-be voters were forced to pony up $2 in poll tax for the privilege of casting their ballot.[163] A ten-cent tax was imposed on transfers of mining stock certificates,[164] and a tax was even levied on such simple luxuries as matches.[165] Property taxation was a separate burden, and a hefty one at that. As the *Bulletin* lamented, the total taxes on real and personal property "amount to over twelve per cent. on every hundred dollars of property in the State. *TWELVE PER CENT!* Just think of it."[166]

With so many saloons in town, liquor licenses became an especially lucrative revenue source for the county. For the quarter ended December, 1867, for example, the county treasury raked in $121.50 from liquor licenses, compared with just $87.75 in merchandise license fees.[167] Distilleries, too, were supposed to pay a tax, although bootleg operations evidently flourished. "It was surmised last year that an illicit distillery was in operation in this county," observed the *Chronicle* in June, 1870, "but all search for its whereabouts proved unavailing" – until a fire in a vacant Fredericksburg house owned by Mrs. Woodford brought the source of the bootleg liquor to light. "The whole establishment was thus unearthed, but the guilty parties have not yet been detected by the revenue officers," reported the newspaper with a touch of glee, "and probably never will be."[168]

A national income tax, adopted by Congress in 1862 as an "emergency" measure to finance the Civil War, was hiked in 1864 from a base rate of three percent and a maximum rate of five percent to practically double those figures; incomes up to $5,000 were now taxed at five percent, with a new top rate of ten percent on income thereafter.[169] This painful levy was eventually reduced in 1870 to just two-and-a-half percent of income, with a $2,000 exemption, but a bill that same year to abolish the "odious" tax entirely was "indefinitely postponed."[170] A full decade after its inception, the "emergency" income tax (but not the tax on whiskey) was finally eliminated in 1872.[171]

At the state level, Alpine was authorized to keep half the revenue from a "migratory stock tax" on animals driven to its meadows for grazing, thanks to the "Barnes Cattle Law."[172] This, too, was apparently a highly lucrative bit of legislation. As late as 1889 the Alpine County Supervisors admonished the Sheriff to hire three new deputies and "to at once proceed to collect the [stock] license due" by arresting one Walter Robie or his herders, and to similarly take prompt legal action "against such other offenders who are in default . . . and who are plotting against the County to avoid the payment of such licenses."[173]

Taxes were occasionally wielded as a business weapon as well. In 1869, a new "license tax" was proposed at the astronomical rate of $4 *per month* on "foreign miners" working mines in Alpine County, a step that may have reflected a covert attack on the Scottish-born Chalmers by his American arch-nemesis, Frank Jones.[174]

Both real and personal property were subject to local tax, with the county assessor meticulously itemizing each resident's assets from the prosperous lawyer's law books to the poorest citizen's pocket-watch. Delinquent tax lists from 1864 disclose that John Lewis owed property taxes on his horse and wagon, while lenders like Johann Miller were even being taxed on the value of the mortgage interests they held, as valuable "solvent debts."[175]

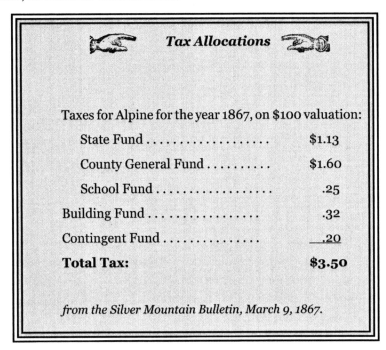

Tax Allocations

Taxes for Alpine for the year 1867, on $100 valuation:

State Fund	$1.13
County General Fund	$1.60
School Fund	.25
Building Fund	.32
Contingent Fund	.20
Total Tax:	**$3.50**

from the Silver Mountain Bulletin, March 9, 1867.

The county assessor wielded a notoriously heavy pen; Chalmers once complained to the State Attorney General that the assessor's valuation for Chalmers' transit and assaying equipment exceeded the price he had paid for them new, and was four times what he could currently sell them for.[176] While disgruntled residents could presumably pack up their pocketwatch and slip out of town, it was not as easy to evade the tax man when it came to real property. Notice after notice in the *Silver Mountain Bulletin* and *Alpine Chronicle* carried long lists of tax-delinquent or tax-defaulted real property.

Miners were entitled to claim a special exemption for $1,000 worth of mining-related property, including:

> *The cabin or dwelling of a miner, not exceeding in value the sum of five hundred dollars; also, his sluices, pipes, hose, windlass, derrick, cars, pumps, tools, implements and appliances necessary for carrying on any kind of mining operations, not exceeding in value the aggregate of five hundred dollars; and two horses, mules, or oxen with their harness, and food for such horses, mules or oxen, for one month, when necessary to be used for any whim, windlass, derrick, car, pump, or hoisting gear.*[177]

But when it came to property taxes on the mines, Chalmers found the Alpine Supervisors "troublesome."[178] It was a sentiment shared by mining speculator F.A.S. Jones, who described the local mining taxes as "verry [sic] high."[179] The main benefit of "a good thundering assessment on the Mining claims," as Chalmers put it, was that it "would materially advance" the value of the County scrip, in which elected officials were paid.[180] And the heavy burden on the mine-owning taxpayer was compounded by the fact that county taxes were required to be paid in gold.[181]

Chalmers objected strenuously to the high tax valuation given to his as-yet-undeveloped mines,[182] arguing the practical fact that "[u]ntil a pay ledge is cut, there is really no mine to tax."[183] After receiving an assessment notice valuing the Imperial Tunnel at $10,000 (producing a tax bill of $1,500),[184] Chalmers dashed off a volley of letters to other county assessors,[185] consulted a noted tax authority for a legal opinion, and vented his dismay in a six-hour speech at a Supervisors' meeting, all without success.[186] Finally in desperation he resorted to what Chalmers called the "Golden Key": a $50 bribe, with which he quickly persuaded County officials to cut the tax assessment in half.[187]

Chalmers's battle with the tax man would prove to be a drama that repeated, year after year. In 1876 he was again dashing off letters, this time to the county Board of Equalization protesting the assessment on the Exchequer Mine and Mill.[188] And in June, 1879, he wrote to the County Assessor in dismay, noting that the assessed value of the Isabella Tunnel had suddenly been raised $21,850.[189]

Other Silver Mountain residents were similarly convinced that assessment values were out of line and Alpine's politicians were for sale. Saloonkeeper Thomas Ogden publicly accused the Board of chicanery in reducing his competitor's tax bill, writing in a scathing letter to the editor:

> [T]he people have no doubt of the honesty of a Board that last year reduced the taxes on Ryan's building (the most valuable property in town) from $1,500 to $500. [190]

The County also fought long and hard to exact tolls on the wood being floated down the Carson River, assessed at up to $1 per cord[191] – the collection of which Judge Eno regularly enjoined and Judge Reed just as routinely upheld, reversing Eno's injunctions.[192] Revenue from the Carson River Wood Bill was significant for the impoverished Alpine. In 1866 alone, the wood tolls amounted to $4,505 – a significant sum for the tiny county's coffers.[193] But as the staunchly anti-Wood Bill *Chronicle* editors would later argue, "The standing tree brings no revenue to our exchequer, but when it falls to the ground it becomes taxable property," adding: "[W]hy hamper this trade by exacting a toll from the enterprise[?]"[194]

The editors' early opposition was vindicated in 1867, when the California Supreme Court struck down the wood toll as an illegal burden on interstate commerce.[195] The county was forced to refund $2,400

Watching the wood drives made a fun – and exceedingly dangerous – outing for these adventuresome children.

Courtesy of Alpine County Historical Society

of the illegally-collected tolls to a wood contractor named Crowe in July, 1872,[196] and perhaps as much as $6,000 to $10,000 to other woodsmen.[197] As the *Chronicle* pointed out, the cut wood itself remained taxable "property" to Alpine owners, however. The Alpine Supervisors voted as late as 1878 to assess one big wood drive at $3 per cut cord, and for good measure raised assessments on land owned by both the Nevada Flume Company and the El Dorado Wood & Flume Company.[198]

The fallout from Alpine's wood tax managed to overflow California's borders and generate interstate tension with Nevada in June, 1870, when Douglas County decided to impose its *own* levy on square timbers and cordwood wending their way down the river from Alpine to Empire. The timber owner, Simpson & Co., stubbornly refused to pay the Nevada tariff, observing that a tax had already been paid once on the same wood to Alpine County. Douglas County's Sheriff decided to hold up the disputed shipment by throwing a boom over the river – doing little to resolve the underlying tax issue but successfully producing a terrific jam as other drives collided with the halted lumber.[199]

In the end the whole wood tax issue became moot, as "stagnation" in the Virginia City wood market killed the golden goose on which the controversial fees were being levied.[200] Alpine would be forced once again to find new geese to pluck.

CHAPTER 11:
FADING TO A GHOST

If "hope springs eternal" was every silver miner's unspoken motto, the perpetual corollary was that richer diggings must be just a mountain away.

News of a "big strike" at Monitor's Tarshish mine in 1867 brought welcome relief from the doldrums that had enveloped the Silver Mountain mines. That April the *Silver Mountain Bulletin* was beside itself, noting the "marvelous stories that reach us almost hourly" and breathlessly comparing the new strike to the wonders of Aladdin's lamp and the riches of the Queen of Sheba.[1] Some 25 pounds of Tarshish ore hurriedly whisked off to Virginia City seemed to confirm the glowing prospects, assaying at an astonishing $1,200 in silver and $200 in gold to the ton.[2] Successive newspaper issues blazed with promoters' confident prognostications of $500 to $2,000 per ton.

By May, the Tarshish superintendent was gleefully displaying a "mammoth silver brick" measuring ten by four inches and another four inches thick, distilled from three and a half tons of this wonderous ore.[3] Nobody seemed inclined to notice that the actual returns from this initial run proved considerably less than first anticipated, at just $300 per ton.[4] By the end of June, the Tarshish had 21 men at work in its mine,[5] and the company was able to quickly raise $40,000 in fresh capital from selling 20,000 shares of its reserve stock.[6]

1868 GLOBE

View of the Entrance to the Tunnel.

Courtesy of California History Room, California State Library, Sacramento CA

the Globe Gold and Silver Mining Co's Mill and Reduction Works.

The Globe, a Monitor-area mine near the Tarshish, was booming in 1868, as shown in these life-like sketches.

Judge Henry Eno captured the prevailing high spirits in Silver Mountain, writing to his brother: "Last year was a gloomy time. But day is beginning to break and the dark clouds that have hung over our snow clad hills are about being dispelled."[7]

The rising fortunes of Monitor quickly drew the luster from the erstwhile star of Silver Mountain and by 1868, that former boomtown had ebbed to between 200 and 300 hardy souls.[8] Prominent merchant S. Reinstein posted a dejected notice in the newspaper confirming his intent to sell off his entire stock, "regardless of cost, within 30 days . . . without reserve, to close business, at extraordinary low prices for cash."[9] By 1870, county-wide real property rolls had plummeted $30,000 from the year before, the sad result of county officials no longer bothering to assess abandoned properties with long-delinquent taxes on them.[10]

The *Chronicle* cannily began hedging its bets by diversifying its base, managing to get itself named the official Litigant Paper for Mono County in October, 1870. "We touch our hats to the Honorable County Officials of Mono, and trust they will not be backward in sending forward their legal advertisements," the editors acknowledged gratefully. "We do not desire to live off of the miseries of others, but so long as the 'chicken pie' is being passed along we will take a small slice."[11] A further sign of the town's much-dimmed prospects was that even the prominent *Chronicle* office at Silver Mountain was apparently in need of a facelift; the landlord finally deigned to install new front doors.[12]

Looking back at year-end 1870 the *Chronicle's* editors found much blame to go around, including the "rebellious character" of the local ores; "incompetent" mining superintendents who "demoralized their companies and then left the county for the county's good"; and the empty pockets of many mining hopefuls. Luckily or unluckily, they noted, a "large number of our most promising claims have passed into the hands of English capitalists."[13]

By 1871, the Exchequer Mill was selling off five yoke of its work oxen,[14] and downtown Silver Mountain was dotted with vacant buildings, flotsam from the initial wave of optimistic overbuilding. As the *Chronicle* explained:

> In the early days of this county the great rush was to Markleeville and Silver Mountain, where every one thought he must get a lot and erect a house, which was no sooner thought of than done, consequently during the crazy excitement of that period buildings sufficient for a population of five thousand were erected at each place, while neither contained over one thousand souls. The majority of these buildings, many unfinished, were allowed to go to wreck [sic] and ruin.[15]

Visitors were in the habit of simply making themselves "at home" in these empty structures, and such casual tenancy was not always gentle. Chided the Folgers:

> We would suggest to outsiders that when they visit our town and are allowed the temporary use of a building, that [sic] when they get ready to return home it would be proper for them to see that the doors of the building aforesaid are properly secured and everything left as found. If this shoe fits any of our readers, we hope it will be put on.[16]

By the Fall of 1871, even the venerable Fisk hotel was standing empty – except for an escaped convict who briefly took shelter there.[17] And by the following year, the hotel's furnishings were being looted: flatware, dishes, chairs, and an octagon clock all were missing, and even a pair of heavy "sad irons" had been taken. A $50 reward was offered.[18]

Although still officially the "litigant paper" for Alpine County, the *Chronicle* was forced to reduce its fee for this service to zero in July, 1871, to keep its title as "official county press."[19] And as if Nature herself was conspiring to see the town extinguished, a landslide descended on Silver Mountain on July 15, 1871, depositing a "large quantity of rocks and earth . . . from the top of the mountain, opposite the Court House."[20] This cataclysmic event was followed one week later by a "cloud burst" causing the river to overflow, piling mud and debris from three to six feet deep over a three-block area from Water to Union Streets. The *Chronicle* estimated the cost to re-open Union Street at a hefty $400.[21]

The town of Monitor, by contrast, was on the up-swing. Silver Mountain entrepreneur Daniel Davidson brought 50 head of sheep over the Big Trees Road and hastily launched a Monitor "branch market" in May, 1870 to serve the growing demand.[22] By 1871, Monitor was enthusiastically described as "more lively than at any time since 1863," with jobs plentiful, new businesses opening,[23] and homes under construction.[24] One perhaps overly-sunny report the following year puffed the town as a "thriving village" of about 600 souls,[25] although a more realistic population figure was probably 200 to 300.[26] Even a devastating fire in 1872, which reduced the entire business district of Monitor to "ashes" within hours and produced losses estimated at $20,000, couldn't quell local spirits. Within weeks, rebuilding efforts were in full swing.[27]

The town of Silver Mountain, too, experienced a brief resurgence in late 1872, thanks to "good results" at the local mines and the growing demand for woodchoppers. The *Chronicle* reported enthusiastically that "[s]everal families came in this week, and we hear of several others preparing to come."[28] But yet another fresh disaster for Silver Mountain's fortunes was brewing – this time, from the direction of Washington.

Demonetization of Silver

In 1873, federal monetary policy stretched long-tentacled fingers to meddle in Alpine mining affairs, with the game-altering death knell for the silver standard.

The U.S. had functioned under a "bimetallic" system since 1792. This meant that the dollar was officially valued in terms of both silver and gold, with a fixed 15-to-1 or 16-to-1 conversion ratio governing the exchange for these metals.[29] The bimetallic currency system was designed to keep dollar-denominated prices relatively stable, since fluctuations in the supply of one metal could be easily offset by the other metal. Thus if gold was plentiful and silver scarce, silver bars would command a higher price in the open market and fewer bars would be minted into coins. With an abundant supply of gold coins circulating as currency, dollar-denominated prices therefore would not be forced to rise – and *vice versa*.

This system functioned well for many years, effectively accommodating fluctuations in the supplies of metals. As the Gold Rush increased the available supply of gold, silver (as the scarcer metal) increased in market value and gold was freely minted for coins at the official government rate. The net practical effect was that the country operated on a *de facto* gold-coin-only standard for much of the 1850s.

But in the 1860s, a series of world events began to swing the pendulum dramatically in the opposite direction. First, the Comstock bonanza swiftly dumped a huge glut of silver on the marketplace, dramatically lowering its price. Sales of gold to the mint at official coinage rates suddenly became much less attractive, with silver so much cheaper and more plentiful.

World events, too, helped to shape U.S. monetary affairs following Germany's victory over France in 1871. Determined to peg its fiscal path firmly to a new gold-only standard, Germany demanded that France atone for its wartime sins through steep "indemnity" payments – in gold. Other European countries, now awash in silver, found themselves forced to fall into line with a similar gold standard. No longer in demand as a currency metal, silver supplies rose while its price continued to drop. Gold, in increasing demand and dwindling supply, escalated in value even farther.

Concerned with the inflationary price effect of a ballooning silver supply, U.S. legislators took drastic steps of their own. As a legislative backlash against cheap silver, Congress adopted the infamous Coinage

Act of 1873, demonetizing silver entirely and leaving gold as the nation's sole legal-tender metal. No longer linked through a fixed ratio to gold and no longer in demand as a coinage metal, the price of silver was left to fluctuate on its own.

The impact on silver mining activity was predictable – and disastrous. With supplies swelling from overseas, the bottom fell out of the silver market. From its original 15-to-1 silver-to-gold conversion rate in 1870, the market forced silver's value down to just 40-to-1 by 1900.[30] Little wonder, then, that the Coinage Act became known among miners as "The Crime of '73".

Adding further chaos to the monetary market, Congress took an additional step to "strengthen" the currency supply in 1875 by removing greenbacks from circulation through the "Specie Resumption Act," which allowed greenback holders to redeem their paper money in gold. Greenbacks, the paper currency issued to carry the country through the Civil War, generally traded at a steep discount from face value, commanding as little as 39 cents in gold coin for a paper dollar in 1864.[31] Fiscal analysts had been looking for a way to reverse the ill-effects of the ruinous "greenback" policy, but the net effect was to further bolster the value of gold at the expense of silver.

Visiting photographer Eliza Withington captured the moment in the summer of 1876, as town notables helped to remove the iron jail cells from Silver Mountain's once-proud stone jail, for transport to the new county seat at Markleeville. On hand for the event were Under-Sheriff (and manager of Ford's Alpine House) George H. Dunlap, Sheriff J.B. Scott, and Supervisor Charles Gregory (presumably the three closest to the camera).

Some blamed the insult to silver as a strategy to artificially prop up the value of gold while California gold production was fading and Nevada silver production skyrocketing. Others saw it as a vast conspiracy by a shadow consortium of international bankers controlling the world's gold supply.[32] Whatever the actual driving forces, the demonetization of silver pushed the entire country into an economic tailspin.

In a sop to outraged mining interests, silver coin was again allowed as legal tender by the 1878 "Bland-Allison Act," but the fixed silver-to-gold ratio was not re-adopted and gold remained the sole official monetary standard. This left silver with no equalizing power in the currency market. Gold, now relatively scarce, commanded a purchasing premium, leading nominal prices to drop. A slow and devastating deflationary spiral would envelop the country for the next two decades.[33]

Moving On

On the local level, a different sort of seismic upheaval took place in 1875, with a county-wide ballot that put Silver Mountain's title as the official county seat on the line. Silver Mountain had survived similar challenges to its dominance in the past, but this time the tides of time had too clearly swung in other directions. Silver Mountain was too cold; too far removed from the center of the county; too inaccessible in winter snows; and most of all, too devoid of loyal voters. By a landslide vote of 129 to 35, Silver Mountain lost the crown of county seat to its long-time rival, Markleeville.[34]

The following November, the Board of Supervisors brusquely ordered the Sheriff to sell the County's buildings at Silver Mountain. Perhaps in hopes the county seat vote would somehow be rescinded or perhaps simply due to a lack of buyers, the sale was twice postponed over the next two years.[35] But in late summer, 1876, one wall of Silver Mountain's proud stone jail was ripped apart to permit the still-sturdy iron jail cells to be extracted and ferried to their new home in Markleeville.[36] There, a fresh wooden jailhouse was erected, using 7,000 feet of lumber furnished by the Exchequer Sawmill.[37] The cost for this crude structure was a mere $603.37, a price lauded by the *Chronicle* (still carrying a grudge over the cost of the original stone jail) as a "just rebuke to the high priced, flimsy jail at Silver Mountain."[38]

Mining interest managed to revive briefly throughout the county in 1876, with work resuming at both the I.X.L. and Advance mines, and "unusual" activity reported in the Silver Mountain district.[39] Lewis Chalmers' Isabella Tunnel also wangled a fresh influx of cash from English investors from 1878 through 1881.[40] But the Isabella never managed to tap the oft-promised lodes, and Chalmers' pleas for further infusions of money eventually fell on deaf ears.

As Silver Mountain's prospects slowly waned, so too did the fortunes of its once-prominent Fisk hotel. In 1876, the Fisks leased the abandoned structure to a pair of optimistic new proprietors, Fearson & McClay, who touted a Christmas turkey dinner that year at the Hotel.[41] A "social dance" at the Fisk also welcomed in the New Year of 1878.[42] But the resurrected enthusiasm did not last long.

The final blow to Silver Mountain came in 1878 in the form of fresh gold discoveries at the mining town of Bodie, just 70 miles away. "Bodie fever" quickly seized Silver Mountainites with a vengeance.[43] Within a matter of months, many of Silver Mountain's most prominent townsfolk packed up their worldly goods and departed. Even Supervisor R.K. Love closed his meat markets in Silver Mountain City and Monitor, and drove his band of hogs over the mountain to make Bodie his new home.[44]

The *Chronicle* reported humorously at first on the "exodus" and "stampede" of citizens for Bodie, predicting: "We may look for a return of some of them next Spring."[45]

Courtesy of Mono County Historical Society

Even the loyal Folger brothers finally abandoned Silver Mountain in 1878 for more promising pastures at Bodie and Bridgeport. Here, A.C. Folger (left) stands with an unidentified man outside his newspaper office at Bridgeport. Robert, A.C.'s brother and journalism partner, died in 1899.

But within just a matter of months, the *Alpine Chronicle* too threw in the towel. After fourteen long years of struggling in Alpine, the Folger brothers put out a bittersweet final paper from Silver Mountain in October, picking up again with an issue from Bodie dated December 7, 1878. One sign of just how rapidly Silver Mountain's population evaporated while Bodie boomed can be found in the Silver Mountain postmaster's salary, which plummeted from $275.84 in 1877 to just $40.67 in 1879.[46]

As if to add insult to Alpine's injury, at least two local buildings were dismantled, packed up and ferried over the mountains for new service in Bodie as well: the "Uncapher House" near Markleeville, and the McBeth Hotel of Monitor.[47] Precious construction lumber milled at the Bemis sawmill near Markleeville was similarly whisked away to Bodie by carpenter Henry C. Ginn to serve the growing demands of this latest mining boomtown.[48]

Bit by bit, Silver Mountain's wooden buildings and its remaining residents slowly vanished. A fire in 1882 "almost annihilated" what was left of the town of Silver Mountain, leaving Ford's beloved Alpine Hotel "in ashes." With both home and livelihood gone, stalwarts R.H. and Almira Ford too departed, moving in with daughter Anna and Judge N.D. Arnot in Markleeville.[49] The stately Fisk Hotel was purchased by A.M. Grover in 1885, disassembled piece by piece, and moved by wagon to Markleeville, where it was re-assembled as the "Hot Springs Hotel" to provide lodging for Grover's resort guests.[50]

By February 1883, just three adults remained living in once-booming Silver Mountain, one of whom was its postmistress; that July, mail service to Silver Mountain was halted entirely and routed instead to Chalmers' slightly more alive but hardly thriving compound of 27 residents at Silver Creek.[51] According to at least one report, pioneering citizen J.J. Rice was the very last hold-out to finally leave Silver Mountain sometime about 1892.[52]

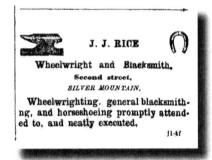

Chalmers himself bade farewell to Alpine County for what would prove to be his final voyage back to London around 1886. Mail service to his Silver Creek compound ceased on November 15, 1890, with all mail thereafter routed to Markleeville. Even Chalmers' spanking-new I.X.L. Mill, which he struggled so hard to finance but never managed to run, was carted off to Mono County about 1896 to work the ore of the Dunderberg Mine.[53] Over time, the boards and timbers of Chalmers' pretty Isabella Boarding House were picked apart and, according to local folklore, made their way into outbuildings at a nearby cow camp.

It was an amazing run for an amazing town. But for all the love and labor lavished on the nearby silver mines, it remains unclear exactly how much profit they paid out in return. One estimate puts the total output of both gold and silver from the Silver Mountain mining district at less than $300,000.[54] Chalmers, by contrast, swore repeatedly that an astonishing $50,000 had been produced from the I.X.L. mine alone as early as 1868,[55] suggesting the district's combined output over two decades could have been considerably more. While exactly how much bullion was produced is impossible to know, if the value of paper shares changing hands is counted it is possible that profits reached into the millions – and that similar amounts were lost by over-eager speculators.

Today, Silver Mountain's streets are silent, with only empty basements to mark where homes and bustling businesses once stood. The heartbeats of a town are gone: no noisy children playing, no barking dogs, no snorting pigs. Square nails and flattened tin-can shingles, their former structure vanished, lie rusting away beneath a blanket of pine needles. The expensive and controversial old stone jail is quietly turning to sand.

Yet a short distance away, bits and pieces of the life of Silver Mountain remain visible. Twelve miles from its original Silver Mountain location, the venerable Fisk Hotel still graces an important corner, albeit now at the intersection of Main and Montgomery Streets in Markleeville. Chalmers' towering brick chimney and tattered letter books remain tangible monuments to his years of hopeful searching. And today's visitors to the Alpine County Museum can experience first-hand the dark confines of Silver Mountain's original iron jail cells.[56] Still legible on the iron walls are the numbers painted in 1867 to help workers assemble the metal cells inside the old stone jail, along with the hand-painted freighting address conveying the pre-made iron sections to Alpine's 1867 treasurer: "T. Carlson, Silver Mountain, care [of] Willie Strumple, Sheriff." And Alpine's Museum and Archives are home to a treasure trove of photos, letters, and documents from those fascinating Silver Mountain days.

But the most important legacy of Silver Mountain is really Alpine County itself – a bequest from those eager silver miners and hard-working timber moguls. Because if not for Silver Mountain's early dreamers, tiny Alpine County would never have been born.

And what of the other Alpine boomtowns during the rambunctious Silver Mountain era – the lumbering and freighting hubs of Markleeville and Centerville; the high-energy mining camps at Bulliona, Monitor, and Mogul; the pioneering settlements of Silver King and Raymond? Well, those are tales still waiting to be told.

Courtesy of Alpine County Historical Society

Courtesy of Alpine County Historical Society

Dustman Collection

The home that Chalmers and Antoinette once loved is still marked by the tall brick chimney of the former Exchequer Mill.

On the south side of Silver Creek, a stone fireplace built to warm a miner's cabin is crumbling back into the earth.

North of the creek, a low stone retaining wall frames the front walkway to a long-gone home on Bluff Street.

Dustman Collection

We hope you have come to love Silver Mountain City as much as we do, and that you will help preserve its legacy for future generations.

Chapter 1 Footnotes:

1   Phyllis Zauner, <u>Virginia City: Its History, Its Ghosts</u> (Zanel Publications 1989), p. 7-9. The initial discoveries were gold, until the "despised" blue clay was assayed and found to contain five times greater value in silver.

2   Remi Nadeau, <u>The Silver Seekers</u> (Crest Publishers 1999), at p. 6.

3   Lincoln's election in 1860 prompted South Carolina to secede just before Christmas – a move soon followed by Mississippi and other states. The Confederate States of America organized itself in February, 1861, with Jeff Davis as president. Two months later, on April 12, 1861, guns were blazing at Ft. Sumter. The war was on.

4   A "John Johnson" was also reportedly part of this group, along with Halver Oleson. *See* Peter Browning, <u>Place Names of the Sierra Nevada</u> (Wilderness Press 1992), at 200.

5   *Monitor Gazette*, January 14, 1865. Other roughly contemporaneous accounts similarly confirm "[t]he first silver-bearing lodes were discovered in this region in 1861." *See* <u>Bancroft Scraps</u> (Bancroft Library), p. 54, containing an Alpine County synopsis. (Although this clipping is not dated or identified, it appears to be from approximately 1864.)

6   R. Nadeau, <u>Silver Seekers,</u> at p. 43.

7   Various sources list the original Mountain Mine claimants as John Johnson, Wesley Poole (or Perry), and V. Harrison (or Harris). *See Monitor Gazette*, January 14, 1865 (identifying the claimants as "John Johnson, __ Harris, and __ Perry"); *see also* Alan H. Patera, "Silver Mountain California," <u>Western Places: A Chronicle of Western Settlement</u>, Vol. 1, No. 3 (September, 1992), at p.43; R. Nadeau, <u>Silver Seekers</u>, at p. 43.

8   *Monitor Gazette*, January 14, 1865. The company apparently was not officially incorporated for another two years. *See infra* note 21.

9   *See, e.g.,* property description in Book "B" of Alpine County Official Records, page 10-11 (indenture from E.W. Adams to Mrs. Mary E. Kent), which references a lot located by G. Francis on July 8, 1861. Other early descriptions show clearly that niceties of land transfers were not always observed; one lot is referenced as having been bought by the seller in 1863 "without any Deed being given for the same until this date." (Book "B", page 115, Robert Fisher to V.R. Hill).

10   The notices of location for both I.X.L. and Buckeye were filed on July 1, 1861. *See* Chalmers Letters, *Private Letters 1871-2*, p. 247 (Abstracts of Title accompanying letter dated August 22, 1871).

11   <u>Western Places</u>, at p. 43; R. Nadeau, <u>Silver Seekers</u>, at p. 43. According to a slightly later report, assays at the Mountain ran from $2 to $181 per ton, "nearly all silver." *Monitor Gazette*, January 14, 1865.

12   *Mining & Scientific Press* article from 1861-62, reprinted in <u>Western Places</u>, at 44-45 ("I have seen the assays of [the Mountain ledge] 672.10 and 860.73 silver per ton. . . ") Other sources cite figures only slightly less grand, *e.g.* $625 per ton. *See* W. Turrentine Jackson, <u>Report on the History of Grover Hot Springs State Park Area and Surrounding Region of Alpine County</u> (Division of Beaches & Parks, Department of Parks and Recreation, State of California 1964), at p. 22.

13   One early legal description references the "Surveys made by the Town Commissioners on October 23, 1862." *See* Book B, page 17-18 (J.H. McConahy to A.C. Phillips dated November 16, 1865).

14   R. Nadeau, <u>Silver Seekers,</u> at p. 44.

15   Silver Mountain (as "Konigsberg") beat Markleeville and Monitor to the post office punch by a matter of months. Markleeville soon had its own post office, on October 21, 1863; Monitor followed suit on November 30, 1863. A. Patera, <u>Western Places</u>, p. 42.

16   R. Nadeau, <u>Silver Seekers</u>, at p. 43.

17   Konig, a defendant (along with "Ed. Booth"), was subjected to a Writ of Attachment to secure a claim by L.S. Wright for $299.99. *See* Attachment Demand dated February 14, 1865, in records of the Alpine County Museum.

18   Among this gentleman's possessions, carefully itemized by a diligent assessor, were two sewing

machines, 1 "poultry", 2 wagons, 3 saddles, 6 half-breed horses, 3 Spanish horses, 3 colts, 30 cows, 20 calves, and 1 watch worth $50. Assessment Records at Alpine County Archives. Possibly the same gentleman, one "F.W. Konig," owned 100 shares ($100 each) of the Colorado No. 2 Gold and Silver Mining Co., issued March 17, 1879. *See* share certificate No. 164 in Alpine County Museum files under "Mines & Mining."

19   Bancroft Scraps, p. 53, clipping dated May 29, 1863 (possibly from the *San Francisco Weekly Bulletin*).

20   Grant turned the tide for the Union by capturing Vicksburg on July 4, 1863, after a six-week siege.

21   *See* Stock certificate featuring incorporation date of June 4, 1863, reprinted in Western Places, at p. 43.

22   Originally a professor of chemistry, Brewer conducted one of the earliest geological surveys of California for State Geologist Josiah D. Whitney. His published journal, Up and Down California in 1860-1864 (University of California Press 1966), makes wonderful reading as a snapshot in time of the places his party visited in their travels.

23   W. H. Brewer, Up and Down California in 1860-1864 (University of California Press 1966), p. 432 (entry for August 4, 1863).

24   Chalmers Letters, *Exchequer Officials 1871-2*, pp. 49-50 (May 22, 1871)(punctuation and paragraph spacing added for clarity).

25   R. Nadeau, Silver Seekers, at p 43.

26   According to one source, Silver Mountain had 200 buildings by October, 1863. R. Nadeau, Silver Seekers, at p. 46.

27   This misconception was fostered, in part, by the hazy description of Nevada Territory itself, which claimed all territory on the Eastern side of the Sierra crest. For a wonderful description of efforts to establish the California-Nevada border, *see* John P. Wilusz, "The Colorful History of the California/Nevada State Boundary," *Professional Surveyor* (January/February 2002), *reprinted online* at www.dot.ca.gov.

28   *See* California County information on Alpine County on www.csac.counties.org. Some 12 counties were created later (Imperial; Glenn; Inyo; Kern; King; Lassen; Madera; Modoc; Orange; Riverside; San Benito; and Ventura), bringing the total to 58.

29   Alpine County beat Lassen in formation by just two weeks (March 16, 1864 versus April 18, 1864), becoming California's 46th County. With fewer than 1,200 current residents, Alpine remains California's smallest county by population.

30   Reprint of "Alpine County Bill," at Alpine County Museum. The "Alpine County Bill" was passed by the Legislature on March 16, 1864, as 1864 Statutes, Chap CLXXX, pp.178-183, but county officers were not seated until August 11, 1864. (*See* Judge Sextus Shearer's essay on the subject of when the county was officially formed, in *Monitor Gazette* of August 27, 1864).

31   Mabel Love, History of the Alpine County Schools (unpublished manuscript, at Alpine County Museum), p. 4. Contemporaneous estimates, however, put the figure at closer to about 2,000 county citizens. *See* Bancroft Scraps, p. 54 (reporting a county-wide population of 2,000 in an undated entry from approximately 1864).

32   Jackson claims that Silver Mountain won the honor by just 40 votes (T. Jackson, *Report*, at p. 53); another source, however, asserts the vote was 824 in favor of Silver Mountain; 729 for Markleeville; 106 for Monitor; and one for Mogul, indicating a total of 1,660 voters (typewritten manuscript *Notes on Early Alpine County* by unidentified source, located in "Alpine County" file at Alpine County Museum).

33   Nevada was admitted to the Union as a free state on October 31, 1864. It has been speculated that Nevada's statehood was conveniently timed to ensure that Nevada silver would benefit Northern forces during the Civil War. But according to Nevada State Archivist Guy Rocha, statehood was unnecessary for control of the Territory's silver, and the tide of war had already turned in favor of the North by the time the statehood issue arose. *See* Rocha's fascinating "Why Did Nevada Become A State?" at www.nevadaweb.com/nevadaca/rocha-2.html.

34   W.T. Jackson, *supra*, p. 2-3.

35   *Alpine Chronicle*, October 1, 1870, *quoting the Amador Ledger. See also Chronicle* issues of January 29 and April 2, 1870.

36   *Chronicle*, January 26, 1878.

37   *Chronicle*, October 1, 1870 (taking issue with the *Ledger*'s characterization).

38   *Alpine Chronicle* of December 31, 1870 and February 18, 1871. However, the year-end *Chronicle* report of December 30, 1871 claimed only that "about $2,700 of the Amador debt" had been discharged within the last 15 months. Accounting irregularities were apparently part of the problem. The *Chronicle* of March 16, 1872, reported that the County debt had suddenly been found to be "$6,000 less than was supposed," due to a failure by the Auditor to adjust totals as warrants were paid, adding: "One who ought to know informs a Supervisor that the Devil himself couldn't make head or tail of the District Attorney's books, from 1864 to 1872."

39   *Chronicle*, February 10, 1872.

40   *Chronicle,* January 26, 1878; *see similarly Chronicle,* August 10, 1878. Property taxes included a 50-cents-per-hundred tax for "Amador." *Chronicle*, October 12, 1872.

Chapter 2 Footnotes:

1   Remi Nadeau, *The Silver Seekers* (Crest Publishers 1999), at p. 45; W. Turrentine Jackson, <u>Report on the History of Grover Hot Springs State Park Area and Surrounding Region of Alpine County</u> (Division of Beaches & Parks, Department of Parks and Recreation, State of California 1964), at pp. 48; 50.

2   *The Mining and Scientific Press*, May 21, 1864, p. 343. *See similarly* <u>Bancroft Scraps</u> (Bancroft Library), p. 54, containing a report dated May 29, 1863 chronicling "three stores, two hotels and a boarding house, one saw-mill in operation and another building; two butcher shops, one blacksmith and one shoemaker shop, one bakery and an assay office, besides divers and other crafts, and places of business."

3   *Chronicle*, April 1, 1871.

4   *Silver Mountain Bulletin*, October 13, 1866.

5   *Silver Mountain Bulletin*, October 13, 1866 and January 5, 1867; *Alpine Chronicle*, October 27, 1866.

6   *See* advertisement for the "40 Drops! Billiard Saloon" in *Bulletin*, January 12, 1867. An "avalanche of snow" from the Court House roof made "a complete wreck" of Patterson's but a heavy counter protected the fixtures and the building itself "was of nominal value" to begin with. *Chronicle*, February 1, 1868.

7   A <u>Bancroft Scraps</u> clipping from May 29, 1863 reports that Konigsburg had "about sixty different places of residence and business, many of which are only tents or the rudest kinds of cabins. There are, however, about a dozen very respectable frame houses, two or three quite spacious and tasty." <u>Scraps</u>, p. 54.

8   <u>Diary of Addison Curtiss</u>, entry for June 15, 1864 (original in Amador County archives).

9   *Id.*; entry for May 6, 1864.

10   *Id.*, entry for May 25, 1864.

11   *Id.*; entries for June 4 and 8, 1864.

12   *Id.*; entry for June 1, 1864.

13   *Id.*, entry for June 3, 1864.

14   *Chronicle,* Feb 2, 1867.

15   <u>Diary of Addison Curtiss</u>; *see* entries for May 6; 8; 9; 10; 15; 16; 22; and 29.

16   *Id.*, entry for May 22, 1864.

17   *Id.*, entries for June 17-18, 1864.

18   Amador County archives, Document ID 25260, File 6488.28.18 (1864 County papers, reflecting bill from District Attorney R.M. Briggs related to the case). *See similarly Sacramento Daily Bee* article of May 14, 1863, noting: "Yesterday, two men went to the Mountain Springs House, between this place [Jackson] and Ione City. One of them commenced hurrahing for Jeff Davis, when Mr. Farmer, proprietor of the house, picked up a club and went after him." (Reproduced at http://www.calarchives4u.com/newspapers/sac-news-other1850-1860s.txt).

19   Bancroft Scraps, p. 56.

20   W.T. Jackson, *supra*, p. 5.

21   *Monitor Gazette*, October 15, 1864.

22   According to "California Place Names," many Summit City inhabitants were Confederate sympathizers. Other sources confirm that Summit City was politically "a stand off between Union men and the rebels." *Daily Alta* of June 15, 1864, quoted by both William M. Maule, "A Contribution to the Geographic and Economic History of Carson, Walker and Mono Basins" (U.S. Forest Service 1938), at p. 29, and W.T. Jackson, p. 55). Exactly how Bull Run Peak got its name is somewhat murkier. While some sources link it to Confederate interests (*see notes excerpted from* California Place Names, *manuscript at Alpine County Museum*, p. 8), others indicate the name was bestowed by the Wheeler Survey team. (Peter Browning, Place Names of the Sierra Nevada From Abbot to Zumwalt (Wilderness Press 1991), at 28).

23   Diary of Addison Curtiss, entry for May 13, 1864.

24   Alpine County remained staunchly Union, with its 87-vote majority helping to secure the election of President Grant in 1868. *Chronicle*, June 24, 1871.

25   Letter dated July 16, 1864 from Royal Fisk to F.H. Smith & Co. (Royal Fisk Letters, at Bancroft Library)(spelling corrected and punctuation added). F.H. Smith appears to have been a business partner of Charles Fisk, owner of the Fisk Hotel in Silver Mountain.

26   Letter dated September 26, 1864 from Royal Fisk to F.H. Smith & Co. (Royal Fisk Letters, Bancroft Library).

27   Bancroft Scraps, p. 52; *see similarly* Henry Eno, Twenty Years on the Pacific Slope (Yale University Press 1965), p. 143 (estimating about 350 inhabitants at Silver Mountain as of April, 1866).

28   *Bulletin*, May 25, 1867. By contrast, there were just 55 voters in Markleeville; 25 at Monitor; 10 at Mogul; and 7 at Silver King.

29   A townsite survey was apparently conducted by the "Town Commissioners" as early as October 23, 1862 (*see* Book "B" of Deeds, p. 17, referencing that survey). It is possible that Theron Reed drew a plat of Silver Mountain, as he did for Markleeville. (*See* J. Marklee Estate, 1864 Inventory and Accounting, *circa* March 10, 1864).

30   "A Map of the Silver Mountain Mining Districts," published by H.H. Bancroft & Co. (copy at Alpine County Museum).

31   *The Mining and Scientific Press*, May 21, 1864, at page 343.

32   Harvey Rice, "Letters From The Pacific Slope; or First Impressions," Letter VII, October 6, 1869 (available on-line at the Library of Congress' "American Memory" website, *http://memory.loc.gov*).

33   We have the *Silver Mountain Bulletin* to thank for this rendition of events and the details that follow; *see Bulletin*, January 19, 1867. At some point, the Court was indeed headquartered at the Mammoth Hotel. *See Chronicle* of April 1, 1871, noting: "The old Mammoth Hotel, lately occupied as a Court House, has been sold to parties in Monitor who will take it down and convert it to what it was originally intended for – a stable. Thus an 'eye sore' will be removed from our town. . . ."

34   The Board of Supervisors Minutes of August 19, 1864 reflect a resolution to lease W.H. Ryan's building for a period of nine months (Book A, p. 24), and the minutes of October 17, 1864 (Book A, p. 57), show a payment to W.H. Ryan for $195.00 "for Rent of Court House."

35   *Chronicle*, February 2, 1867.

36   *Bulletin*, January 19, 1867.

37   *Chronicle*, March 25, 1871. As noted in a footnote above, apparently the old Mammoth Hotel was also briefly used as a court house circa 1870-71; *see Chronicle* April 1, 1871, indicating that the building "lately occupied as a Court house" had been sold.

38   *Chronicle*, March 25, 1871.

39   *See Chronicle*, October 8, 1870.

40   Decrees of foreclosure were granted by Judge Theron Reed in the cases of *Watson v. Hadley* and *Wycoff v. Fisher. Bulletin*, March 9, 1867, reporting the District Court proceedings for Monday, March 4, 1867.

41   In 1872, for example, Elizabeth Smith commenced a divorce action against J.B. Smith for "cause too numerous to mention." *Chronicle*, March 9, 1872.

42   *Chronicle*, January 7, 1871.

43   *Bulletin*, May 25, 1867.

44   *Chronicle*, October 12, 1872. Vollem, a native of Norway, owned a ranch near Woodfords.

45   Hay, formerly of Quebec, filed his Declaration of Intention to become a citizen on October 19, 1868, and received his final naturalization papers on October 7, 1872. *See copies* at Alpine County Museum.

46   Torgrim Olson was admitted to citizenship on March 4, 1867; Daniel Davidson and John Johnson were admitted to citizenship the following day. *Bulletin*, March 9, 1867.

47   Board Minutes of August 26, 1864 (Book "A", page 31).

48   *See* Board Minutes of October 17, 1864, which include an item submitted for payment by store-keeper E.A. Coursen for candles, and Minutes of November 7, 1864, with an $18 bill for "making shackles and ironing chairs."

49   Board Minutes of October 19, 1864 (Minutes, Book "A" p. 59), rejecting a bid of E. Alexander for "Boarding Prisoners."

50   According to a summary of the case in the files of the Alpine County Museum, William Harris was indicted by the Alpine Grand Jury for the murder of Saxon Williams after shooting Williams below the right eye with a five-barrelled Colts pistol on December 28, 1864. Harris was promptly arrested and did not manage to post bail until October, 1865, nearly a year later. Harris was eventually acquitted of the crime in September, 1866, the jury finding that Harris actually intended to shoot "Dutch Pete" Christeson, who had threatened to kill Harris on sight, and that the killing of S. Williams was an accident. *See "Jail" file* at Alpine County Museum; *see also* "Births/ Marriages/Deaths" Index at Alpine County Museum, p. 31, *citing Alpine Miner* of September 8, 1866.

51   Dr. M.T. Moore testified by affidavit at what appears to be a bail hearing, noting that "said Harris has been and now is affected with the chronic pleuracy, and severe and constant neuralgia . . . [and also] is affected with tape worms in the intestines, for which he has also been under my treatment and [is] in present need of medical attention." The doctor's affidavit went on to aver that "the general health of said Harris is now very poor, and that close confinement for the space of seven months in the character of prison he now occupies would be very injurious to his health, and would greatly endanger his life." Harris' lawyer J.C. Robinson testified similarly that "said jail is very uncomfortably constructed and illy suited for the purpose of keeping a prisoner during the winter months of the climate in which it is situated." *See "Jail" file* at Alpine County Museum.

52   *See* Alpine County: Bear Valley, Kirkwood, and Markleeville (Images of America series, Arcadia Publishing, 2005), captions on pp. 118, 125.

53   Supervisors Minutes of May 4, 1865; *see also Chronicle* of Feb. 24, 1872 ("The County owns half a block, where the jail is, donated by citizens of Silver Mountain for county purposes.")

54   *Chronicle*, March 9, 1867; *Bulletin* March 16, 1867.

55   *Bulletin*, March 16, 1867.

56   *Chronicle*, March 16, 1867.

57   *Bulletin*, May 11, 1867, reporting that the ceremony was held the previous Monday, May 6, 1867.

58   *Bulletin,* May 18, 1867.

59   *Chronicle*, Feb. 3, 1872. ("[F]inding about $1,400 in the Hospital Fund [the Board] conceived the brilliant idea of building a jail; one of them being a carpenter and another a blacksmith, and another official owning an old boiler, it was too good a thing to let slip, and, against the protest of the taxpayers and District Attorney, it was erected and the county involved in a further debt of $7,000.")

60   *Bulletin*, May 18, 1867, noting a rumor that "one of the Supervisors was interested in the contract"; *see also Chronicle*, February 3, 1872 (quoted in footnote above).

61   *Bulletin,* May 18, 1867.

62   *Bulletin,* May 18, 1867.

63   Diary of O.S. Adams, entry for August 12, 1867 (Dustman collection).

64   *Chronicle,* Feb. 24, 1872.

65   *Chronicle*, September 21, 1867.

66   *Chronicle*, December 14, 1867.

67   *Chronicle*, December 14, 1867.

68   *Chronicle*, May 30, 1868.

69   *Chronicle*, February 3, 1872.

70   *Chronicle*, May 7, 1870.

71   *Chronicle*, February 3 and March 9, 1872.

72   *Chronicle,* December 7, 1872.

73   *Chronicle*, February 24, 1872.

74   W.T. Jackson, p. 49.

75   "Reports of the County Superintendent of Public Schools for Alpine County to the Superintendent of Public Instruction, State of California, 1863-1914" (extracted from California State Archives and published by the Alpine County Museum, 1995), at page 2 (Summary for 1864-5) shows 324 children.

76   *Bulletin*, February 23, 1867.

77   Mabel Love, History of The Alpine County Schools (manuscript donated to Alpine County Museum 1989, and transcript published 1990), p.4.

78   "Reports of the County Superintendent of Public Schools," *supra*, p. 15 (1875-76).

79   "Reports of the County Superintendent," *supra*, p. 10 (1871-2).

80   "Reports of the County Superintendent," *supra*, pp. 8 and 16 (1870-71 and 1876-77).

81   Spencer petitioned the Board of Supervisors on August 5, 1878 for a 60-day leave, and left Silver Mountain on September 5 of that year, supposedly to visit her mother in Kansas. *Chronicle*, August 10 and September 7, 1878. Whether or not she ever made it to Kansas is unclear, but Spencer evidently soon joined the throngs headed for Bodie as she reportedly died there on February 17, 1880. *See* "Births/Marriages/Deaths" Index p. 42, *citing Monitor Argus* of March 1, 1880.

Chapter 3 Footnotes:

1   *See* advertisement in *Silver Mountain Bulletin*, December 22, 1866.

2   Diary of Addison Curtiss, entries for May 5 and 6, 1864 (original in Amador County archives).

3   According to family tradition the name was originally "Fiske," but Charles dispensed with the final 'e' because "he did not want any frills in his name." *Las Calaveras*, Calaveras County Historical Society bulletin, Vol. XVI, No. 3 (April, 1968).

4   *See Las Calaveras*, Calaveras County Historical Society's quarterly bulletin, Vol. XVI, No. 3 (April, 1968).

5   *See* Calaveras County Historical Society bulletin (April, 1968).

6   Amador Assessment Roll of 1864 (Alpine County Archives). This pricey valuation is consistent with a hotel rather than a single family dwelling, but the description of "house and other improvements" suggests its initial use was as a family home. Fisk also was listed as the owner of Lot 12 of Block 25 in Silver Mountain in 1864.

7   *Alpine Heritage: One Hundred Years of History, Recreation, Lore in Alpine County, California, 1864-1964*, published by the Alpine County Museum (Revised edition May 1987), at p. 24.

8   William Kent advertised "Private Rooms for Oyster Suppers" as early as 1866, while the Oriental Hotel advertisement used images of oysters the following Christmas. *See Bulletin*, December 22, 1866; *Chronicle*, December 7, 1867. Fisk offered similar fare at his hotel, judging by remnants of oyster shells still evident at the site.

9   *Bulletin*, April 13, 1867.

10   Letter of Royal Fisk dated January 7, 1865, to F.H. Smith & Co., of which Charles Fisk was a co-partner (Royal Fisk Letters, Bancroft Library).

11   "Reports of the County Superintendent of Public Schools for Alpine County to the Superintendent of Public Instruction, Sate of California, 1863-1914" (extracted from California State Archives and published by the Alpine County Museum, 1995), at page 6 (Summary for 1868-9).

12   *Chronicle*, Feb. 22, 1868.

13   Fisk served as a Trustee of the Mountain Company (*Chronicle*, Jan 12, 1867), and was an initial Trustee and incorporator of the Onondaga G&SM, incorporated September 1, 1863 (Certificate of Incorporation at Amador County Archives). The *Las Calaveras* article (cited above) also suggests Fisk was part of a group that unsuccessfully "drove a long prospect tunnel into Silver Mountain," possibly a reference to Chalmers' Isabella Tunnel.

14   *Chronicle*, January 1, 1870 (delinquent tax summons).

15   *Las Calaveras*, Calaveras County Historical Society's quarterly bulletin, Vol. XVI, No. 3 (April, 1968).

16   *Chronicle*, May 7, 1870 (anticipating the Fisk family's return from Murphys).

17   As Charles "Fiske," he purchased two lots in Town of Murphys on September 8, 1877; the deed was recorded 11 years later at the request of Frank W. Fisk. *See* copy of deed recorded in Book 15 of Deeds, Page 504, Calaveras County Records, a copy of which is located at the Calaveras County Historical Society. *See also Las Calaveras* issue of April, 1968.

18   *Monitor Gazette*, June 18, 1864 (emphasis added).

19   Owner L.M. Goodwin borrowed $4,000 from A. Constine and Jonas Lincoln, issuing a mortgage against the Mammoth dated April 11, 1864; the mortgage was assigned to John Agnew July 14, 1864. *See* original Assignment of Mortgage in Amador County Archives.

20   *Chronicle*, April 1, 1871.

21   *Chronicle,* April 1, 1871. The adjacent Mammoth *stable* was later demolished and the lumber recycled to construct the IXL boarding house. *Chronicle*, September 9, 1876.

22   *Chronicle,* August 26, September 2 & 9, 1876. Withington died of cancer just a few short months later, in March, 1877.

23   *Chronicle,* February 18, 1871.

24   *Chronicle,* December 2, 1871.

25   Ford filled the vacancy as Superintendent of Schools in 1882 after P.W. Parker's departure (Mabel Love, <u>History of Alpine County Schools</u>, p. 7), and served as the Acting Coroner, assembling a coroner's jury for the inquest investigating the shooting death of E.H. Errickson (*Chronicle,* December 21, 1872).

26   Chalmers Letters, *Private Letters 1880-81,* p. 634 (February 16, 1881).

27   Chalmers Letters, *Private Letters 1880-81,* p. 778 (April 17, 1881).

28   Chalmers Letters, *Private Letters 1880-81,* p. 55 (April 5, 1880)("another Sack of Coffee for Boarding House"); p. 138 (May 3, 1880)(ordering "1 Barrel of Coffee Sugar" for boarding house). For his *own* use, however, Chalmers ordered "good Cube Sugar" by the barrel. *Private Letters 1880-81,* p. 343 (August 30, 1880).

29   Chalmers Letters, *Private Letters 1880-81,* p. 304 (August 11, 1880)(ordering 4,000 pounds of flour).

30   Chalmers Letters, *Private Letters 1880-81,* p. 657 (February 15, 1881)(remitting $235.33 for "Boarding House Beef"); previous payments to the same were $63 (p. 361, September 13, 1881) and $182.55 (p. 447, October 6, 1880); and on December 16, 1880, Chalmers had written "send no more beef," suggesting the February $235 payment covered beef supplies from October 6 through December 16.

31   Chalmers Letters, *Private Letters,* p . 363 (September 14, 1880). Chalmers also apparently utilized Chinese household help; *see* Chalmers Letters *Private Letters,* p. 861 (June 8, 1881), requesting a "good China servant" to cook, wash, iron, "make beds, sweep, scrub, brush shoes, and do exactly as Mrs. C. tells him."

32   Chalmers Letters, *Private Letters,* p. 363-64 (September 14, 1880)(punctuation added).

33   Chalmers Letters, *Private Letters,* p. 805 (April 27, 1881).

34   Chalmers Letters, *Private Letters,* p. 805-806 (April 27, 1881)(punctuation added; emphasis in original).

35   Chalmers Letters, *Isabella Officials 1878-79,* pp. 36, 38, 40, 252 (December 15 and 20, 1878; June 9, 1879)($3/day for miners; $2.50/day for car men or graders; $1/day Board); *see also* <u>Id.</u> at p. 824 (July 28, 1880) (indicating the men had to pay $2/month for the "doctor and washman."). At the Exchequer Mine, Chalmers was forced to reduce his shifts from ten hours to eight, as the men "could not stand it in water (drip from above <u>cold ice</u> water) for 10 hours as formerly." Chalmers Letters, *Private Letters 1871-2,* p. 503 (February 12, 1873).

36   Chalmers Letters, *Exchequer Officials 1873,* p. 69 (April 11, 1873).

37   Chalmers Letters, *Exchequer Officials 1873,* p. 111 (August 25, 1873).

38   Chalmers Letters, *Exchequer Officials 1873,* p. 69 (April 11, 1873).

39   *Chronicle,* April 15, 1871.

40   *Chronicle,* March 12, 1870.

41   At least one of Chalmers' buildings at the I.X.L. Mine apparently caught fire "while in the Sheriff's Custody" (apparently due to an attachment), resulting in a loss of $125 worth of candles; *see* Chalmers Letters, *Exchequer Officials 1873,* p. 447 (May 26, 1874)(microfilm version at Alpine County Museum; original at Bancroft Library).

42   *Chronicle,* December 1 and 15, 1866 (reporting an organizational meeting of the grandly-named "Alpine Hook & Ladder Company No. 1").

43   *Chronicle,* October 21, 1871.

44   *Chronicle,* May 31, 1873.

45   *Chronicle*, December 17, 1870.

46   *Chronicle*, May 27, 1871.

47   *Chronicle*, March 30, 1872.

48   The *Chronicle* edition of March 30, 1872, lists satisfied local sewing machine owners including Mrs. D. Davidson, Mrs. W.P. Merrill, Mrs. A.M. Wade and Mrs. Charles Folger, indicating "We have sold in the past seven months $855 worth of machines" and adding, "If any good man, morally and financially, wants to buy a sewing machine[,] call upon us, as we have a few more of the same sort left."

49   *Id.*

50   *Chronicle*, July 22, 1871.

51   *Chronicle*, Dec. 15, 1877 (No stranger to hyperbole, Dr. Kissner's ad boldly proclaimed: "[T]he only preparation known that will cure Consumption and all diseases of the Throat and Lungs. . . . If your life is worth saving, don't delay in giving these Powders a trial, as they will surely cure you!").

52   *Chronicle*, March 30, 1872.

53   *Chronicle*, March 30, 1872.

54   *Chronicle,* November 4 and 11, 1871.

55   Addison Curtiss diary, entry for June 20, 1864 (punctuation added).

56   Addison Curtiss diary, entry for June 13, 1864.

57   Diary of O.S. Adams, entry for September 8 and November 28, 1867.

Chapter 4 Footnotes:

1   Peter Browning, Place Names of the Sierra Nevada (Wilderness Press 1991), at p. 72. The *Territorial Enterprise* was actually the first newspaper on the entire Eastern slope, commencing publication at Genoa in December, 1858, but it was located in Utah Territory. Stanley W. Paher, Nevada Ghost Towns & Mining Camps (Nevada Publications 1970), p. 56.

2   William M. Maule, "A Contribution to the Geographic and Economic History of Carson, Walker and Mono Basins" (U.S. Forest Service 1938), at p. 12, *reprinting* copy of the *Chronicle*'s April 23, 1864 first edition. According to the 1864 Assessment Roll, R.M. Folger was taxed on a printing press valued at $800. (Alpine County Archives). The *Chronicle* office was conveniently located on Montgomery Street, "opposite the City Hall" in Markleeville (*Chronicle* masthead, June 16, 1866).

3   *The Monitor Gazette* began publication about June, 1864, with offices at the corner of Monitor and South Streets in the town of Monitor; publishers were S.J. Noble, S.G. Lewis, and W.O. Hayes; the latter would later reopen the *Silver Mountain Bulletin*. *See* microfilm of *Monitor Gazette* at Alpine County Museum; (the first issue preserved is June 11, 1864, identified as "Volume I, No. 2"); *see also* W. Turrentine Jackson, Report on the History of Grover Hot Springs State Park Area and Surrounding Region of Alpine County (Division of Beaches & Parks, Department of Parks and Recreation, State of California 1964), at p. 37.

4   According to its competitor, the original *Bulletin* was launched about 1864 but folded after a year in operation, only to be re-launched in 1865 and die again within the next 12 months. *Chronicle*, June 29, 1878.

5   *Chronicle*, March 9, 1867.

6   *Bulletin,* February 2, 1867.

7   *Bulletin*, March 30, 1867.

8   *Bulletin,* March 30, 1867 (emphasis in original).

9   *Monitor Gazette*, October 15, 1864.

10   *Bulletin,* May 4, 1867.

11   *Chronicle*, August 24, 1872; *see also* September 23, 1876; *and* August 31, 1878.

12   *Chronicle*, July 1, 1876. Alex Folger was the one to take the books and records of the Mountain No. 1 to San Francisco, when its offices were moved there in 1876. *Chronicle*, September 9, 1876.

13   Chalmers Letters, *Exchequer Officials 1871-2*, p. 68 (May 17, 1871).

14   *Chronicle*, July 1, 22, and 29, 1976 (a time during which the Mountain Mine increased its capital stock and moved its offices to San Francisco); Robert Folger was re-elected to the Board the following year, according to the *Chronicle* of January 13, 1877.

15   *Chronicle*, July 15, 1876.

16   *Chronicle*, September 23, 1876. He was re-elected a Director of the Pennsylvania Gold & Silver Mining Company in 1878. *Chronicle*, August 31, 1878.

17   *Chronicle*, July 29, 1876.

18   According to W. Turrentine Jackson, Silver Mountain was chosen "by the slim majority of forty votes, amidst cries of fraud at Monitor and Markleeville." (Henry Eno, Twenty Years on the Pacific Slope (Yale University Press 1965), p. 68, *citing* articles from the *Sacramento Daily Union* and *Daily Alta*). In another source, Jackson observes that from 1865 on, "almost every year" Markleeville or Monitor organized a movement to claim the title. (W. Turrentine Jackson, Report on the History of Grover Hot Springs State Park Area and Surrounding Region of Alpine County (Division of Beaches & Parks, Department of Parks and Recreation, State of California 1964), at pp. 4, 6, and 32). The issue certainly came up in 1866, with the *Chronicle* observing that "the county seat question has divided the Union party," to be decided (again) in the coming September election. (*Chronicle*, October 27, 1866).

19   Interestingly enough, O.S. Adams was hired to pack up and load the printing press and type for the *Bulletin*. Diary of O.S. Adams, entries for July 5 through July 11, 1867.

20   *Chronicle*, August 31, 1867.

21   When a fresh petition to move the county seat began circulating in 1871, the *Chronicle* noted tartly that its rival, the *Miner*, was in favor and called Monitor the "hotbed of this movement" (*Chronicle,* September 16, 1871), protesting it was "not true" that fewer than 25 people supported keeping the county seat at Silver Mountain. (*Chronicle*, December 23 and 30, 1871). The editors boldly asserted that the petition for removal had "only 65 signatures" (January 20, 1872); it turned out to have 140 (February 10, 1872). The *Chronicle* published a list of twenty reasons that the county seat bill (introduced in response to the petition) should not be passed, the last item of which read simply, "Leave well enough alone." (February 24, 1872). The editors blamed "leading Democrats" in Monitor for instigating the attempted upheaval (March 16, 1872). Ultimately, the Governor vetoed the 1872 removal bill. (April 6, 1872).

22   *See Chronicle*, November 9, 1867 (indicating that D.C. Riddell was the newspaper's next-door neighbor). Riddell's offices were located in "Francis's Block" (*Chronicle,* December 28, 1867), likely a reference to John H. Francis, who owned Lots 1 and 7 of Block 4 (*Chronicle*, January 7, 1871). Careful comparison of old photographs also suggests that the *Chronicle*'s original location was on this same corner.

23   The *Chronicle*'s original masthead listed just R.M. Folger as publisher. *See, for example, issue of* June 16, 1866.

24   Robert Folger sailed from New York on January 11, 1849, aboard the schooner *Anthem*, arriving at San Francisco five months later after an "adventurous" journey. Frank S. Wedertz, Mono Diggings (Community Printing 2001), p. 81-82.

25   F. Wedertz, Mono Diggings, at p.82-83.

26   Robert supposedly "drifted into journalism" with his brother Charles, in 1851, but the dates would suggest he wasn't in Sacramento at the time. F. Wedertz, Mono Diggings, at p. 82.

27   *Chronicle*, June 16 and December 29, 1866.

28   Amador Assessment Roll of 1864 (Alpine County Archives).

29   Whether he was *the* first postmaster is unclear, although some sources give him that distinction (*see, e.g.,* P. Browning, Place Names of the Sierra Nevada, at p. 72). He was clearly among the earliest postmasters; the *Silver Mountain Bulletin* identifies A.C. Folger as Markleeville's postmaster in 1866 (December 22, 1866 issue).

30   *Chronicle*, February 16, 1867; June 22, 1867.

31   *Chronicle*, December 28, 1867.

32   *Chronicle,* June 6, 1868, and January 1, 1870 (insurance agent); May 31, 1873 (notary).

33   *Chronicle*, June 18, 1870.

34   *Chronicle*, December 31, 1870 (Deputy County Clerk); and October 28, 1871 (Justice of the Peace).

35   *Chronicle*, August 12, 1876. Parties wishing to be enrolled on the Great Register of Voters were directed to "apply at the Chronicle Office."

36   *Chronicle*, August 12 and November 4, 1876.

37   Robert Folger is listed as a Board member for 1874-75. There was no school held in the Franklin (Silver Mountain) District that school year, however. *See* "Reports of the County Superintendent of Public Schools for Alpine County to the Superintendent of Public Instruction, State of California, 1863-1914" (extracted from California State Archives and published by the Alpine County Museum, 1995), at p. 14 (Summary for 1874-75). Folger resigned his post in 1876, forcing Superintendent Ford to appoint a new Trustee in his place. *Chronicle,* July 1, 1876.

38   *Chronicle*, July 20, 1872. At least one source identifies the Folgers as Quakers, a religious persuasion that also would have led them to shun military duty. F. Wedertz, Mono Diggings, p. 84 (indicating that both Folger brothers were active in the Society of Friends while living in Bridgeport).

39   *Chronicle*, August 26, 1876.

40   *See Chronicle* of November 2 and November 9, 1872.

41   Possibly occupying a building owned by Levi Miller just West of their original location; *see Chronicle* issues of January 1, 1870 (identifying the *Chronicle*'s location as on Main Street, between First and Second Streets), and December 17, 1870 (indicating that "Architect Miller" was putting new doors on the property).

42   The *Chronicle* of May 31, 1873, still identifies the *Chronicle*'s location as Main Street between 1st and 2nd. The *Alpine Miner* congratulated the *Chronicle* on its move to "better quarters" in its June 6, 1874 issue. The August 28, 1875 issue of the *Chronicle* identifies its new location as the corner of Fifth.

43   *Chronicle*, August 28, 1875.

44   *Chronicle*, November 19, 1870.

45   *Chronicle*, January 28, 1871.

46   *Chronicle*, January 28, 1871

47   *Chronicle*, May 27, 1871.

48   *Chronicle*, October 15, 1870.

49   *Chronicle*, November 5, 1870.

50   *Chronicle*, November 26, 1870.

51   *Chronicle*, January 13, 1872.

52   *Chronicle*, June 17, 1871.

53   *Chronicle*, December 15, 1877.

54   *Chronicle*, September 14, 1878. The editors of the *Chronicle* (probably correctly) attributed the "stampede" for Bodie to "suspension of mining operations at Monitor" (*i.e.,* the Advance Mine, which had recently closed). *Chronicle,* August 31, 1878.

55   *Chronicle*, September 7, 1878.

56   *Chronicle*, May 11, 1878.

57   *Chronicle*, June 22, 1878; *see also* August 10, 1878.

58   *Chronicle*, September 28, 1878, and October 5, 1878.

59   *Chronicle*, June 15 and 22, 1878; August 10 and 17, 1878. The *Chronicle* had apparently omitted 14 delinquent taxpayers from the list whose taxes were "virtually paid," as it claimed was "customary." *Chronicle*, August 17, 1878.

60   *Chronicle*, October 5, 1878. (Peter Curtz had been appointed District Attorney in February, in place of Thomas J. Orgon, who had died. *Chronicle*, February 2, 1878.)

61   *Chronicle*, August 24, 1878.

62   *Chronicle*, October 19, 1878.

63   *Chronicle*, October 12 and 19, 1878. Their new quarters at Bodie were hardly lavish; for their first three months in Bodie, the Folgers were forced to make do with the only vacant house in town, a "one story shanty, 10 x 14, in, or [we] may say out of town" (that is, on Mills Street, opposite the noisy South Standard hoisting works); in February, 1879, they happily moved to a new office on the second floor of Goodson's building, on the east side of Main Street between Standard Avenue and Green Street (*Mono Alpine Chronicle*, December 28, 1878, and February 22, 1879).

64   *Mono Alpine Chronicle,* May 3, 1879.

65   P. Browning, <u>Place Names of the Sierra Nevada</u>, at p. 72.

Chapter 5 Footnotes:

1   *Chronicle*, January 27, 1872 (reporting 12 below zero, "the oldest ever known in this town").

2   *Chronicle*, March 18, 1871 (punctuation corrected).

3   *Chronicle*, September 16, 1876.

4   William H. Brewer, <u>Up and Down California in 1860-1864</u> (University of California Press 1966), p. 430 (entry for July 3, 1863).

5   *Chronicle*, May 7, 1870.

6   Chalmers Letters, *Private Letters 1868-9*, p. 268 (January 18, 1869); *see similarly* p. 274 (January 24, 1869).

7   Chalmers Letters, *Private Letters 1880-81*, p. 2 (March 16, 1880)(punctuation added).

8   <u>Diary of O.S. Adams</u>, entry for April 14, 1867 (Dustman collection).

9   *Chronicle*, February 1, 1868.

10   William H. Brewer, <u>Up and Down California</u>, *supra*, p. 434 (entry for August 8, 1863).

11   <u>Diary of O.S. Adams</u>, entry for February 13, 1867 (Dustman collection).

12   The body of 28-year-old Nils Magnus August Drake was found in Indian Valley, about 8 miles from Silver Mountain, after he had tried to cross the mountains via the Big Tree Road in early February. He apparently had sought refuge in C.L. Thompson's barn, but let his fire go out. *Chronicle*, June 13, 1868. In an odd twist of fate, each the three stalwart citizens who went out to bring Drake's body back to Silver Mountain for burial would themselves pass away within a short span: Errickson was shot in 1872; and Norton and Snowshoe Thompson both died in 1876.

13   *Chronicle*, December 29, 1866 and December 28, 1867.

14   William H. Brewer, <u>Up and Down California</u>, p. 435 (entry for August 8, 1863).

15   *Chronicle*, January 13, 1872 (describing Alex Folger).

16   Tahoe Nuggets #136, www.thestormking.com.

17   Snowshoe Thompson's heavy oak skis reportedly tipped the scales at 25 pounds. *See* Snowshoe Thompson: Legendary Skiing Mailman, www.thestormking.com.

18   Chalmers Letters, *PrivateLetters 1871-2*, pp. 342, 351, and 361 (January 9, 12, and 15, 1872).

19   *Chronicle*, February 23, 1867.

20   *Chronicle*, February 1, 1868.

21   *See, e.g., Chronicle* January 26, 1867; March 9, 1867; and December 26, 1868.

22   *Chronicle*, March 9, 1867.

23   *Chronicle*, January 27, 1877.

24   *Silver Mountain Bulletin*, March 23, 1867.

25   *Monitor Gazette*, February 4, 1865.

26   *Monitor Gazette*, February 4, 1865.

27   *Bulletin*, March 23, 1867.

28   *Bulletin*, February 23, 1867.

29   *Bulletin*, February 23, 1867.

30   Henry Eno, <u>Twenty Years on the Pacific Slope</u> (Yale University Press 1965), p. 152 (punctuation added).

31   *Chronicle*, April 6, 1867.

32   During the winter of 1871-2, Silver Mountain was inaccessible by stage for 109 days. *Chronicle*, March 30, 1872.

33   *Chronicle*, June 6, 1868.

34   For the six months ending January 1, 1867, McBeth reported $2,560.08 in fees. *Bulletin*, February 23, 1867.

35   *Bulletin*, March 2, 1867 (spelling corrected).

36   *Bulletin*, March 9, 1867.

37   Excerpt from "Overland Journey to California," by Mrs. James Caples May, reprinted in *Alpine Heritage: One Hundred Years of History, Recreation, Lore in Alpine County, California 1864-1964*, published by the Centennial Book Committee (1964), p. 31 (punctuation added).

38   Marshall Fey, <u>Emigrant Trails: The Long Road to California</u> (Western Trails Research Association 2008), p. 155.

39   As late as 1871, tolls charged on the Amador & Nevada Wagon Road were 75 cents for each loaded wagon. *Chronicle*, September 9, 1871.

40   Eric Jung, <u>Bulls, Bears and Highway Fares: A History of Alpine County, California</u> (Cub Reporter Publishing 2004), pp. 47-54; *see also* W. Turrentine Jackson, <u>Report on the History of Grover Hot Springs State Park Area and Surrounding Region of Alpine County</u> (Division of Beaches & Parks, Department of Parks and Recreation, State of California 1964), p. 49.

41   William H. Brewer, <u>Up and Down California</u>, *supra*, p. 431 (entries for July 31 and August 4, 1863).

42   *The Mining and Scientific Press*, April 23, 1864.

43   *The Mining and Scientific Press*, May 21, 1864.

44   Toll Road Permit, Utah Territory, dated December 1, 1852. The original of this document is located in the Nevada State Archives in a book quaintly titled "First Records of Carson Valley, Utah Territory." The "First

Records" book is reproduced on-line at the Nevada State Library and Archives website; for this toll road permit, *see* http://dmla.clan.lib.nv.us/docs/NSLA/archives/1record/page14.htm.

45   W.T. Jackson, *supra*, p. 52.

46   *Chronicle*, January 26, 1867.

47   *Chronicle*, February 2, 1867.

48   *Chronicle*, February 2, 1867.

49   *Monitor Gazette*, June 18, 1864. Over time, tolls dropped significantly. Seven years later, passage for a loaded wagon along the same route cost 75 cents. *Chronicle*, September 9, 1871

50   *Monitor Gazette*, October 29, 1864.

51   *Chronicle*, June 16, 1866, reporting a summons in the suit by Silver Mountain Toll Road Co. against · Isaac Stewart "for tolls for passage over the toll road of Plaintiff in the months of February and March, 1866."

52   Official Records Book "B", p. 113-114 (Deed from Anselm Tash to John M. Johnson, dated February 3, 1866).

53   Official Records Book "B", p. 614-615 (Sheriff's Deed to N. Osgood dated September 14, 1867, conveying a one-third interest in the Silver Mountain Toll Road from Markleeville to Mount Bullion, to satisfy judgment against the former owners of $3,357.33. Osgood apparently paid only $1000 for their interest at the execution sale.).

54   *Monitor Gazette*, March 11, 1865.

55   *Chronicle*, January 26, 1867.

56   *Board of Supervisors Minutes,* September 3, 1866 (Book A, p. 193)(Archives microfilm #60).

57   *Chronicle*, December 23, 1871; *see also* February 3, 1872.

58   *Chronicle*, March 16, 1867.

59   *Chronicle*, November 16, 1872.

60   *Chronicle*, December 22, 1866.

61   *Chronicle*, November 18, 1876.

62   William H. Brewer, Up and Down California, *supra*, p.118 (entry for June 18, 1861).

63   William H. Brewer, Up and Down California, *supra*, p. 247 (entry for February 22, 1862). This leg of the journey was apparently near San Jose, California.

64   *Monitor Gazette,* June 18, 1864.

65   Letter from Royal Fisk to F.H. Smith & Co., October 8, 1864 (Royal Fisk Letters, Bancroft Library) (punctuation added).

66   *Silver Mountain Bulletin*, October 13, 1866 (advertisement for Matteson & Garland's stage service).

67   *Chronicle*, June 16, 1866.

68   *Silver Mountain Bulletin*, March 23, 1867.

69   *Chronicle*, May 7 1870; December 17, 1870.

70   *Chronicle*, April 8, 1871. Other stage lines operating during at least a portion of this period included the Thornburg, Alpine, and Pioneer Omnibus lines serving Carson City and all points in between, while Wellington's Stage Line ferried passengers between Silver Mountain and Aurora (per Humboldt-Toiyabe National Forest history of Silver Mountain City).

71   *Chronicle*, October 28, 1871.

72   *Chronicle*, February 3, 1872.

73   *Chronicle*, February 3 and 24, 1872.

74   Letter from Royal Fisk to F.H. Smith & Co., October 8, 1864 (Royal Fisk Letters, Bancroft Library) (spelling corrected).

75   Sam P. Davis, <u>The History of Nevada</u>, vol. I, Chapter VIII (1912), "The Lawless Element," p. 242-243 (reprinted on-line at <u>www.nevadaobserver.com</u> under "Reading Room" tab).

76   *Chronicle*, October 27, 1866. The victim's account was printed intact, atrocious spelling and all.

77   *Chronicle*, November 3, 1866. Sandy Bowers, of Bowers Mansion fame, reportedly offered to pay $250 for the return of his gold watch, "but the offer was not accepted." Three of the Geiger Grade robbers were later arrested. One was identified as James W. Crum, a name curiously similar to that of a former Alpine Sheriff (James Krum), who had recently been described as "repudiated; the people had lost confidence as to his honesty as a public officer; he was spending too much money, for a poor man. . ." *Chronicle*, November 17 and December 22, 1866.

78   Sam P. Davis, <u>The History of Nevada</u>, *supra*, p. 243.

79   *Chronicle*, March 16, 1867.

80   *Chronicle*, May 11, 1878.

81   *Chronicle*, December 2, 1871.

82   *Chronicle,* October 12, 1878.

83   *Chronicle*, April 2, 1870.

84   *Chronicle*, October 1, 1870.

85   *Chronicle*, July 2, 1870; October 1, 1870.

86   Snowshoe Thompson: Legendary Skiing Mailman, <u>www.thestormking.com</u>.

87   Elma S. Bradshaw, "Our Man of the Mountains," p. 3 (undated typescript prepared approximately 1967), copy at Nevada Historical Society, Reno.

88   Snowshoe Thompson: Legendary Skiing Mailman, <u>www.thestormking.com.</u>

89   Elma S. Bradshaw, *supra*, p. 6.

90   Elma S. Bradshaw, *supra,* p. 6, *quoting* article by Herbert Hamlin.

91   Elma S. Bradshaw, *supra*, at p. 6.

92   Douglas McDonald, <u>Nevada Lost Mines & Buried Treasures</u>, p. 65-66 (Nevada Publications 1981).

93   William H. Brewer, <u>Up and Down California</u>, *supra*, p. 122-23 (entry for July 2, 1861).

94   Chalmers Letters, *Private Letters 1868-9*, p. 194 (December 21, 1868)(punctuation added); *see also Private Letters 1868-9,* p. 339 (April 11, 1869), bluntly advising: "Wells Fargo & Coy. Don't; -- They are more insecure than by regular Mail."

95   William M. Maule, "A Contribution to the Geographic and Economic History of Carson, Walker and Mono Basins" (U.S. Forest Service 1938), at p. 30, *quoting* Capt. J.H. Simpson's "Report of Explorations Across Great Basin of Utah in 1859."

96   Humboldt-Toiyabe National Forest history of Silver Mountain City, indicating that a private telegraph line was connected in 1863; according to the local newspaper, however, the actual date of completion was in 1864. *See* footnote 92, *infra*, and accompanying text.

97   *Monitor Gazette*, June 18, 1864.

98   *Monitor Gazette*, June 18, 1864.

99   *Monitor Gazette*, June 18, 1864.

100   *Bulletin,* December 22, 1866; *Chronicle,* December 28, 1867. "Francis' Block" was likely named for John H. Francis, the owner of several lots in Block 4, situated between 2nd and 3rd Streets.

101   *Chronicle*, May 30, 1868.

102   *Chronicle*, February 8, 1868.

103   *Chronicle*, December 14, 1867.

104   *Chronicle*, January 4, 1868.

105   *Chronicle*, December 14, 1872.

106   *Chronicle*, April 6, 1878.

107   Chalmers Letters, *Private Letters 1878-1881*, p. 74 (April 13, 1880).

108   Chalmers Letters, *Private Letters 1878-1881*, p. 199 (June 25, 1880).

109   Chalmers Letters, *Private Letters 1878-1881*, p. 63 (April 8, 1880).

110   *See* Harvey Rice, "Letters from the Pacific Slope; or First Impressions," Letter VII, October 6, 1869 (indicating that the longest tunnel was an astonishing (for the time) 1,700 feet)(available on-line at the Library of Congress' "American Memory" website, *http://memory.loc.gov*).

111   *Chronicle*, March 4, 1871. According to the *Chronicle*, this survey was for a *narrow-gauge* railroad between Reno and Virginia City. As actually constructed, however, the Virginia & Truckee line was standard-gauge.

112   *Chronicle* September 16, 1871; November 11, 1871.

113   *Chronicle*, April 6, 1872.

114   *Chronicle*, July 20, 1872; August 17, 1872.

115   *Chronicle*, August 17, 1872.

116   *Chronicle*, July 1, 1876 and January 27, 1877.

117   *Chronicle*, November 24, 1866.

118   *Chronicle*, September 28 and November 2, 1872.

119   *Chronicle*, December 23, 1876.

120   *Chronicle*, September 30, 1876.

121   Chalmers Letters, *Private Letters 1878-1881*, p. 532 (December 8, 1880)(writing to Mrs. Searight in San Francisco).

122   Chalmers Letters, *Private Letters 1878-1881*, p. 497 (November 1, 1880).

123   Chalmers Letters, *Private Letters 1878-1881*, p. 244 (July 13, 1880)(punctuation added).

124   The Silver Mountain stage departed from Carson on Mondays, Wednesdays, and Fridays about 10 a.m., arriving at Silver Mountain at 8 or 9 p.m. Chalmers Letters, *Private Letters 1878-1881*, p. 209 (June 26, 1880).

125   *Chronicle*, November 30, 1872.

126   *Chronicle*, January 20, 1877.

127   Sam P. Davis, *supra*, at p. 245. According to Davis, what may have been the world's first train robbery took place on November 1, 1870, when the Overland Express train was held up west of Reno and lightened of $40,000 in gold.

128   *Chronicle*, November 30, 1872.

129   *Chronicle*, February 10 and March 9, 1872. The *Chronicle* reported that Snowshoe, tiring of the wait, made himself a pair of "snowshoes"; other sources suggest that he actually *walked* the 75 miles through the snow. Elma S. Bradshaw, *supra*, at p. 8.

130   *Chronicle*, February 10, 1872.

Chapter 6 Footnotes:

1   *Chronicle*, March 23, 1867; *see similarly* F.A.S. Jones Letter to James Jones, January 20, 1869 (at Alpine County Museum), indicating the Mountain Tunnel extended some 1,523 feet at the extravagant cost of $51.96 per foot, with "[n]o indications of a ledge" in sight. The original Mountain Company mine was commenced 1,000 feet above the level of the town, but costs for hoisting machinery and other improvements proved too much for the value of the ore, so a second tunnel was begun at the base of the mountain. Rossiter W. Raymond, <u>Mineral Resources West of the Rocky Mountains</u>, 1873 (transcription of Lewis Chalmers' report pertaining to Alpine County, at Alpine County Museum), p. 1.

2   *Chronicle*, January 4, 1868 (noting progress of 580 feet in the "hardest kind of rock"); Chalmers Letters, *Imperial Officials 1867-70*, pp. 212-213 (January 25, 1869) (reporting size of the tunnel and progress of just 5-1/2 feet a week, working two shifts); Rossiter W. Raymond, <u>Mineral Resources West of the Rocky Mountains</u>, 1873 (transcription of Lewis Chalmers' report pertaining to Alpine County, at Alpine County Museum), p. 2-3 (1,000-foot tunnel through "solid granite" had pierced the vein at the 800-foot level, but produced only "limited quantities" of ruby silver ore).

3   *Chronicle*, February 4, 1871.

4   Around 1867, bullion from the Silver Mountain mining district was averaging $7,000 to $8,000 a <u>month</u>. <u>Bancroft Scraps</u> (Bancroft Library), p. 55. One source cites estimates putting the total gold and silver production from Alpine County to be between $3 and $5 million, but notes that recorded output from 1880 to 1948 shows just $143, 769 in gold and roughly half that in silver. William B. Clark, <u>Mines and Mineral Resources of Alpine County</u> (Calif. Division of Mines and Geology, 1977), p. 14.

5   The Tarshish in Monitor District was perhaps the richest of the three. A report from soon after its location in 1863 indicated ore had been found there yielding "with careful treatment" more than $200 per ton. (<u>Bancroft Scraps</u>, p. 53-55). Henry Eno relayed rumors of a vein from 8 to 12 feet wide of the "richest silver ore I ever saw," with assays as high as $1400. (Henry Eno, <u>Twenty Years on the Pacific Slope</u> (Yale University Press 1965), p. 161). A "mammoth silver brick" was produced from some 7,100 pounds of Tarshish ore in 1867, with the brick valued at over $1,200. (*Chronicle*, May 4, 1867). Chalmers reported in 1869 that the mine had taken out ore yielding from $2,000 to $3,000 per ton. Chalmers Letters, *Imperial Officials 1867-70*, p. 300-302 (April 19, 1869). A large body of "first class ore" was reportedly struck in 1872. (*Chronicle*, March 9, 1872). And as late as 1880, the lode – now renamed "Colorado No. 2" – was "shipping bullion pretty regularly." (Chalmers Letters, *Isabelle Officials*, p. 570 (February 25, 1880)).

6   Letter from C.H. Wakelee (at San Francisco) to Capt. James Jones, June 10, 1865 (Alpine County Museum).

7   Chalmers Letters, *Private Letters 1871-72*, pp. 43 and 50-51 (May 1 and 22, 1871).

8   Rossiter W. Raymond, <u>Mineral Resources West of the Rocky Mountains</u>, 1872 (transcription of Lewis Chalmers' report pertaining to Alpine County, at Alpine County Museum), p. 2.

9   *See Bulletin* of March 23, 1867, noting that the Pennsylvania Company had run its tunnel some 525 feet, but with progress of just 7 to 11 feet per week, with two shifts.

10   <u>Bancroft Scraps</u>, p. 54 (unattributed clipping from approximately 1864).

11   A "Eugenia" claim in the Silver Mountain District is listed in William B. Clark's <u>Mines and Mineral Resources of Alpine County</u> (p. 16); *see also* Indenture dated August 30, 1878, between N.D. Arnot Jr. and Henry Syme, conveying (among other interests) a Tunnel Right known as 'The Eugenie Tunnel,' including an old existing tunnel "on the Isabelle Company's ground" (Calif. State Library).

12   *Mono-Alpine Chronicle*, December 21, 1878.

13   *Mono-Alpine Chronicle*, December 21, 1878; Chalmers Letters, *Isabelle Officials 1880-82*, p. 206-208 (January 22, 1881).

14   Chalmers Letters, *Private Letters 1878-81*, p. 15 (March 22, 1880).

15   Chalmers Letters, *Isabella Officials 1878-80*, p. 98 (January 29, 1879).

16   Chalmers Letters, *Isabella Officials 1880-82*, p. 210 (January 22, 1881).

17   Jackson called it "4400 feet of fruitless tunneling." W. Turrentine Jackson, <u>Report on the History of Grover Hot Springs State Park Area and Surrounding Region of Alpine County</u> (Division of Beaches & Parks, Department of Parks and Recreation, State of California 1964), at p. 92.

18   *Alpine Miner*, April 27, 1867.

19   *Chronicle*, April 13, 1867.

20   *Chronicle*, May 30, 1868.

21   *Chronicle*, April 13, 1867.

22   *Bulletin*, January 5, 1867.

23   Michigan Tunnel and Mining Company Prospectus, *circa* 1864 (Dustman collection). The Prospectus also contains a number of such gems of hyperbole, including: "It is confidently believed that the Company will be able to declare *dividends* before the amount realized by the sale of stock has been expended, in which case it will prove one of the finest pieces of financial speculation of the times." (Emphasis in original.)

24   Rossiter W. Raymond, <u>Mining Statistics West of the Rocky Mountains</u>, 1869 (transcription of report pertaining to Alpine County, at Alpine County Museum), p. 1.

25   *Chronicle*, May 11, 1867.

26   *Chronicle*, June 29, 1878 (suggesting the *Bulletin* had resumed publication in 1865, but folded in just twelve months); *see also* Indenture dated April 20, 1866, Book "B" of Alpine County Official Records, p. 207, indicating the *Bulletin*'s publishing equipment was sold by publishers W.O. Hayes and J.W. Ballard to Daniel Latimer and Robert Epperson of Calaveras County for the sum of $1500.

27   *Chronicle*, February 10, 1872 ("It is well known that our little cotemporary is nothing but a 'dodge' published to sell its innumerable 'rich mines,' and, although small, its lying proclivity is big."); and February 24, 1872 ("We could fill our columns with items from our cotemporary, extending through a period of nearly eight years, in proof of its being the meanest kind of a 'wildcat.'")

28   *Chronicle*, October 8, 1870.

29   *Chronicle*, December 30, 1871.

30   Remi Nadeau, <u>The Silver Seekers</u> (Crest Publishers 1999), at p. 48.

31   *Bulletin*, January 26, 1867.

32   *Chronicle*, October 21, 1871.

33   Chalmers Letters, *Exchequer Officials 1873-74*, p. 447 (May 26, 1874)(Bancroft Library microfilm).

34   Chalmers Letters, *Exchequer Officials 1873-74*, p. 463-64 (June 8, 1874)(Bancroft microfilm).

35   <u>Diary of Addison Curtiss</u>, entry for June 1, 1864 (original in Amador County archives).

36   <u>Diary of Addison Curtiss</u>, entry for June 3, 1864.

37   For a fascinating look at the history of explosives and blasting and a historical timeline, *see* <u>www.explosives.org/HistoryofExplosives.htm</u>. For the chemical composition of various powders, *see* technical notes at <u>www.bodiehistory.com/drilling-blasting.htm</u>.

38   *Bulletin*, March 23, 1867.

39   *See* <u>www.bodiehistory.com</u>. An alternate powder was called Tonite Patent, which supposedly had no fumes. Chalmers Letters, *Isabella Officials 1878-80*, p. 373. (September 12, 1879).

40   *See supra* Note 37, history of explosives.

41   Chalmers Letters, *Imperial Officials 1867-70*, p. 283 (March 8, 1869).

42   Chalmers Letters, *Private Letters* 1868-69, p. 132 (August 24, 1868).

43   Chalmers Letters, *Isabelle Officials 1878-80,* pp. 261; 277; 285; 287; 373; 406-7 (June - October, 1879).

44   Chalmers Letters, *Isabelle Officials 1878-80*, p. 279; 285-86; 289-92 (July 11- 14, 1879).

45   Chalmers Letters, *Isabelle Officials 1878-80*, p. 407 (October 20, 1879).

46   Chalmers Letters, *Isabelle Officials 1878-80*, p. 492; 496; 509-10 (January 12-19, 1880).

47   Chalmers Letters, *Isabelle Officials 1878-80*, p. 620; 638 (March 17 and 24, 1880).

48   Chalmers Letters, *Isabelle Officials 1878-80*, p. 509-10; 532-33 (January 19 and February 2, 1880) (describing it as a "Baker No. 5-1/2 Blower").

49   Chalmers Letters, *Isabelle Officials 1878-80*, p. 711 (May 5, 1880)(Chalmers may have substituted a larger blower later, as his original report indicates the Baker was purchased "conditionally" for just $800; but 2,000 feet of pipe with freight cost $2,000. *See* Chalmers Letters, *Isabelle Officials 1878-80* at 533-34 (February 2, 1880)).

50   *See* www.bodiehistory.com/drilling-blasting.htm, endnote 5.

51   For a fascinating and detailed history of the development of mechanical rock drills, *see* www.americanheritage.com/articles/magazine/it/1999/1/1999_1_56.shtml.

52   Chalmers Letters, *Exchequer Officials 1870-73*, p. 352 (March 28, 1871).

53   *Monitor Gazette*, October 15, 1864.

54   *Monitor Gazette*, October 8, 1864.

55   *See* Book "B" of Alpine County Official Records, p. 638-640 (October 18, 1867 Sheriff's Deed to D.E. and G.H. Swinerton of the Whiteside's Star Mill).

56   *Monitor Gazette*, February 18 and 25, 1865; *see also* Rossiter W. Raymond, <u>Mining Statistics West of the Rocky Mountains</u>, 1869 (transcription of report pertaining to Alpine County, at Alpine County Museum), p. 2.

57   *Chronicle*, February 4 and 11, 1871 (reporting the Globe's Mill was preparing to commence operations, with a mill building 58' x 61' in size, and 18' high); and April 20, 1872 (noting that the mill and furnaces had been started up at the Tarshish).

58   Rossiter W. Raymond, <u>Mineral Resources West of the Rocky Mountains</u>, 1873 (transcription of Lewis Chalmers' report pertaining to Alpine County, at Alpine County Museum), p. 26.

59   Rossiter W. Raymond, <u>Mining Statistics West of the Rocky Mountains</u>, 1869 (transcription of report pertaining to Alpine County, at Alpine County Museum), p. 3.

60   *Bulletin*, March 23, 1867.

61   *Chronicle*, August 24, 1878 (describing the Rivot erected at Markleeville in 1865 as one of the "scores" of failures); Rossiter W. Raymond, <u>Mineral Resources West of the Rocky Mountains</u>, 1873 (transcription of Lewis Chalmers' report pertaining to Alpine County, at Alpine County Museum), p. 25.

62   The first "Stetefeldt" furnace was erected at Reno, Nevada by Charles A. Stetefeldt about 1869. *See* C.A. Stetefeldt, "The Stetefeldt Furnace," published in vol. 24, Transactions of the American Institute of Mining Engineers (February 1894 to October 1894)(New York 1895)(available on-line through Google books).

63   Chalmers Letters, *Private Letters 1871-2,* p. 135 (June 18, 1871) *and* pp. 171; 240 (July 16 and August 12, 1871). *See similarly* Chalmers Letters, *Exchequer Officials 1870-73*, p. 319 (February 23, 1871), noting that he had recommended the purchase of the much-desired Stetefeldt (and estimated the cost at $5,000 to $6,000) as early as February, 1870.

64   Rossiter W. Raymond, <u>Mineral Resources West of the Rocky Mountains</u>, 1874 (transcription of Lewis Chalmers' report pertaining to Alpine County, at Alpine County Museum), p. 15-16.

65   Chalmers Letters, *Exchequer Officials 1870-73*, p. 306 (February 23, 1871).

66   Chalmers Letters, *Exchequer Officials 1870-73*, p. 312 (February 23, 1871).

67   Chalmers Letters, *Exchequer Officials 1870-73*, p. 319 (February 23, 1871).

68   Chalmers Letters, *Exchequer Officials 1870-73*, p. 385 (May 5, 1871). Chalmers did, apparently, succeed in having a new O'Hara Furnace installed at the old Exchequer Mill. The O'Hara was a long masonry affair with two parallel furnaces, one above the other, using chain-driven "plows" to move the ore slowly from one opening to the other, with salt added to chlorodize the ore during the roasting process. The Exchequer's new "O'Harra roasting furnace" would be one of the assets subject to execution sale listed in the notice of Sheriff's Sale in December, 1877. *See* footnote 72, *infra*.

69   Chalmers Letters, *Exchequer Officials 1870-73*, p. 408 (June 26, 1871).

70   Chalmers Letters, *Exchequer Officials 1870-73*, p. 499-500 (December 4, 1871).

71   *Chronicle*, September 2; 23; and 30, 1876.

72   *Chronicle*, December 16 and 30, 1876; December 15, 1877. Creditors of the Exchequer included A.S. Hallidie, the maker of a wire tramway. *Chronicle*, December 15, 1877.

73   W.T. Jackson, *supra*, at p. 89; Frank S. Wedertz, <u>Mono Diggings</u> (Community Printing 2001), p. 140-142 (suggesting the $60,000 I.X.L. mill that had "never been run" was purchased in 1896 and moved to the Dunderberg Mine, near Bridgeport).

74   *Monitor Gazette*, July 2, 1864.

75   Chalmers Letters, *Imperial Officials 1867-70*, pp. 451-453; 524 (November 1 and December 1, 1869).

76   Chalmers Letters, *Private Letters 1871-72*, p. 503 (February 12, 1873).

77   *Chronicle*, February 1, 1868 (reporting the death of William Bastian, "one of our most esteemed citizens").

78   *Chronicle*, November 12, 1870.

79   *Chronicle*, December 10, 1870.

80   *Chronicle*, December 16, 1876. (Although reported in the *Alpine Chronicle*, this "Imperial" was likely a vertical shaft somewhere on the Comstock, and not Chalmers' similarly-named horizontal tunnel.)

81   Chalmers Letters, *Exchequer Officials 1870-73*, p. 367 (April 18, 1871). It is hard to imagine the man survived, as the inclined winze and sump were by this time over 150 feet in length, according to an earlier letter at p. 361 (April 3, 1871).

82   Chalmers Letters, *Imperial Officials 1867-70*, p. 363-365 (August 9, 1869).

83   *Bulletin*, May 18, 1867.

84   *Chronicle*, November 11, 1876.

85   *Chronicle*, November 4, 1876.

86   *Chronicle*, December 16, 1876.

87   *Chronicle*, July 29, 1876.

88   W.H. Brewer, <u>Up and Down California in 1860-1864</u> (University of California Press 1966), p. 142-43 (entry for July 24, 1861).

89   *Chronicle*, November 19, 1870.

90   *Chronicle*, September 28, 1872 (railroad associated with Blue Lakes water project would pass within three miles of Silver Mountain); and November 2, 1872 ("John Horsley . . . was in town a few days since and assured us that everything in connection with the contemplated canal for supplying San Francisco with water from our Blue Lakes and the narrow guage [*sic*] railroad from Carson Valley and Silver Mountain to Oakland, is progressing finely, and that it will be built.").

91   *Chronicle*, December 10, 1870.

92   *Chronicle*, March 9, 1872 (describing ore taken from the I.X.L. "last Saturday").

Chapter 7 Footnotes:

1   William H. Brewer, <u>Up and Down California in 1860-1864</u> (University of California Press 1966), p. 432. The early mining records for Great Mogul District similarly reflect one female claimant as early as May, 1863: Florence Williams, possibly the wife of J.O. Williams, another of the company's eleven founders. Great Mogul Mining District Book "B", page 9 (notice of location for the Genoa Ledge dated May 8, 1863).

2   "Births/Marriages/Deaths" Index, compiled by Kim Summerhill (Skinner) (manuscript containing extracts from various newspapers 1864-1886, at Alpine County Museum), p. 2 (*citing Monitor Gazette* of September 10, 1864).

3   "Births/Marriages/Deaths" Index, p.3 (*citing Monitor Gazette* of December 17, 1864).

4   "Births/ Marriages/Deaths" Index, p. 3 (*citing Monitor Gazette* of August 26, 1865).

5   *For more details of the story of* "Silver Mountain's First Baby," *see Alpine Review*, Vol. XII, No. 2 (Summer/Fall 2005). Note that Alpine had not officially become a separate county by the time "Vady" was born in May, 1864. Thus, at least one other baby has been given credit as the Alpine "first" – although actually entering the world at Genoa, in Nevada Territory. *See* note 7, *infra*. Whether Alpine was officially a county even then is a separate question.

6   "Births/ Marriages/Index" Index, p. 16 (*citing* Monitor Gazette of December 17, 1864).

7   The *Monitor Gazette* reported that a son was born in Genoa, Nevada Territory on July 17, 1864, to the wife of James McLane, gleefully pronouncing him "Our First Baby" (*per* "Births/Marriages/Deaths" Index, p. 16, *citing* Monitor Gazette of July 23, 1864).

8   *See* <u>Diary of Addison Curtiss</u>, entry for May 19, 1864 (original in Amador County archives), reporting that Curtiss "[c]hopped wood below the burying ground" at Silver Mountain that day.

9   "Births/Marriages/Deaths" Index, p. 31 (*citing Alpine Signal* of June 20, 1879, describing the drowning death of the 15-month-old son of John Peterson, of Fredericksburg).

10   "Births/Marriages/Deaths" Index, p. 34 (*citing Monitor Gazette*, January 14, 1865).

11   *Chronicle*, February 1, 1868 (reporting the death of William Bastian, whose leg had been crushed by a wall collapse at the I.X.L. mine).

12   Henry J. Ritter met a "frightful and almost instantaneous death at the Diamond Sawmill" in November, 1885 ("Births/Marriages/Deaths" Index, p. 29 (*citing Alpine Argus* of November 21, 1885)). Similarly, Canadian John Hill, age 21, was killed instantly by a "log saw" near Woodfords. ("Births/Marriages/Deaths" Index, p. 25 (*citing Monitor Argus* of September 11, 1882)).

13   Lewis Anderson, age 30, died at Temple's Wood Camp on the East Carson when a log rolled over him, crushing his skull (*Chronicle*, January 5, 1878). Logger Andrew Dardis was crushed "so severely in the hips that if the injury be not mortal, he will be disabled for life," after falling into the East Fork of the Carson River while trying to free a log jam (*Carson Daily Appeal*, May 17, 1865). And in what may also have been a logging-related incident, F.E. Young drowned "at the falls above Silver King" (*Chronicle*, August 17, 1878).

14   *Chronicle*, May 28, 1870.

15   *Chronicle,* June 13, 1868 (report on finding the body of Nils Magnus August Drake about eight miles from Silver Mountain).

16   "Births/Marriages/Deaths" Index, p. 34 (*citing Alpine Miner* of July 9, 1870).

17   "Births/Marriages/Deaths" Index, p. 38 (*citing Alpine Miner*, June 18, 1870).

18   *Chronicle,* January 5, 1878. An accompanying article noted that "[t]he mutilation of the body of the

late Peter Peterson by hogs has created a great feeling against hogs running at large in our town. They go in droves and parents are fearful that if anything should happen to their children while playing on the street, that they would be attacked by the brutes and killed."

19   *Chronicle*, November 5, 1870.

20   *Chronicle,* October 29, 1870.

21   *Monitor Gazette*, February 18, 1865.

22   *Chronicle*, September 7, 1872.

23   *Chronicle*, April 13, 1878.

24   "Births/Marriages/Deaths" Index, p. 42 (*citing Monitor Argus* of May 15, 1882).

25   *Chronicle*, February 8, 1868.

26   *Monitor Gazette*, July 2, 1864.

27   *Chronicle,* October 14, 1871; Coroner's Jury Testimony & Verdict in the Matter of Inquest, Mrs. H.W. Bagley, filed October 9, 1871 (Alpine County Archives, Box 8D3).

28   Remi Nadeau, <u>The Silver Seekers</u> (Crest Publishers 1999), at p. 55. This story appears to have come from the Oral History of Harry Hawkins (manuscript at Alpine County Museum, p. 15). It is possible the person referred to was the similar-sounding "W.L. Flippen," who had a dry goods store in Silver Mountain about 1878 (*Chronicle*, January 5, 1878).

29   Chalmers wrote to Mrs. Neddenreip inquiring about her fees as a midwife, and also asked Genoa's Dr. Luce for his charge "for being here on the 25th & remaining until all is well" and the name of a "skillful female *accoucheur.*" (Chalmers Letters, *Private Letters 1881-84,* pp. 23 and 56 (July 13 and 31, 1881)). By January, 1882, he still owed money to Dr. Luce, although whether for medicine or obstetric services is unclear (Chalmers Letters, *Private Letters 1881-84*, p. 261 (January 27, 1882)).

30   Letter from A.B. Fleming of Oakland to Miss Nellie Barnum of Monitor, California, dated November 16, 1879 (California State Library, Barnum family correspondence)(punctuation added).

31   *Silver Mountain Bulletin*, January 19, 1867.

32   *Chronicle*, January 22, 1870 (scarlet fever); December 16, 1871 (smallpox).

33   "Lewie" (as Chalmers called him) apparently contracted tuberculosis in England in early 1868, and finally died at the Exchequer Mill house beside Silver Creek on May 10, 1872. *See* Chalmers Letters, *Private Letters 1868-1869,* p. 11 (March 25, 1868)(expressing "how much shocked" Chalmers was by news of Lewie's illness, directing him to "obey implicitly the Doctor's Prescriptions" and advising him not to "get down hearted – very few indeed there are whose lungs are unaffected"); *see also Chronicle*, May 11, 1872 (obituary, noting the death of Lewis W.J.C. Chalmers, age 20, "[a]fter many years of poor health and a few weeks of a rapid decline"); *see also* December 28, 1872.

34   Charles A. Ford died at Silver Mountain on April 16, 1871, of "consumption" (*Alpine Chronicle*, April 22, 1871; *see also* "Births/Marriages/Deaths" Index, pp. 34-35); "pioneer citizen" Orrin Grey passed away at Walley's Warm Springs Hotel from "hasty consumption" (*Chronicle,* May 27, 1871); *see also* death notice for Seth E. Winchester, who similarly died of "consumption" at Lower Lake on March 3, 1873, (per "Births/Marriages/Deaths" Index, p. 49, *citing Alpine Miner* of March 15, 1873).

35   "Births/Marriages/Deaths" Index, p. 49 (*citing Alpine Miner* of September 24, 1864).

36   *Monitor Gazette*, October 8, 1864.

37   *Chronicle*, January 13, 1877 (Uncapher, a former resident of Markleeville, was then living in Salinas City).

38   Roland E. Johns, a month shy of 3, passed away on February 17, and his tiny brother, John D. Johns, 1 year 3 months, died the following day. *Chronicle*, February 23, 1878.

39   "Births/Marriages/Deaths" Index, p. 3 (*citing Monitor Gazette*, October 21, 1865).

40   "Births/Marriages/Deaths" Index, p. 3 (*citing Silver Mountain Bulletin*, October 13, 1866).

41   *Chronicle*, September 17, 1870.

42   *Chronicle*, January 5, 1878.

43   *Chronicle*, January 19 and 26, 1878.

44   *Monitor Gazette*, February 4, 1865.

45   *Monitor Gazette*, February 11, 1865.

46   *Chronicle*, June 25, 1870 and December 24, 1870. Ford also purchased "Treat's Hotel" (*aka* "The Oriental") in April, 1871 (*Chronicle*, April 22, 1871), followed by the "Severson" (probably Seaverson) property next door to the Alpine House in 1876 (*Chronicle*, July 29, 1876).

47   Born about 1811 in New Hampshire (according to the 1870 census), Ford would have been in his mid-fifties at the time he came to Silver Mountain. The 1864 Amador Assessment Roll (Alpine County Archives) shows Ford owning Lot 9 of Block 13, with a small house, and also Lot 6 of Block 35.

48   Eldest daughter Ella became a teacher in 1871-2, and soon was married to George H. Dunlap in Carson City. (*See* "Reports of the County Superintendent of Public Schools for Alpine County to the Superintendent of Public Instruction, State of California, 1863-1914" (extracted from California State Archives and published by the Alpine County Museum, 1995), at p. 9 (Summary for 1871-72); *Chronicle* of May 11, 1872.) The Fords' only son, Charles, passed away in 1871 of consumption. (*Chronicle*, April 22, 1871.) However, the Fords' youngest daughter, Anna, was just 15 in 1870 and likely helped in the hotel. She would grow up to marry N.D. Arnot at Silver Mountain on October 30, 1877. (*See* Arnot Family Bible entries, copy at Alpine County Museum).

49   *Chronicle*, June 25, 1870; December 24, 1870. Not surprisingly, Ford himself was the Postmaster for Silver Mountain; *see Chronicle*, January 8 and June 25, 1870.

50   *Chronicle*, February 18, 1871 (indicating Ford was selling tickets for the "Anchor" line of steamers to New York and European ports, "at short notice.").

51   *Chronicle,* March 26, 1870; June 10, 1871; October 28, 1871 (listing Ford as a Justice of the Peace for Township No. 2). Ford officiated at the funerals of County Treasurer Thomas Legget and District Attorney Thomas J. Orgon, in January, 1878. *See Chronicle*, January 19 and January 26, 1878.

52   Ford served as a justice of the peace from at least 1867 through 1878. He was Acting Coroner at the inquest into the death of E.H. Errickson (shot by Reusch). *Chronicle*, December 21, 1872. He also served as a member of the coroner's jury inquiring into the unfortunate death of Peter Peterson, then officiated at his funeral at the Alpine House. *Chronicle*, January 5, 1878.

53   Ford was a member of the Board of Education for the Franklin (Silver Mountain) School District from 1867-68 and 1877-78; he served as Superintendent of Schools from 1872-73; 1875-76; 1876-77; and 1881-82. "Reports of the County Superintendent of Public Schools," *supra*, at pp. 5; 11; 15; 16; 17; and 21; *see also Chronicle*, July 6, 1878 (announcing Ford's election to the Board of Trustees); when he and fellow Trustees "cast lots" to choose the length of their terms (a process deemed illegal), the Superintendent simply appointed them to their positions. *Chronicle*, July 13, 1878; *and see* Mabel Love, <u>History of the Alpine County Schools</u> (manuscript donated to Alpine County Museum 1989, and transcript published 1990), at p. 4-5, citing Ford as a "fine, commendable citizen" for pitching in whenever a vacancy needed to be filled.

Ford pitched in as well as an examiner on the Board of Examiners, testing those seeking a teaching credential. *Chronicle*, April 27, 1872. And in July, 1876, it was Ford who shouldered the burden of appointing Trustees for both the Silver Mountain and Woodsfords school districts. *Chronicle*, July 1, 1876. He also served as a fill-in Superintendent as late as 1881-82. "Reports of the County Superintendent of Public Schools," *supra*, at 21; *see also* M. Love, *supra*, <u>History of the Alpine County Schools</u>," at pp. 5-7.

54   *Chronicle*, August 3 and 31, 1878.

55   Other housewives certainly did. Spending seven winters at Silver Mountain was described as "very hard on Mrs. Fisk," for example, causing the Fisk family eventually to move to Murphys. *See Las Calaveras*, Calaveras County Historical Society's quarterly bulletin, Vol. XVI, No. 3 (April, 1968).

56   *Chronicle*, October 5 and 19, 1878.

57   M. Love, History of the Alpine County Schools, *supra*, p. 7.

58   *See* Arnot family Bible, copy at the Alpine County Museum.

59   *See* Arnot family Bible, copy at the Alpine County Museum.

60   *Chronicle*, December 23, 1876.

61   *Chronicle,* December 7, 14, 21, and 28, 1867.

62   *Chronicle,* December 28, 1872.

63   *Chronicle,* December 23, 1876.

64   *Mono-Alpine Chronicle*, January 4, 1879; *Chronicle*, December 23, 1876.

65   *Chronicle,* December 28, 1872.

66   *Chronicle,* November 16, 1872.

67   *Chronicle,* December 7, 14, and 28, 1867. The editors of the *Chronicle* received a pair of "well-appointed snow-shoes" from Rice, light-heartedly promising to "favor our citizens with an entertainment of a gymnastic character before Winter passes away." *Chronicle*, December 28, 1867.

68   *Chronicle*, December 29, 1866.

69   *Chronicle*, December 28, 1867.

70   No tree was planned for Monitor or Woodfords in 1876, for example. *Chronicle*, December 23, 1876.

71   *Chronicle,* December 7, 21, and 28, 1867.

72   *Chronicle,* December 14, 21, and 28, 1872.

73   *Chronicle,* December 21 and 28, 1872.

74   *See, e.g., Chronicle*, December 23 and 30, 1876; January 6 and 13, 1877, describing not only the Christmas "hop" at Silver Mountain but a New Year's "social dance" at Silver Mountain's Occidental Hall and another dance at Woodfords.

75   *Chronicle,* July 8, 1876.

76   *Chronicle,* July 8, 1876.

77   *Chronicle,* July 8, 1876.

78   *See* advertisement for the event in *Chronicle* of June 22, 1878, and report of July 6, 1878.

79   *Chronicle,* December 1, 1866.

80   *Chronicle,* November 30, 1872.

81   *Chronicle,* November 30, 1872.

82   *Chronicle,* August 24 and September 7, 1872.

83   *Chronicle,* January 5, 1878.

84   *Chronicle,* September 7, 1872 (describing the "excellent vocal and instrumental music handsomely rendered" at the Exchequer boarding house, some 2,000 feet above town in Scandinavian Canyon).

85   *Chronicle,* January 12 and 19, 1878.

86   In the 1870 census, for example, there were only 34 females listed among Silver Mountain's total population of 146 – and 19 of those 34 were children.

87   Diary of O.S. Adams, entry for July 1, 1867.

88   *Chronicle,* May 4, 1878.

89   *Chronicle,* November 11, 1876.

90   *Chronicle*, November 18, 1876.

91   *Boston Semi-Weekly Advertiser*, October 28, 1871.

92   *Boston Semi-Weekly Advertiser*, October 28, 1871.

93   *Kennebec Reporter*, April 1, 1876 (Gardiner, Maine).

94   *Daily Alta California*, May 31, 1870.

95   *Chronicle*, November 4, 1876.

96   *Chronicle*, November 4, 1876.

97   Viscount James Bryce, <u>The American Commonwealth</u> (MacMillan & Co., 1889), *reprinted at* <u>www. sfmuseum.org</u>. Bryce notes, however, that a variety of bills attempting to carry out those sentiments were defeated.

98   *Boston Evening Transcript*, September 19, 1877 (*quoting* a San Francisco dispatch of September 18, 1877).

99   *Chronicle*, September 2, 1876.

100   *Chronicle*, April 15, 1876.

101   W. Turrentine Jackson, <u>Report on the History of Grover Hot Springs State Park Area and Surrounding Region of Alpine County</u> (Division of Beaches & Parks, Department of Parks and Recreation, State of California 1964), p. 49.

102   W. T. Jackson, *supra*, p. 41 (*quoting Alpine Miner* of April 6, 1872).

103   "Births/Marriages/Deaths" Index, p. 27 (*citing Alpine Signal*, October 2, 1878).

104   Justice was swift for this offense; the crime occurred on Monday, and the offender was convicted on Wednesday. *Chronicle*, May 4, 1878. The *Chronicle* also reported "hostilities" in Virginia City between rival factions of the Hop Sing and Sam Sing groups in which three men suffered gunshot wounds, two of them likely fatal. In a departure from the *Chroncle's* usual gentle style, the editors added cynically: "So long as the whites are not injured their little pastimes should not be disturbed." *Chronicle*, January 13, 1877.

105   *Chronicle*, July 27, 1878. Apparently because it was an involuntary homicide, Wah Kee was allowed to plead guilty to the reduced charge of "selling liquor to Indians" and received a jail sentence of just 90 days and a $100 fine – further evidence, it would seem, of the era's tragic disregard for the rights of Native Americans.

106   *Chronicle*, January 13, 1877.

107   Chalmers Letters, *Private Letters 1871-72*, p. 517 (March 17, 1873).

108   Oral history information from Gary Coyan.

109   Chalmers Letters, *Private Letters 1880-81*, p. 31 (March 25, 1880).

110   Chalmers Letters, *Private Letters 1880-81*, p. 688 (February 24, 1881); *see also* Chalmers Letters, *Private Letters 1880-81*, p. 861 (June 8, 1881), seeking another "good China Servant" for his household, and offering a glimpse of the life awaiting the unfortunate employee, with the following job description: "Must be a good cook, washer & Ironer & general servant, make beds, sweep, scrub, brush shoes, and do exactly as Mrs. C tells him."

111   Chalmers Letters, *Private Letters 1880-81*, p. 363 (September 14, 1880).

112   Letter from W.P. Merrill to Bullion & Exchange Bank in Carson City, dated July 18, 1899 (Dustman collection).

113   W. T. Jackson, *supra*, at p. 26 (*quoting Sacramento Daily Union*, August 13, 1863).

114   This road superintendent may have been William A. Johnson. *See infra* note 111.

115   W. T. Jackson, *supra,* at pp. 26-27 (*quoting Alpine Chronicle* of April 23, 1863, itself reprinted in *Calaveras Prospect*, September 23, 1933).

116   William M. Maule, "A Contribution to the Geographic and Economic History of Carson, Walker and Mono Basins" (U.S. Forest Service 1938), under section "Washoe Tribes", *citing Chronicle* of January 16, 1869

and April 23, 1864. If Maule is correct, this Captain Jim served as chief of the "central" Washoe Tribe, a 300-member group with territory from Steamboat Springs in Truckee Meadows all the way south to Double Springs and west to Markleeville. Captain Jim reportedly died at the age of 48, just two years after his encounter with the road superintendent, and was interred in an old mining shaft near Mountain House. W. Maule, *id.*

117   Bancroft Scraps (Bancroft Library), p. 53 (apparently clipped from the *San Francisco Weekly Bulletin* of April 7, 1871).

118   *Chronicle*, October 19, 1872. Quipped the editors, "So we may rest content in regard to the severity of the coming Winter, for we must admit that our Indians have generally been very correct in their predictions," adding cynically, "We do not intend to provide any less quantity of wood and beans, however."

119   *Chronicle*, November 30, 1872.

120   I am indebted to a member of the Washoe Tribe (who wishes to remain anonymous) for this insightful observation. For a wonderful history of the Washoe people, *see* Wa She Shu: "The Washoe People" (compiled by Lissa Guimaraes Dodds as her senior thesis at University of California at Santa Cruz), *available online at* www.washoetribe.us.

121   *Monitor Gazette*, March 18, 1865.

122   *Chronicle*, November 18, 1876. The words "lah poo" may have been an effort to render the Washoe expression "le bu' u"– a polite request, roughly translated "May I have – ." (Translation courtesy of a Washoe speaker who wishes to remain anonymous.) Such visits were likely part of the generous Indian custom of sharing food. Wa She Shu, *supra*, at 29.

123   *Chronicle*, January 27, 1877.

124   Chalmers Letters, *Isabella Officials*, p. 490 (January 9, 1882).

125   *Chronicle*, July 13, 1878; *San Francisco Chronicle*, February 9, 1893 (*quoting the Genoa Courier*). *See also* Wa She Shu, *supra*, describing the piñon harvest as lasting four to six weeks, with a 4-5 day celebration known as "goom sa bye" marking the ripening of the pine nuts.

126   Chalmers Letters, *Private Letters 1868-69*, p. 58 (April 29, 1868).

127   *Chronicle*, August 26, 1876.

128   *Chronicle*, November 10, 1866.

129   *Chronicle*, August 3, 1878.

130   *Monitor Gazette*, March 18, 1865.

131   *Board of Supervisors Minutes*, July 10, 1889 (Book B, p. 422-423).

132   *Chronicle*, August 28, 1875.

133   *Chronicle*, December 30, 1876 ("Knives and pistols were flourished around very carelessly, resulting in the stabbing of Indian Bob.")

134   *Chronicle*, April 22, 1871.

135   *Chronicle,* April 22, 1871; *see also* "Births/Marriages/Deaths" Index, pp. 29-30 (*citing Alpine Miner*, April 22 and 29, 1871).

136   *Chronicle*, September 16, 1871. Indian/white tensions were high elsewhere, as well. The *Chronicle* of November 18, 1871 reported that the Army was being dispatched to negotiate with the Apaches bearing "propositions of peace which, if rejected, will be followed by war." As late as 1878, similar rumors were circulating regarding efforts by the Bannack tribe to enlist the Piutes and Washoes in a brewing "Indian war" against the whites. *Chronicle,* July 6, 13, and 20, 1878.

137   *Merced County Argus*, September 30, 1871.

138   The *Alpine Miner* observed that "the family are in constant fear of the getting even process of the Indians, though the shootist himself has departed for Utah," and "it is bad policy to kill an Indian unless you are

ready at once to leave the country forever." "Births/Marriages/Deaths" Index, pp. 29-30 (*citing Alpine Miner*, April 22 and 29, 1871). A similarly-named "James Stevens," age 38, eventually committed suicide near Lewiston, Idaho Territory, according to the *Alpine Argus* of February 27, 1886. "Births/Marriages/Deaths" Index, p. 30.

139   *Chronicle*, July 13, 1878.

140   Frank S. Wedertz, Mono Diggings (Community Publishing 2001), p. 81-84. Speculation continued that "Bobby and Alex" were Quakers after they had moved to Bridgeport, driven perhaps by their "high, starched collars," polite manners, and gentle speech – plus the "white kerchief" always quaintly worn around the neck of Alex's wife. *See* Ella M. Cain, The Story of Early Mono County (Fearon Publishers 1961), p. 58. If they were Quakers, however, it is hard to explain why both names appears on the membership list of the local Alpine Rifles. *See* "Muster Roll" dated April 2, 1864 (listing both Alex. and Robert Folger) and "Muster Roll" dated March 15, 1866 (listing Alexander Folger), Alpine Rifles Materials from California Archives Foundation (copies at Alpine County Museum, pp. 92 and 100).

141   Peter Browning, Place Names of the Sierra Nevada (Wilderness Press 1992), at p. 72.

142   *Chronicle*, June 16, 1866.

143   P. Browning, Place Names of the Sierra Nevada, *supra*, at p. 72 (incorrectly identifying Alexander C. Folger as "Andrew"); *see also Chronicle*, March 16, 1867 and June 1, 1867, showing Alex. Folger as Markleeville's postmaster.

144   F. Wedertz, Mono Diggings, at 84.

145   E. Cain, The Story of Early Mono County, *supra*, at p.58.

146   E. Cain, The Story of Early Mono County, *supra*, at p.47.

147   E. Cain, The Story of Early Mono County, *supra*, at 58.

148   E. Cain, The Story of Early Mono County, *supra*, at p. 59.

149   *Silver Mountain Bulletin*, May 18, 1867. *See also "Jail Travail"* in Chapter 2, *infra*.

150   *See, e.g., Chronicle*, February 10, 1872 and February 24, 1872, calling the competing *Miner* "nothing but a 'dodge' published to sell its innumerable 'rich mines,'" a "swindle," and "the meanest kind of a 'wildcat.'"

151   W. M. Maule, *supra*, at p. 28; *see also Chronicle*, August 24, 1872; July 1 and 22, 1876; September 9 and 23, 1876; January 13, 1877.

152   *Chronicle*, July 29, 1876.

153   *See* Chalmers Letters, *Exchequer Officials 1871-2*, p. 67-68 and 74 (Abstract of Title for Buckeye No. One transmitted with Chalmers' letter of May 19, 1871, indicating that Folger, McBeth and others had acquired their interests in Buckeye from George Wiseman on an unspecified date in 1871 (presumably prior to May 19th)); *see also* Chalmers Letters, *Private Letters 1871-2*, p. 152 ("Memorandum of Agreement" dated July 3, 1871, committing to sell the same Buckeye Company claims to Chalmers' close associates, Lord Ranelagh and Henry Syme).

154   Henry Eno, Twenty Years on the Pacific Slope (Yale University Press 1965), p. 82 n.32 (*citing the Silver Mountain Bulletin* of May 18, 1867).

155   *Chronicle*, May 11, June 15 and 22, 1878.

156   F. Wedertz, Mono Diggings, at 84.

157   *Chronicle*, November 5, 1870.

158   *Chronicle*, April 29, 1871 (reprinting an article from the "Journal of Chemistry").

159   *Bulletin*, April 13, 1867.

160   *Chronicle*, July 20, 1878.

161   *Chronicle*, November 26, 1870.

162   *Chronicle*, February 17, 1872. Anna Ford, daughter of Rev. R.H. Ford, was referred to as the "angel" of the *Chronicle* office in the May 11, 1872 issue; some five years later, Anna would become the wife of Judge Arnot. The egalitarian Folgers also proudly hired "lady compositors" after the paper moved to Bodie. *See Bodie Chronicle*, February 14, 1880.

163   *See Chronicle*, August 26, September 2 and 9, 1876, observing that Withington was in town, with rooms at Ford's Hotel.

164   *Chronicle*, January 27, 1872.

165   *Chronicle*, March 9, 1872. It is possible the warring couple eventually managed to make up, however; the case was subsequently "[s]tricken from the calendar," according to the *Chronicle* of October 19, 1872.

166   *Chronicle*, December 15, 1877.

167   *Chronicle,* February 16, 1878.

168   *Chronicle,* March 2, 1878.

169   *Chronicle*, July 16, 1870 (a theft which netted the adulterer two and a half years' imprisonment at San Quentin – and his female accomplice the same sentence).

170   An 1871 comment reproduced in *The Idaho Statesman*, October 26, 2004.

171   *Chronicle*, September 18, 1875. In addition, the person had to reside within the precinct for at least six months prior to the election, have his name "enrolled on the Great Register of such county," and could not have been "convicted of any infamous crime."

172   *Chronicle*, August 5, 1871. The issue of women's suffrage was being litigated elsewhere, as well. In Boston, Mrs. Sarah Spencer and Mrs. S.E. Miller were suing the voting registrar and superintendent of election for $500 in damages for refusing to allow them to register and vote. *Boston Semi-Weekly Advertiser*, October 28, 1871.

173   *Bulletin*, April 27, 1867 [punctuation added].

174   *Chronicle*, March 2, 1878.

175   *Chronicle*, August 5, 1876.

176   *Chronicle*, August 26, 1876.

177   One source cites an estimate that each load of laundry required hauling some 50 gallons of water – perhaps an overstatement, although it probably felt that way. Beth & Bill Sagstetter, <u>The Mining Camps Speak</u> (Benchmark Publishing 1998), at 142.

Chapter 8 Footnotes:

1   *Monitor Gazette*, September 10, 1864.

2   William M. Maule, "A Contribution to the Geographic and Economic History of Carson, Walker and Mono Basins" (U.S. Forest Service 1938), p. 27 (recounting the October 12, 1867 grand jury proceedings in People v. Thomas Ogden).

3   *Monitor Gazette*, October 15, 1864.

4   *Monitor Gazette*, March 4, 1865.

5   W. Turrentine Jackson, Report on the History of Grover Hot Springs State Park Area and Surrounding Region of Alpine County (Division of Beaches & Parks, Department of Parks and Recreation, State of California 1964), p. 33, cited a newspaper report blaming "strangers in the county" for a burglary and robbery in Markleeville. *See also Chronicle*, September 23 and 30, 1871 and October 21, 1871 (advising that escaped Nevada State prisoners were thought to be "skulking" around Carson Valley and "two or three [may] have made their way into Hope Valley.").

6   *Chronicle*, January 7, 1871.

7   Marklee was shot on May 14, 1863 by a man named Henry Tuttle. *See* Jacob Marklee Probate File at Alpine County Museum, including copy of newspaper article from Taylors Falls Reporter, May 28, 1864 (a year after the killing); and Affidavit by Gilbert H. Clement dated September 3, 1863, Amador County Archives document 5274.118.38, stating that Marklee was killed by "a pistol ball." At least two people were present at the time, besides Marklee. According to the Taylors Falls newspaper, a violent dispute had initially ensued between Marklee and a party named Gould, after Gould claimed half of Marklee's property. (Gould's claim may have had some basis in reality; a short receipt signed "Jacob J. Marklee" dated November 25, 1861 states: "Received of Gould payment in full for one half of the Merkly claim and road running from Wade's mill to Silver Mountain" (copy at Alpine Museum Archives)). During the dispute, Marklee "put [Gould] out doors," then buckled on a pistol. There appears to be no question that Tuttle then fired the fatal shot at Marklee. But the Amador County jury found Tuttle "not guilty" of murder on March 24, 1864, apparently finding the shooting was in self-defense. *See* Court Minutes of People v. H.W. Tuttle, Case No. 1026, 11th Judicial District Court, Amador County Book "C", page 469 (copy at Alpine County Museum).

8   Peltier and A.T. Lee were co-proprietors of Markleeville's Empire Market, an inauspicious locale for a violent dispute. Lee punched Peltier, and Peltier retaliated by applying a cleaver to Lee's shoulder; though wounded, Lee grabbed a butcher knife and delivered a fatal slice to Peltier's throat. *Monitor Gazette*, July 2, 1864.

9   *Chronicle*, September 10, 1870.

10   *Chronicle*, September 10, 17, and 24, 1870.

11   *Chronicle*, September 17 and 24, 1870; Alpine Miner, September 17, 1870.

12   *Chronicle*, June 3, 1871.

13   *Chronicle*, October 8, 1870.

14   *Chronicle*, August 24, 1872. The wedding was conducted by none other than Judge C.P. Goff, who just four months later would also hold Reusch to answer on the charge of murder. *Chronicle*, December 28, 1872.

15   *Chronicle*, December 21, 1872.

16   *Chronicle*, October 26, 1872.

17   *Chronicle*, December 21, 1872.

18   *Chronicle*, December 21, 1872.

19   Testimony on Inquest of E. Reusch, filed with County Clerk on April 27, 1874.

20   Testimony on Inquest of E. Reusch, filed with County Clerk on April 27, 1874 [punctuation added].

21   Testimony on Inquest of E. Reusch, supra.

22   Coroner's Jury Report dated April 18, 1874 (and filed April 20, 1874), which is appended to Testimony on Inquest of E. Reusch, supra.

23   *Monitor Gazette*, July 9 and 23, 1864; September 3, 1864.

24   *Monitor Gazette*, November 5, 1864.

25   *Monitor Gazette*, September 17, 1864. The now ex-constable, George Thomas, was charged with grand larceny for $150 of missing "tobacco, segars, perfumery, etc."

26   *Chronicle*, November 17, 1866.

27   *The Free Press*, November 18, 1865. One further fascinating tidbit: one of the infamous Geiger Grade robbers caught in 1866 was identified as "James W. Crum". *Chronicle*, December 22, 1866.

28   McBeth served as a trustee in 1863 for the Monitor-based "Wild Yankee Gold & Silver Mining Co.," and the articles of incorporation for the "Desplain Mining Company" (another Monitor company) were recorded in 1863 at his request. Amador County Archives document 5264.A62 (Certificate of Incorporation of Wild Yankee Gold & Silver Mining Company) and document 5264.A19 (Certificate of Incorporation of the Desplain Mining Company).

29   Amador Assessment Roll of 1864 (Alpine County Archives).

30   McBeth made the slog on "snowshoes" through 3- to 5-foot depths, after "the greatest snow storm" in local memory (*Chronicle*, February 23 and March 2, 1867; *Silver Mountain Bulletin*, March 2 and 9, 1867; *see also Alpine Miner*, March 2, 1867).

31   *Chronicle*, June 16, 1866.

32   *Bulletin*, April 13, 1867.

33   The escapade was reported under "Local Intelligence" in the *Chronicle*, July 16, 1870.

34   "Births/Marriages/Deaths" Index, compiled by Kim Summerhill (Skinner)(manuscript containing extracts from various newspapers 1864-1886, at Alpine County Museum), p. 35 (*citing Alpine Chronicle* and *Alpine Miner*, both August 21, 1869).

35   *Chronicle*, October 15, 1870, reporting the birth of Mac's son on October 12, 1870, at Silver Mountain.

36   *See* Abstract of Title of The Sam Brannan claim (showing deed from Daniel Davidson to McBeth and others dated October 11, 1870, and a Memorandum of Agreement & Sale dated February 3, 1871), contained in Syme Collection, California State Library (SMC, Box 21, Folder 1).

37   *Chronicle*, May 28, 1870.

38   *Chronicle*, March 25, 1871.

39   McBeth owned a saloon worth $2,000 that burned in the 1872 Monitor fire. Chronicle, April 6, 1872. By September, however, he had evidently rebuilt as he was listed as proprietor of a "new and commodious" hotel in Monitor known as the "National Hotel." *Chronicle*, September 7, 1872.

40   *Chronicle*, September 2, 1871.

41   *Chronicle*, February 3, 1872.

42   *Chronicle*, March 2, 1872.

43   Testimony on Inquest of E. Reusch, filed with County Clerk on April 27, 1874.

44   In 1872, McBeth was sued by "Wright & Parmer." *Chronicle*, October 12 and 19, 1872. And in 1876, creditors Adams and Wells Fargo & Co. both successfully sued McBeth and won judgments. *Chronicle*, October 14, 1876.

45   Chalmers Letters, *Private Letters 1871-1872*, pp. 462-463 (November 8, 1872).

46   *Chronicle*, December 23, 1876 (notice of Sheriff's Sale).

47   *Chronicle*, October 12, 1878.

48   *See Alpine Argus*, August 8, 1885.

49   Chalmers Letters, *Private Letters 1880-1881*, pp. 83 and 95 (April 14 and 16, 1880).

50   *Alpine Argus*, August 8, 1885.

51   *Chronicle*, October 22 and 29, 1870.

52   *Chronicle*, October 22, 1870.

53   *Chronicle*, November 5, 1870.

54   *Chronicle*, October 29, 1870.

55   *Chronicle*, February 4, 1871.

56   *Chronicle*, May 13 and June 24, 1871.

57   *Chronicle*, February 11 and May 20, 1871.

58   *Chronicle*, March 4, 1871.

59   *Chronicle*, September 2, 1871.

60   *Chronicle*, May 30; June 6 and 13, 1868.

61   *Chronicle*, March 26, 1870.

62   Legget was one of the original trustees of the Silver Mountain Quarrying & Mining Co. in September, 1863. See Certificate of Incorporation dated September 24, 1863 (Amador County Archives, document 5264.84); *see also* Book "B" of Deeds, p. 167-168 (land deed dated September 24, 1863, from T.W. Legget and others to the Silver Mountain Quarrying & Mining Co.).

63   Chalmers described Legget as "a great rogue," reporting that Legget – a shareholder of the Lady Franklin mine – had refused to record a relocation of that mine by "jumpers" acting for Chalmers. Chalmers Letters, *Private Letters 1871-1872*, p. 485 (copy of document dated August 10, 1872, transcribed in Chalmers copybook circa November 20, 1872, bearing pencil notation, "There was an objection & it was not recorded"), and p. 504 (February 12, 1873)("I had Franklin jumped . . . but the Recorder Leggett [sic], the mastermind and a great rogue, being a Shareholder, refused to put [it] on record.")(punctuation altered).

64   *See* "Reports of the County Superintendent of Public Schools for Alpine County to the Superintendent of Public Instruction, State of California, 1863-1914" (extracted from California State Archives and Published by the Alpine County Museum, 1995), at p. 11 (Report for 1872-73, made by R.H. Ford), stating: "I have been obliged to depend upon such information as I could gather from the county treasurer's books: and strictly they are not correct as some warrants cancelled during the year belonged to the former year. . . "

65   "Reports of the County Superintendent," supra, at p. 15 (Report for 1875-76, by R.H. Ford): "The Super[intendent]'s account and the county treasurer's books do not tally and I have been unable to get them rectified as the Treasurer has been absent from the county when I had an opportunity of visiting his office."

66   *Chronicle*, September 11, 1875.

67   *Chronicle*, April 20, 1878.

68   Alpine Co. Board of Supervisors Minutes, Book B, pp. 59 and 68 (September 10, 1877 & March 6, 1878).

69   Chalmers Letters, *Private Letters 1880-1881*, p. 10 (March 7, 1880).

70   *See Chronicle*, May 11 and June 22, 1878, concerning People v. Legget; *see also* notes concerning the Legget investigation at Alpine County Museum, referencing Grand Jury Report of June 30, 1882.

71   Legget was 61 years old at his death; R.H. Ford conducted the services. *Chronicle*, January 19 and 26, 1878.

72   As late as 1889, the County was still dealing with the mess. A judgment for $5,976.75 was entered on January 5, 1887, in favor of the County and against Legget's estate, no part of which had been paid as of July, 1889

(Book "A" of Judgments, p. 392, arising out of State v. John P. Elliot, Executor), referenced in Board of Supervisors Minutes, Book "B", p. 426-427 (Minutes of July 22, 1889).

73   *Chronicle*, October 13, 1866 ("The late Grand Jury reported in favor of having a suitable person appointed to examine the books of the Board of Supervisors but we presume there will be no more attention paid this suggestion than there was to a like recommendation made by the previous Grand Jury; it is not the policy of that body to have its manner of doing business inquired into.").

74   *Chronicle*, March 16, 1872. Alpine County wasn't alone in having its treasury pilfered; Nevada's first state Treasurer, Ebenezer Rhoades, embezzled roughly $100,000 from its general fund and permanent school fund between the time he took office 1864 and his death (by suicide) in 1869, leaving that new state unable to pay its territorial debt until well after the turn of the century. Oral presentation by Patty Cafferata, former Nevada State Treasurer, 7/24/2010, at Dangberg Ranch (Nevada State Parks).

75   *Chronicle*, November 16, 1872.

76   *Chronicle*, February 3, 1872.

77   *Chronicle*, October 26, 1872.

78   *Chronicle*, August 12, 1871 (emphasis in original).

79   *Chronicle*, September 2, 1871.

80   Henry Eno, <u>Twenty Years on the Pacific Slope</u> (Yale University Press 1965), pp. 108; 143-144.

81   *Monitor Gazette*, August 27, 1864. August 1st was, however, the commencement of Shearer's term of office.

82   Competitors for the Union Party ticket convention alone included attorneys Henry Eno; Robert Thompson; I. Marshall; C.P. Goff; Moses Tebbs; H.Cook; and the incumbent, Sextus Shearer. H. Eno, Twenty Years on the Pacific Slope, p. 137 n.31.

83   *See* Alan H. Patera, "Silver Mountain California," Western Places: A Chronicle of Western Settlement, Vol. 1, No. 3 (September 1992), at p.43 (stock certificate for the Mountain Gold and Silver Mining Co. issued July 27, 1866, bearing Sextus Shearer's signature as president).

84   *Chronicle*, August 3, 1867.

85   *Chronicle*, December 14 and 28, 1867.

86   H. Eno, <u>Twenty Years on the Pacific Slope</u>, p.108 [punctuation added].

87   H. Eno, <u>Twenty Years on the Pacific Slope</u>, p. 36.

88   H. Eno, <u>Twenty Years on the Pacific Slope</u>, p. 37 [punctuation added].

89   H. Eno, <u>Twenty Years on the Pacific Slope</u>, pp. 44; 47.

90   H. Eno, <u>Twenty Years on the Pacific Slope</u>, p. 47-52.

91   H. Eno, <u>Twenty Years on the Pacific Slope</u>, p. 53-55. According to Eno biographer W. Turrentine Jackson, the Mokelumne Canal was among the three largest canal projects in California at the time, with its initial cost projected to be $100,000 but a final tally of more than twice that. *Id.*

92   H. Eno, <u>Twenty Years on the Pacific Slope</u>, p. 65.

93   H. Eno, <u>Twenty Years on the Pacific Slope</u>, pp. 107; 124.

94   H. Eno, <u>Twenty Years on the Pacific Slope</u>, p. 135. Interestingly enough, had Eno lost, he contemplated making a voyage to China via the Sandwich Islands as a roving reporter "for some newspaper." *Id.*

95   H. Eno, <u>Twenty Years on the Pacific Slope</u>, pp. 69-70; 137 [punctuation added].

96   H. Eno, <u>Twenty Years on the Pacific Slope</u>, pp. 143-44 [punctuation added].

97   H. Eno, <u>Twenty Years on the Pacific Slope</u>, p. 134 [punctuation added].

98   H. Eno, <u>Twenty Years on the Pacific Slope</u>, p. 144 [punctuation added].

99   The legislation was apparently an annual franchise; a similar bill was introduced in February, 1867, permitting Alpine to collect tolls on wood floated down the East Carson River. *See Chronicle*, February 2, 1867.

100   *Chronicle*, July 20, 1872, recounting the legal saga. According to that issue, the wood choppers offered to pay half that amount, threatening to otherwise test the law in court, but the Board reportedly refused. Nevertheless, earlier newspaper articles suggest the rate being collected on cordwood in 1867 was only 37½ cents. *See Bulletin* of March 30, 1867; *see also Alpine Miner*, July 6, 1867, indicating Tax Collector Robert Patterson was announcing a "collector's sale" to collect the tax against "Holenback's Camp on the main Carson River" and others. Later tax rates would run as high as $3 a cord. *See Chronicle*, August 10, 1878, indicating that wood in the "big wood drive" would be assessed at $3/cord.

101   *See* notices published by the Board of Supervisors in both the *Chronicle* and *Bulletin*, March 16, 1867.

102   "Upper Carson Watershed Report" (June 2004), *available on-line*. According to this source, an estimated 14 million board-feet of lumber were floated down Alpine rivers in 1866 alone.

103   *Chronicle*, October 13, 1866 (noting that $4,505 had been collected in tolls, although $1,900 of that figure was in the form of a note); *see also* November 3, 1866 (showing income from "Carson River Tolls" for the quarter ending September 3, 1866 of $1,760.00).

104   *Chronicle*, June 29, 1867 ("Thus far the star of the woodmen appears to be in the ascendent, and it seems to be a foregone conclusin that the citizens of this county will have to bleed pretty freely for the acts of their officials in bidding defiance to reason, justice and fair dealing.").

105   H. Eno, <u>Twenty Years on the Pacific Slope</u>, p. 78.

106   *Chronicle*, June 29, 1867; February 22, 1868; and September 2, 1871.

107   *Chronicle*, June 22 and 29, 1867, indicating that Reed (apparently tired of the repetitious injunctions) ruled precipitously from Sacramento, without holding a hearing. *See also* October 20, 1866, in which Judge Reed decided wood cases for the county.

108   *Chronicle*, June 29, 1867.

109   Reports concerning the amount of the repayment differ. One 1872 article mentions the sum of $2,405.37 (apparently for just one claimant). (*Chronicle*, July 20, 1872.) An 1868 story estimates costs and damages of between $6,000 and 10,000. (*Chronicle*, February 22, 1868).

110   H. Eno, <u>Twenty Years on the Pacific Slope</u>, p. 79-80, 144, 149.

111   H. Eno, <u>Twenty Years on the Pacific Slope</u>, p. 80-81 (*quoting the Chronicle* of October 19, 1867). District Judge Reed may have reversed himself, however, before the California Supreme Court ultimately settled the issue; the *Chronicle* of May 27, 1871 indicates Reed had ruled County officers must be paid in gold, a decision likely to be tested in the state Supreme Court.

112   H. Eno, <u>Twenty Years on the Pacific Slope</u>, pp. 71, 85.

113   H. Eno, <u>Twenty Years on the Pacific Slope</u>, p. 89.

114   H. Eno, <u>Twenty Years on the Pacific Slope</u>, pp. 85, 89.

115   H. Eno, <u>Twenty Years on the Pacific Slope</u>, pp. 85, 87.

116   *See Chronicle*, December 21, 1867.

117   H. Eno, <u>Twenty Years on the Pacific Slope</u>, p. 89.

118   H. Eno, <u>Twenty Years on the Pacific Slope</u>, p. 164.

119   H. Eno, <u>Twenty Years on the Pacific Slope</u>, pp. 93-94, 180-181, 190-191.

120   H. Eno, <u>Twenty Years on the Pacific Slope</u>, pp. 93-97, 191, 194.

121   H. Eno, <u>Twenty Years on the Pacific Slope</u>, pp. 205-206.

122   H. Eno, <u>Twenty Years on the Pacific Slope</u>, p. 97.

123   H. Eno, <u>Twenty Years on the Pacific Slope</u>, p. 110 [punctuation added].

124   H. Eno, <u>Twenty Years on the Pacific Slope</u>, p. 147 n.37.

125   H. Eno, <u>Twenty Years on the Pacific Slope</u>, p. 147, n.37.

126   *Inyo Register*, August 26, 1909 (indicating that Reed was 77 when he passed away).

127   Catalogue of Phi Alpha Society, 1845-1890, vol. 23, p. 48 (*reprinted online by* Google Books).

128   Possessory claim of H.D. Coon to a town lot in Silver Mountain, at the corner of Main and Fourth Streets, dated July 3, 1863, and filed with the Amador County Recorder on July 8, 1863 (original in Amador County Archives, document 7914.354).

129   Articles of Incorporation for the "Bell & Curts Gold & Silver Mining Co." (notarized by Reed on August 17, 1863); the "Black Hawk Gold & Silver Mining Co." (notarized in Markleeville on October 19, 1863, but requesting that the recorder's bill be sent to Reed at Sacramento); the "Onondaga Gold & Silver Mining Co." (notarized September 2, 1863); and the "Three Sisters Gold & Silver Mining Co." (notarized October 28, 1863) (originals in Amador County Archives, document nos. 5264.A14; 5264.A16; 5264.A49; and 5264.A88). Reed also notarized a possessory claim by James E. White in a 160-acre parcel of property in the Silver Mountain Mining District (November 2, 1863)(Amador County Archives, document 7914.363) .

130   Reed was formally appointed as a Notary for Alpine County at Silver Mountain in 1864 (*Monitor Gazette*, September 17, 1864). He notarized a complaint by J.W. Saunders on June 1, 1864 (Amador County Archives document 6674.1050); a Preemption claim by David S. Hutchinson for property located approximately two and a half miles south of the town of Silver Mountain on June 26, 1864 (Amador County Archives document 7914.425); and a Deed of property in the Town of Silver Mountain on August 29, 1864 (Book "A" of Deeds, pp. 38-38)(referencing a "plat and survey" of the South Park Addition to Silver Mountain made by T. Reed on May 1, 1864), suggesting a law practice at Silver Mountain extending for more than a year.

131   *See* "Inventory & Accounting" dated approximately March 10, 1864, for the Marklee Estate (Amador County Archives, document 5274.118, copy at Alpine County Museum).

132   H. Eno, <u>Twenty Years on the Pacific Slope</u>, p. 147.

133   *See, e.g., Chronicle*, March 16, 1867, indicating that District Court was scheduled the first Mondays of March and September.

134   *Inyo Register*, August 26, 1909.

135   *Chronicle*, March 30, 1867.

136   One newspaper mention indicates his home was at Havilah, a brief-lived gold mining boomtown and the original county seat of Kern County. *Chronicle*, May 11, 1867.

137   H. Eno, <u>Twenty Years on the Pacific Slope</u>, p. 80, n.24.

138   *Mono-Alpine Chronicle*, January 4, 1879.

139   *Chronicle*, February 16, 1867.

140   *Chronicle*, October 12 and 19, 1872.

141   H. Eno, <u>Twenty Years on the Pacific Slope</u>, p. 80, n.24; *see similarly* detailed recounting of the incident by Willie Arthur Chalfant, The Story of Inyo (Hammond Press, 1922), p. 236 (*reprinted online by* Google Books).

142   The death of Saxon Williams occurred on December 28, 1864. Although the case took nearly two years to get to trial, the jury ultimately acquitted William Harris, issuing a verdict of "Not Guilty" on September 6, 1866. Williams' defense was that he was actually shooting at Peter Christeson, not Williams, with whom he was "on the best terms of friendship." *See* summary of the Harris case at Alpine County Museum.

143   For a longer discussion of the wood tax, *see* H. Eno, <u>Twenty Years on the Pacific Slope</u>, pp. 78-79, and section on Henry Eno, *infra*.

144   H. Eno, <u>Twenty Years on the Pacific Slope</u>, p. 80.

145   *Chronicle*, July 15, 1876.

146   *Chronicle*, May 25, 1878.

147   *Chronicle*, May 25, 1878 (*quoting the Bodie Standard*).

148   *See* "The New Constitution" by Viscount James Bryce, The American Commonwealth (MacMillan & Co., 1889) and related materials, reprinted online at www.sfmuseum.org.

149   *Bodie Chronicle*, January 3, 1880.

150   *See* Letters of Henry Eno, p. 80 n.24, *citing* the *Yreka Journal* of March 24 and 31, 1909; *see also Inyo Register*, August 26, 1909.

151   Amador County Assessment Roll of 1864, showing that Goff owned a lot and house on Webster Street.

152   *See Chronicle*, March 12 and 26, 1870, identifying Goff as judge. Goff's advertisements (as a lawyer) appeared as early as December 9, 1865, and he apparently continued to practice law as late as 1873, despite his position on the bench as a judge. *See* Goff Chronology (manuscript of newspaper references compiled by Kim Summerfield (Skinner)) (copy at Alpine Museum) at p. 1, noting that newspapers in 1873 showed Goff's availability as an "Attorney at Law" during the same period he was identified as the county Judge.

153   *Chronicle*, March 4, 1871. It is unclear whether this last reference ("General Machinist") was intended in the literal or figurative sense.

154   *Chronicle*, June 10, 1871.

155   *Chronicle*, April 2, 1870.

156   The newspaper grumbled over the judge's failure to reside at the county seat of Silver Mountain, issuing decisions from his Markleeville office instead, and opined that chambers should be open in Silver Mountain at least once a week. *Chronicle*, September 23, 1871; January 20, 1872. In lawyerly fashion, Goff produced "authority" for holding chambers at Markleeville, at least sufficient to silence such editorial quibblings. *Chronicle*, January 27, 1872.

157   *Chronicle*, April 6, 1872. *See similarly Chronicle*, February 10, 1872.

158   *Chronicle*, May 11, 1872. Coincidentally (or not), Mrs. Brown journeyed back from San Francisco to Silver Mountain that same week and announced plans to reopen Brown's Hotel. *Id.*

159   *Chronicle*, September 21 and October 19, 1872.

160   Goff Chronology at p. 1 (*citing* Board of Supervisors Minutes, Book "A", minutes of October 20, 1873) recording the vote at the October 15, 1873 election at 185 (for S.W. Griffith) to 116 (for Goff)). But it took a citizens' petition before Goff vacated the Judge's chambers (See Goff Chronology, citing Board of Supervisors Minutes Book "A", May 4, 1874).

161   Goff Chronology, p. 2 (reflecting citizen's petition in the Board of Supervisors Minutes for May 4, 1874, Book "A").

162   Goff Chronology, p. 3 (*citing Alpine Miner*, May 16 and May 23, 1874). Goff himself also wrote to a friend that he intended to marry Mrs. Britton. (Letter by C.P. Goff to O.F. Thornton dated May 14, 1874 (Thornton Letters collection at Alpine County Museum)("You say they think I am going to marry Mrs. Britton. That is so. I am going to be married on Sunday. . .")). Goff's former wife, Hannah, divorced him in 1873, receiving the sum of $500 in alimony. *See Alpine Miner*, October 11, 1873, *cited by* Goff Chronology, p. 1. The relationship with Britton apparently scandalized the town of Silver Mountain; at Genoa, Goff reportedly asked a friend about the "safety of his putting in an appearance" in Silver Mountain and was told "not to do it," while Mrs. Britton was advised that a visit to town "would be worse for you than the Judge." Goff Chronology, p. 3 (*citing Alpine Miner* of May 16,1874).

163   In 1873, Brown (Britton) was appointed by Goff as guardian of her young niece, Wilhelmina Jonberg. After Goff lost the 1873 election (see supra note 158), the new Judge Griffith swiftly removed Britton as guardian. *See* Goff Chronology at p. 3 and 4, *citing* Probate Court records from 1873-74 (April 20, 1874), and *Alpine Miner* of May 16, 1874.

164   By June, 1874, Goff was being sued by the Folgers for printing; by merchant John Sauquet; liveryman J.J. Rice; and Thomas Orgon; similar suits had also been filed against the former Mrs. Britton. Goff Chronology, p. 4.

165   Goff Chronology, p. 5-6.

166   *Chronicle*, January 13, 1877 (citing the *San Francisco Chronicle* and *Call*). Goff and a "private detective" named Frederick W. Gradville reportedly tried to extort money from one C.S. Ladd, owner of "a Cearney [sic] street shooting gallery," threatening to have Ladd arrested for improperly using ball-and-powder cartridges in his establishment "unless he paid twenty dollars" – the extorted cash being split between Goff and Gradville.

167   Goff died Friday, August 6, 1886, at his office at 625 Merchant Street, Room 3, San Francisco, at the age of 70. *Alpine Argus*, August 14, 1886.

168   *Chronicle*, September 2, 1876.

169   Raymond Arnot was born on September 29, 1873, in San Franciso; Eugenie passed away on August 29, 1875, at the age of just 26. *See* Arnot family history material at Alpine County Museum.

170   *Chronicle*, December 15, 1877.

171   *See* Arnot family history material at Alpine County Museum.

172   *Chronicle*, August 17, 1878. The Arnot home appears to have been located at "4th and Union" in Silver Mountain, according to "Births" information in Arnot family history material (at Alpine County Museum); this address was also given for the offices of the Silver Creek Gold & Silver Mining Co., of which Arnot was Secretary. (*Chronicle*, June 22, 1878.) Anna appears to have been a tolerant wife; the middle name of baby "Mary Eugenie" seems to have been chosen to honor Arnot's deceased first wife.

173   Mabel Love, History of the Alpine County Schools (manuscript donated to Alpine County Museum 1989, and transcript published 1990), p. 7.

174   Chalmers Letters, *Private Letters 1880-1881*, p. 7 (March 16, 1880).

175   Chalmers Letters, *Private Letters 1880-1881*, p. 7 (March 16, 1880).

176   *Chronicle*, December 15, 1877. It would appear that Arnot Sr. advanced money to the newly-incorporated Isabella Company to purchase the Northern Extensions of the Adolphus Lode from Peter Olson and Peter Schlytter, and others. *See* Chalmers Letters, Private Letters 1880-1881, pp. 88-89 (April 15, 1880). The Arnots may also have been owed money for the newly-completed I.X.L. mill.

177   *Chronicle*, April 13, 1878.

178   *Chronicle*, December 15, 1877. It is unclear whether Chalmers successfully finished the installation of a tramway at the Exchequer mine, but he was contemplating it in 1873. *See* Rossiter W. Raymond, Mineral Resources West of the Rocky Mountains, 1873 (transcription of Lewis Chalmers' report pertaining to Alpine County, copy at Alpine County Museum), p. 7-8 ("So soon as [Mr. Chalmers] can turn out 30 tons a day, he will recommend the construction of a wire tramway which will cost, complete, per mile, $10,000.00, according to Mr. Hallidie, the patentee . . ."). Oddly enough, Hallidie's judgment was obtained June 26, 1877, nearly a month after five other judgments were rendered on May 29, 1877. Yet Hallidie was first to execute on the Exchequer/I.X.L. properties.

179   *Chronicle*, December 15, 1877.

180   W.T. Jackson, *supra*, at p. 72 (quoting Alpine Signal of August 14, 1878). Since Halladie and Gregory both held senior encumbrances, it would appear that Arnot arranged to pay off their $4,834.38 combined debt, perhaps at a substantial discount. This might explain Chalmers' later assertion that syndicate funds went to Arnot "to acquire Exchequer debt." *See infra* n. 180.

181   Chalmers Letters, *Private Letters 1880-1881*, p. 325 (August 24, 1880).

182   Chalmers Letters, *Private Letters 1880-1881*, p. 230 (July 12, 1880). In an even more convoluted story, Chalmers asserted that money sent to Arnot by the London Syndicate had been advanced only to acquire Exchequer debt – and thus that Arnot's acquisition of the Isabella gave investors no rights to the property. "[A]t the time [Arnot] bought in the Isabelle he had no funds of Exchequer [Company] at his command. They were there for *another purpose, e.g. to buy out claims ag[ainst] The Exchequer Co." Chalmers Letters,* Private Letters 1880-1881, p. 297-298 (August 10, 1880).

Chalmers also claimed that Arnot Sr. foreclosed a lien on the Isabelle Company's Pine Tree and Adolphus mines, purchasing them at the foreclosure sale, and that Arnot Jr. "who was not then on the best of terms with his father" stepped in to "jump" the locations, claiming them as his own. Chalmers Letters, *Private Letters 1880-1881*, p. 91 (April 15, 1880).

183   *Chronicle*, April 13, 1878.

184   Chalmers Letters, *Isabella Officials 1878-1880*, pp. 281-3; 299 (July 11 and 17, 1879).

185   *See* Chalmers Letters, *Isabella Officials 1878-1880*, p. 283 (July 11, 1879); and Quitclaim from N.D. Arnot Jr. to Henry Syme, dated September 30, 1879 (California State Library, Syme Collection, SMC, Box 21, Folder 1). The Quitclaim recites a nominal consideration of just "One dollar in Gold Coin" paid to Arnot.

186   *See* Sheriff's Deed dated February 7, 1900, conveying Chalmers' property to N.D. Arnot (Jr.)(Book "H" of Deeds, p. 197-203); *see also* quitclaim deed from Arnot to Nettie dated July 30, 1900, also in Book "H", pp. 292-293. Interestingly enough, this transfer of the homesite was recorded "at the request of D. Bari," Antoinette's "boarder."

187   According to son Philip, Arnot served in place of Placerville's Judge Williams, who was ill. *See* Letter from Philip H. Arnot dated December 28, 1971, in Arnot family history material at Alpine County Museum.

188   Frank S. Wedertz, Mono Diggings (Community Printing & Publishing, 2001), p. 145.

189   Judge Arnot officiated at the January 11, 1902 wedding of Markleeville residents Charles Barrett (age 23) and Clara Mayo (age 19) at Mayo's Ranch. *See* Marriage License, in the Nevada Historical Society Archives, University of Nevada at Reno.

190   The Arnot family moved to Placerville on October 12, 1904, after "many people wrote to [Arnot] from Placerville, begging him to come over there and run for judge." *See* Letter from Philip H. Arnot dated December 28, 1971, in Arnot family history material at Alpine County Museum.

Chapter 9 Footnotes:

1   Chalmers Letters, *Private Letters 1871-72*, p. 284 (September 13, 1871)(punctuation altered).

2   *Testimonials in Favour of Lewis Chalmers, M.A. (1865)*, copy at Sutro Library (San Francisco), p. 5.

3   Correspondence from researcher Gordon Harland to the author dated July 16, 2010, indicates the senior Chalmers died September 20, 1850. Other information, however, indicates the father handed over at least some of his affairs to Lewis (junior) in 1847, so it is possible the elder Chalmers was ill for several years. *Testimonials, supra,* at p. 8.

4   *Testimonials, supra,* at p. 10.

5   John Crenna, Fraserburgh Past & Present (1914). Chalmers himself mentioned that he "could have wished before leaving the good Burgh that I had been able to see the outer breakwater finished for the reception of steamers." *Testimonials, supra,* at p. 2. The North Pier would prove an "unlucky one," according to Crenna, being poorly positioned on a reef, and was badly damaged in the storms of 1851-52.

6   *Testimonials, supra*, at pp. 10-11 (indicating that the railway had opened to Fraserburgh in April, 1865).

7   *Testimonials, supra*, at p. 12.

8   John Crenna, <u>Fraserburgh Past & Present</u> (1914).

9   *Testimonials, supra*, at pp. 10-11.

10   They were married June 25, 1850. Some sources show her name as "Eliza." *See* correspondence from Gordon Harland dated July 2 and 6, 2010, in files of the author.

11   Chalmers Letters, *Private Letters 1868-69*, p. 13 (March 25, 1868).

12   Ellen Miller McEwen was born November 24, 1833, in Dundee, Scotland, and married Chalmers on July 7, 1853, when she was not quite twenty. *See* correspondence dated July 2 and 6, 2010, with Gordon Harland in possession of author.

13   Remi Nadeau, <u>The Silver Seekers</u> (Crest Publishers 1999), at p. 49. Ellen died at Witch Hill on July 23, 1863, of "Phthisis upwards of seven months" (tuberculosis)(correspondence dated July 6, 2010, from Gordon Harland).

14   Chalmers Letters, *Private Letters 1868-69*, p. 268 (January 18, 1869); *see also* correspondence dated July 2, 2010, from Gordon Harland.

15   Chalmers Letters, *Private Letters 1868-69*, p. 160 (September 14, 1868); *see also* correspondence dated July 2, 2010, from Gordon Harland.

16   Chalmers Letters, *Private Letters 1868-69*, pp. 171 and 268 (November 22, 1868 and January 18, 1869); *see also* correspondence dated July 2, 2010, from Gordon Harland.

17   Chalmers Letters, *Private Letters 1868-69*, pp. 52; 103; 136; 169; and 325 (April 27, 1868; August 10, 1868; August 28, 1868; November 22, 1868; March 26, 1869); *see also* correspondence dated July 2, 2010, from Gordon Harland.

18   Chalmers Letters, *Private Letters 1868-69*, p.58; 82 (April 29, 1868; June 24, 1868). Elleny may also have been known as "Nellie"; *see* Chalmers Letters, *Exchequer Officials 1871-72*, p. 113 (May 29, 1871). Another baby, Ellen MacEwen Chalmers, born August 25, 1855, apparently did not survive. Correspondence from Gordon Harland dated July 2 and 6, 2010, in possession of author.

19   *Testimonials, supra*, at p. 5. This is indirectly confirmed by a remark in Chalmers' obituary that he "became involved in some financial speculations which ended badly, and a crash followed." *Fraserburgh Herald*, March 8, 1904.

20   Letter by George A. Dey, Fraserburgh, dated November 2, 1995, citing anecdotal report from Dr. David Morrison, "the best in local history" (copy at Alpine County Museum)(emphasis in original; punctuation added).

21   *Fraserburgh Herald* obituary, March 8, 1904.

22   *Testimonials, supra*, at p. 12. Johnson, Matthey & Co. were "assayers and melters to the Bank of England," with offices at Hatton Garden, London.

23   *See, e.g.,* Chalmers Letters, *Private Letters 1871-72*, p. 498 (December 23, 1872), in which Chalmers notes: "[M]y friends were sorry they could not do anything with [a mining investment] at present . . . in consequence of the stand which the *Times* and other influential Journals are making against everything in the shape of an American Mine. . . ." Even the local Alpine paper acknowledged, "[I]t is notorious that the affairs of many of our [mining] companies have been outrageously conducted; that the officers have lined their own pockets at the expense of the shareholders." *Chronicle*, November 17, 1866.

24   *Monitor Gazette*, September 10, 1864, *quoting* a "sarcastic advertisement" in the Virginia Enterprise.

25   Chalmers Letters, *Imperial Officials*, p. 199 (date illegible, but approximately January 11, 1869).

26   Chalmers Letters, *Private Letters 1868-69*, p. 62; 157; and 270 (May 18, 1868; September 14, 1868; January 24, 1869).

27   Letter from F.A.S. Jones to his brother, Capt. James Jones, dated September 29, 1864 (Jones Letters, Alpine County Museum document 94.21.02)(punctuation added).

28   The lien by Petiss may actually have been fraudulent; Chalmers claimed that James Jones "trump[ed] up a claim for salary to himself as Superintendent" for $910 and manufactured a similar claim by Thornton (as Secretary) for $902, then assigned both claims to Petiss, who obtained judgment as a straw man. Chalmers Letters, *Private Letters 1868-69*, pp. 19-20 (April 4, 1868).

29   Chalmers Letters, *Imperial Officials*, pp. 7 and 12 (December 9, 1867; January 17, 1868); *see similarly* Chalmers Letters, *Private Letters 1868-69,* pp. 4-5 (February 29, 1868).

30   Chalmers Letters, *Imperial Officials*, p. 4 (December 3, 1867)(threatening to sue B. Petiss for damages for withholding possession).

31   Chalmers Letters, *Imperial Officials*, p. 7 and 12 (December 9, 1867 and January 17, 1868) (suggesting that London hold up issuing shares to Jones until he relinquished possession, and hinting that Jones' own brother had received funds that he failed to pass on). Ultimately, the London Syndicate may have paid $5000 themselves to clear up the liens, despite the Jones' assertion that it had already been paid. Chalmers Letters, *Private Letters 1868-69*, p. 5 (February 29, 1868).

32   Chalmers Letters, *Private Letters 1868-69*, p. 3 (February 29, 1868)(indicating that Chalmers had paid Mercer to run the first 25 feet of the Tunnel, a step he could take only after obtaining possession).

33   Chalmers Letters, *Imperial Officials*, p. 20 (March 17, 1868).

34   Chalmers Letters, *Private Letters 1868-69*, pp. 100-101; 149 (July 15, 1868; September 5, 1868).

35   Chalmers Letters, *Private Letters 1868-69,* pp. 71-3; 92 (June 18-29, 1868); Chalmers Letters, *Imperial Officials*, p. 131; 233 (September 21, 1868; February 8, 1869).

36   Chalmers Letters, *Imperial Officials*, p. 54 (May 30, 1868).

37   Chalmers Letters, *Private Letters 1868-69*, p. 324 (March 27, 1869).

38   Chalmers Letters, *Private Letters 1868-69*, p. 272 (January 24, 1869).

39   Chalmers Letters, *Imperial Officials*, p. 195 (December 28, 1868).

40   Chalmers Letters, *Imperial Officials*, p. 172 (November 3, 1868)(emphasis in original).

41   Chalmers Letters, *Imperial Officials*, p. 279 (March 3, 1869) and p. 286 (March 15, 1869).

42   Chalmers Letters, *Imperial Officials*, pp. 342; 346 (July 1 and 3, 1869). According to the Michigan Tunnel Prospectus, the multiple mineral lodes shown on the surface in the form of a "massive out-crop of veins" were: Fashion; Senate; Triumph; Cosmopolitan; Monitor Coal; Monitor Coal #2; Ocean Wave; Glasgow; Halvetia [*sic*]; Florence; Manchester; Neosho; Nimekeequa; Constitution; Abe Lincoln; Hercules; Worden; Chicago; Michigan; and American. The Triumph would have been the third of these lodes; Chalmers offered no explanation for the non-appearance of the first two.

43   Chalmers Letters, *Imperial Officials*, p. 547 (February 5, 1870).

44   Chalmers Letters, *Imperial Officials*, p. 548-51; 568-572 (February 10, 1870; and undated lien claim of approximately April 21, 1870). *Similarly,* the *Alpine Chronicle* of November 5, 1870 noted that a Sheriff's sale had been set for November 28, 1870, with Chalmers as plaintiff suing for $5,951.81 plus some $149.30 in costs.

45   Chalmers Letters, *Imperial Officials,* p. 549 (February 10, 1870)(noting that the tunnel was now in 1,406 feet, and adding hopefully "and about 230 feet from the foot wall of the Florence Ledge.").

46   *Chronicle*, February 19, 1870; *see also* Chalmers Letters, *Private Letters 1869-71*, p. 167 (February 14, 1870), indicating that John had "arrived here this evening safe and sound."

47   Chalmers Letters, *Private Letters 1869-71*, p. 309 (April 6, 1870)(indicating the bullion was .901 fine); p. 315 (April 9, 1870)("Brick. Sent"); pp. 321 and 331 (April 13 and 18, 1870)("Bar Bullion, value $287, shipped

9th"); and *Imperial Officials 1867-70*, p. 576 (April 21, 1870)(confirming that "Captn. Chalmers of The Exchequer Coy. . . . made his first bullion shipment to London on the 9th instant.").

48   W. Turrentine Jackson, <u>Report on the History of Grover Hot Springs State Park Area and Surrounding Region of Alpine County</u> (Division of Beaches & Parks, Department of Parks and Recreation, State of California 1964), at p. 64-65 (quoting the *Alpine Miner* of July 23, 1870).

49   *Chronicle*, October 22, 1870.

50   Chalmers Letters, *Imperial Officials*, p. 555-57 (April 18, 1870).

51   Chalmers Letters, *Private Letters 1869-71*, p. 522 (July 30, 1870)("Lewie arrived 29th").

52   *Chronicle*, October 8, 1870.

53   Chalmers Letters, *Private Letters 1868-69*, p. 155 (September 14, 1868)(mentioning a "very valuable property" including a timber ranch, saw, and quartz mill, which "should go with IXL.").

54   Chalmers noted as early as March, 1870 that acquisition of the Davidson 16-stamp mill "with a large Timber Ranch" would require "only" $20,000. Chalmers Letters, *Private Letters 1869-71*, p. 306 (March 30, 1870). Later negotiations were for $10,000 in cash and $5,000 in stock. Chalmers Letters, *Private Letters 1869-71*, p. 440 (June 25, 1870). Another source suggests that the final purchase price was closer to $20,000, half paid in cash and half in Exchequer stock. W.T. Jackson, *supra*, at p. 64. The negotiation apparently took some months to arrange; the mill's purchase was finally reported in the *Chronicle* of September 3, 1870, with the Exchequer Co. "taking possession Monday last."

55   1870 Census for Alpine County Township No. 2, p. 3 (enumerated July 13, 1870).

56   *Chronicle*, November 26, 1870.

57   *Chronicle*, January 14, 1871 (*quoting the Sacramento Bee).*

58   Chalmers Letters, *Private Letters 1871-72*, p. 168 (July 9, 1871).

59   Chalmers Letters, *Private Letters 1871-72*, p. 160 (July 4, 1871).

60   Chalmers Letters, *Exchequer Officials 1870-73*, p. 428 (November 8, 1871).

61   Chalmers Letters, *Exchequer Officials 1870-73*, p.499 (December 4, 1871).

62   Chalmers Letters, *Exchequer Officials 1870-73*, p. 500 (December 4, 1871).

63   Chalmers Letters, *Exchequer Officials 1870-73*, p. 508 (December 15, 1871). Chalmers noted the bar was .967 fine, but that the returns represented just over 45 per cent of the ore's assay value – an abysmally low performance which he attributed to an insufficient number of settling pans.

64   Chalmers Letters, *Private Letters 1871-72*, pp. 155; 159; 203 (July 3 and 4, 1871; August 1, 1871).

65   Chalmers Letters, *Private Letters 1871-72*, p. 181 (July 24, 1871)(emphasis in original; punctuation added).

66   Chalmers Letters, *Private Letters 1871-72*, pp. 366 and 368 (January 15 and 16, 1872).

67   Chalmers Letters, *Private Letters 1871-72,* pp. 383 and 385 (February 26, 1872 and March 5, 1872) (indicating Chalmers left Alpine on January 24, 1872, arriving in New York on February 24, leaving again that same night for England aboard the White Star Line's "Atlantic").

68   *Chronicle*, May 11, 1872 (citing Lewie's "many years of poor health").

69   *Chronicle*, May 11, 1872.

70   Letter from George Lowe to O.F. Thornton dated May 5, 1872, in Judy Wickwire Collection.

71   Chalmers Letters, *Private Letters 1871-72*, p. 403 (June 19, 1872).

72   Letter from Mary Hanson to O.F. Thornton, dated June 17, 1872 (Thornton Letters, Alpine County Museum document 81.04.36C)(spelling corrected); *see also Chronicle*, June 8, 1872 ("We understand that [Chalmers] has purchased hoisting works for both the Exchequer and I.X.L. mines, and that henceforth energetic mining operations will be the order of the day in and around Silver Mountain.").

73   Chalmers Letters, *Private Letters 1871-72*, pp. 470; 493 (November 8 and 29, 1872); *see also* *Chronicle*, September 14, 1872 (noting John's departure from San Francisco on the Panama steamer on September 7).

74   Chalmers acknowledged receipt of a remittance of £1650 in October, 1872, and mentions another £8100 Stg. that he was apparently expecting to receive. Chalmers Letters, *Exchequer Officials 1870-73*, p. 625; 631 (October 28 and November 15, 1872).

75   Chalmers Letters, *Exchequer Officials 1873-74* (Bancroft Library), p. 126 (September 15, 1873). Reconstruction of the old mill included $1,100 worth of new settling pans. Chalmers Letters, *Exchequer Officials 1870-73*, p. 624 (October 23, 1872).

76   *See* Chalmers Letters, *Exchequer Officials 1870-73*, pp. 617; 627; 632 (October 14 through November 15, 1872), referencing the new I.X.L. hoisting works.

77   Rossiter W. Raymond, Mineral Resources West of the Rocky Mountains, 1873 (transcription of Lewis Chalmers' report pertaining to Alpine County, at Alpine County Museum), p. 5 ("The lode was struck on the 6th of August. . . ."); *see similarly Alpine Miner*, September 6, 1873, *cited by* W.T. Jackson, *supra*, at p. 70.

78   For a longer discussion of the demonetization issue, *see* Chapter 11. *See also* William Miller, A New History of the United States (George Braziller, Inc., 1958), p. 272-73; Allan Nevins and H.S. Commager, A Pocket History of the United States (Pocket Books 1992), p. 323; 330-333.

79   Chalmers Letters, *Exchequer Officials 1873-74* (Bancroft Library), p. 156 (October 17, 1873).

80   Markleeville became the new county seat thanks to a lopsided vote in October, 1875, in which Silver Mountain received just 35 votes, compared to 129 for Markleeville ("Notes on Early Alpine County," unpublished typescript at Alpine County Museum).

81   *Chronicle*, September 9, 1876.

82   Chalmers mentioned acquisition of the site in his 1871-2 *Private Letters*, p. 539 (March 21, 1873); completion of the mill in late 1876 received newspaper attention in the *Chronicle*, December 16, 1876. Other sources indicate, however, that the brand-new mill never ran, and that I.X.L. ore was actually treated at the Exchequer Mill. *See* William B. Clark, "Mines & Mineral Resources of Alpine County CA" (1977); *see similarly* Frank Wedertz, Mono Diggings (Community Printing & Publishing, 2001), p. 140, indicating the I.X.L. mill "had never been run," despite costing some $60,000 to build, and was later purchased by an English syndicate in 1896 and hauled to the Dunderberg Mine site in Mono County; *and see* Roger Mitchell, High Sierra SUV Trails, Vol. 1, p. 111 (Track & Trail Publications, 2002), also indicating the IX.L. Mill equipment was moved to the Dunderberg in Mono County by a British syndicate in 1896.

83   Antoinette Laughton was in the Silver Mountain area as early as 1876; a newspaper story mentions that she was thrown by her horse and dislocated an ankle. *Chronicle*, October 14, 1876. A doctor was procured to treat her from Genoa — suggesting the possibility that Chalmers's deep pockets were already being tapped.

84   According to the Shaws Flat Cemetery Record at Columbia State Historical Park, Depuy was a "blacksmith from New York." The 1880 Alpine Census, however, identifies Antoinette's father as "French" and her mother as "Prussian." Bavia was 75 years old when he died, and his much-younger wife Catharine S. (Burger) Depuy only 44 years old at her death the following year.

85   Antoinette and Laughton were married on July 16, 1872, in San Francisco. *See San Francisco Morning Call*, July 19, 1872 (misspelling her name "Annette De Prey").

86   R. Nadeau, *supra*, at p. 55.

87   Chalmers mentions a San Francisco landlady named Laughton in his 1878 letters. Chalmers Letters, *Isabella Officials 1878-80*, p. 35; 38 (December 15, 1878). By then, however, Nettie was already living at Silver Mountain.

88   *Chronicle*, February 2, 1878 (noting that Chalmers had "arrived safe in England about the 15th January" and expressing "hopes he will soon arrange matters with a view to the extinguishment of [Exchequer's] liabilities here, and that work will soon be resumed.").

89   *Chronicle*, February 16, March 16, and March 23, 1878.

90   *Chronicle*, March 23, 1878.

91   *Chronicle*, June 29, 1878.

92   *Isabella Officials 1878-80*, p. 139 (February 15, 1879).

93   Chalmers Letters, *Exchequer Officials 1871-72*, p. 12 (April 18, 1871).

94   Rossiter W. Raymond, <u>Mineral Resources West of the Rocky Mountains</u>, for 1870 (transcription of Lewis Chalmers' report pertaining to Alpine County, at Alpine County Museum), pp. 3-4.

95   It is unclear where the name "Isabella" originated, as the tunnel apparently was known originally the "Eugenie" Tunnel. The transfer by N.D. Arnot, Jr. to Henry Syme identifies the tunnel right as the "Eugenie Tunnel," with a legal description referencing an "old tunnel on the Isabelle Company's ground." (*See* Indenture dated August 30, 1878, from N.D. Arnot Jr. to H. Syme, at California State Library, Syme Collection). "Isabella" was a common enough woman's name at the time; Daniel Davidson had both a sister (Isabella Small) and a daughter (born about 1870) named Isabella.

96   Chalmers anticipated that other mining companies would use the tunnel (and pay a fee) to access their veins. The Isabella Company eventually purchased its own "sett" of mining claims in Scandinavian Canyon, including the Hamilton; Jefferson; Pine Tree; Adolphus; Mendocino; Sandy Gulch; Sam Brannan; Richmond; Ben Nevis; Boone Co., and an adjoining mill site known as O. Tanner's Mill Site. *See* Chalmers Letters, *Isabella Officials 1878-80,* p. 31; 97-8; 514 (December 15, 1878; January 29, 1879; January 27, 1880); *see also* County Clerk's Affidavits dated March 8, 1880 (California State Library, Syme Collection).

97   *Isabella Officials 1878-80*, pp. 97-98 (January 29, 1879). Other lodes being targeted were the "Adolphus" and "Pine Tree." *Id.*

98   *Mono-Alpine Chronicle*, December 21, 1878.

99   Chalmers Letters, *Isabella Officials,* p. 41; 45; 54 (December 21, 25, and 30, 1878).

100   Chalmers Letters, *Isabella Officials,* p. 123 (February 4, 1879).

101   Chalmers Letters, *Isabella Officials,* pp. 30 and 40 (December 15 and 20, 1878).

102   Chalmers Letters, *Isabella Officials,* p. 30 (December 15, 1878). The *Mono-Alpine Chronicle* of January 4, 1879 confirmed that the boarding house was new, reporting: "Lewis Chalmers returned to this town [Silver Mountain] several weeks ago, and now has a boarding house started at the I X L Mill, and eight or ten men employed building a bridge across Silver [C]reek . . . and grading a road and place for building at the mouth of the tunnel . . . ."

103   *Mono-Alpine Chronicle*, December 21, 1878; Chalmers Letters, *Isabella Officials,* p. 30 (December 15, 1878).

104   *Mono-Alpine Chronicle*, December 21, 1878; Chalmers Letters, *Isabella Officials,* p. 59 (January 6, 1879).

105   Chalmers Letters, *Isabella Officials,* p. 79 (January 18, 1879).

106   Chalmers Letters, *Isabella Officials,* p. 31; 35; 87 (December 15, 1878; January 25, 1879).

107   Chalmers Letters, *Isabella Officials,* p. 88 (January 25, 1879). The boilers would occupy most of a 20 x 32-foot boiler room.

108   Chalmers Letters, *Isabella Officials,* p. 40 (December 20, 1878); pp. 52-53 (December 30, 1878).

109   Chalmers Letters, *Isabella Officials,* p. 89 (January 25, 1879).

110   Chalmers Letters, *Isabella Officials,* p. 38 (December 15, 1878)(punctuation altered).

111   Chalmers Letters, *Isabella Officials,* p. 53 (December 30, 1878).

112   Chalmers Letters, *Isabella Officials,* p. 38 (December 15, 1878); p. 44 (December 25, 1878); p. 67 (January 9, 1879).

113   Chalmers Letters, *Isabella Officials*, p. 67 (January 9, 1879).

114   Chalmers Letters, *Isabella Officials*, p. 85 (January 18, 1879).

115   Chalmers Letters, *Isabella Officials*, pp. 61-6 (January 8-9, 1879).

116   Chalmers Letters, *Isabella Officials*, p. 92 (January 25, 1879).

117   Chalmers Letters, *Isabella Officials*, p. 58 (January 6, 1879)(indicating that the blacksmith's shop was 16' x 32' while the carpenter's shop was 18' x 32'); p. 88-89 (January 25, 1879).

118   Chalmers Letters, *Isabella Officials*, p. 204; 213 (March 31 and April 28, 1879).

119   Chalmers Letters, *Isabella Officials*, p. 241 (May 21, 1879).

120   Chalmers Letters, *Isabella Officials*, p. 52 (December 30, 1878).

121   Chalmers Letters, *Isabella Officials*, p. 52 (December 30, 1878).

122   Chalmers Letters, *Isabella Officials*, p. 100 (January 30, 1879); pp. 132 and 134 (February 12, 1879).

123   Chalmers Letters, *Isabella Officials*, p. 137 (February 12, 1879).

124   Chalmers Letters, *Isabella Officials*, p. 147 (February 18, 1879).

125   Chalmers Letters, *Isabella Officials*, p. 155 (February 19, 1879).

126   Chalmers Letters, *Isabella Officials*, p. 160 (February 24, 1879).

127   Chalmers Letters, *Isabella Officials*, p. 160 (February 24, 1879).

128   Chalmers Letters, *Isabella Officials*, p. 175-6 (March 8-10, 1879).

129   Chalmers Letters, *Isabella Officials*, p. 176-7 (March 10, 1879)(punctuation altered).

130   Chalmers Letters, *Isabella Officials*, p. 166 (February 28, 1879).

131   Chalmers Letters, *Isabella Officials*, pp. 212; 214; 225; 258; 263; 269; 300-301; 311; 328; 330; 383 (April 28 – Sept 27, 1879).

132   Chalmers Letters, *Isabella Officials*, unnumbered page following p. 97 (January 29, 1879)(punctuation and spelling corrected).

133   Chalmers Letters, *Isabella Officials*, p. 184 (March 14, 1879)(punctuation altered).

134   Chalmers Letters, *Isabella Officials*, p. 185 (March 17, 1879)(punctuation altered).

135   Chalmers Letters, *Isabella Officials*, p. 593 (March 8, 1880).

136   Chalmers Letters, *Isabella Officials*, p. 184 (March 14, 1879).

137   Burleigh's drill was used on the Sherman Mountain tunnel at Georgetown, Colorado, in 1870. *See* Michael H. Piatt, "If Hell is Below, It Wouldn't Take Long To Go There," available online at www.bodiehistory.com/drilling-blasting.htm. An earlier but less durable Burleigh design had been used as early as 1866 in the Massachusetts Hoosac Tunnel. For a wonderful history of the development of the rock drill, *see* www.americanheritage.com/articles/magazine/it/1999/1/1999_1_56.shtml.

138   *See* M.H. Piatt mining article, n.5, at www.bodiehistory.com, and American Heritage article, *supra*.

139   American Heritage article, *supra*.

140   Chalmers Letters, *Isabella Officials*, p. 203 (March 31, 1879)(emphasis in original).

141   Chalmers Letters, *Isabella Officials*, p. 277 (July 7, 1879).

142   Dynamite was developed by Swedish chemist Alfred Nobel in 1866, a mixture of nitroglycerine and kieselguhr. The Giant Powder Company opened its plant – the first in the U.S. to manufacture dynamite – in 1870. *See* History of Explosives, www.explosives.org. *See also* Chapter 6.

143   Chalmers Letters, *Isabella Officials*, p. 357 (September 8, 1879).

144   Chalmers Letters, *Isabella Officials*, p. 346-47 (August 24, 1879).

145   Chalmers Letters, *Isabella Officials*, p. 338; 341; 343; 368 (August 19 through September 10, 1879).

146   Chalmers Letters, *Isabella Officials*, pp. 296; 303; 308; 317; 323; 333; 338; 343; 351; 361; 382 (July 18 through September 24, 1879).

147   *Mono-Alpine Chronicle*, January 18, 1879.

148   Chalmers Letters, *Isabella Officials*, pp. 428-433 (November 10, 1879).

149   Chalmers Letters, *Isabella Officials*, p. 455; 466-67; 478 (December 8, 22, and 29, 1879).

150   "The Hoosac Tunnel," *reprinting* article from Scribner's Magazine of December, 1870, *on-line* at www.catskillarchive.com/rrextra/htstory1.html.

151   Chalmers Letters, *Isabella Officials*, p. 210 (April 7, 1879)(punctuation altered).

152   Chalmers Letters, *Isabella Officials*, p. 407 (October 20, 1879).

153   Chalmers Letters, *Isabella Officials*, pp. 490-91 (January 12, 1880).

154   Chalmers Letters, *Isabella Officials*, pp. 496, 509-10; 532-34 (January 12 – February 2, 1880). Installation of the 13" vent pipe was "quite a job," requiring cutting a channel into the roof of the tunnel, but it provided immediate relief. He employed a tinner to make up the air pipe on-site. *See* pp. 609*ff*; 621; 638; 668-69 (March 15 – April 5, 1880). At least initially, however, Chalmers apparently kept his Sturtevant blower. *See* p. 604 (March 13, 1880). He later acknowledged the new blower and pipe "ran away with" $2,267.17 in costs and shipping. *See* p. 711 (May 5, 1880).

155   Chalmers Letters, *Isabella Officials*, p. 492, 496, 509-10; 532-34 (January 13 – February 2, 1880).

156   Chalmers Letters, *Isabella Officials*, p. 492; 496 (January 12 – 13, 1880).

157   Chalmers Letters, *Isabella Officials*, p. 181 (March 14, 1879).

158   Chalmers Letters, *Isabella Officials*, pp. 98; 181 (January 29, 1879; March 14, 1879).

159   Chalmers Letters, *Isabella Officials*, pp. 599-607 (March 13, 1880). This letter began, "I am sorry to find that my utmost exertions here give so little satisfaction."

160   Chalmers Letters, *Isabella Officials 1878-80*, p. 619 (March 17, 1880)(punctuation added).

161   Chalmers Letters, *Isabella Officials 1878-80*, p. 634 (March 22, 1880)(spelling corrected).

162   Chalmers Letters, *Isabella Officials 1878-80*, p. 776 (June 30, 1880).

163   Chalmers Letters, *Isabella Officials 1878-80*, pp. 696-97 (April 21 – 26, 1880); *see similarly* p. 683 (April 12, 1880), noting that he was into the "meanest kind of blasting rock" with a single blast requiring 100 cartridges.

164   Chalmers Letters, *Isabella Officials 1878-80*, p. 698 (April 26, 1880).

165   Chalmers Letters, *Isabella Officials 1878-80*, p. 664 (April 3, 1880).

166   Chalmers Letters, *Isabella Officials 1878-80*, p. 711 (May 5, 1880).

167   Chalmers Letters, *Isabella Officials 1878-80*, p. 708 (May 3, 1880).

168   Chalmers Letters, *Isabella Officials 1878-80*, pp. 716; 733; 739*ff*; 758 (May 8 – June 24, 1880)

169   Chalmers Letters, *Isabella Officials 1878-80*, p. 739 (May 29, 1880)(no money for payday); 755-56 (June 14, 1880)(regarding Diamond Drill).

170   Chalmers Letters, *Isabella Officials 1878-80*, p. 858 (August 17, 1880); and Chalmers Letters, *Isabella Officials 1880-82*, p. 2 (August 25, 1880).

171   Chalmers Letters, *Private Letters 1880-81*, p. 312 (August 17, 1880)(punctuation added)(indicating he presently had one mule hauling seven cars at a time at Exchequer, and expected soon to have two mules hauling five cars each); *see also* interest in locomotives Chalmers Letters, *Isabella Officials 1878-80*, at pp. 535; 761-63; 847-50 (February 1, 1880 – August 16, 1880). At the Isabella Tunnel, he apparently had a pair of "Tunnel mules"

superintended by boys about age 16, paid $60 per month including Board. *Isabella Officials 1878-80*, p. 341 (August 22, 1879).

172   Chalmers Letters, *Isabella Officials 1878-80,* p. 798 (July 13, 1880).

173   Chalmers Letters, *Private Letters 1880-81*, pp. 476; 528 (October 27 and December 7, 1880).

174   Chalmers Letters, *Isabella Officials 1878-80,* unnumbered page following p. 811 (July 2, 1880), and Chalmers Letters, *Isabella Officials 1880-82,* p. 18 (August 31, 1880)(telegram). Surprisingly, the additional money was apparently sent; *see* Chalmers Letters, *Isabella Officials 1880-82*, p. 46 (September 13, 1880), acknowledging receipt of another £500 remittance.

175   Chalmers Letters, *Isabella Officials 1880-82*, p. 97 (October 4, 1880).

176   Chalmers Letters, *Isabella Officials 1880-82*, p. 116 (October 11, 1880).

177   *Id.* at p. 116.

178   Purchased from L. Reynolds & Co. in San Francisco. Chalmers Letters, *Private Letters 1880-81*, p. 468 (October 25, 1880); *see also* Chalmers Letters, *Isabella Officials 1880-82*, p. 173 (December 16, 1880).

179   Chalmers Letters, *Isabella Officials 1880-82*, p. 206-8 (January 22, 1881).

180   Chalmers Letters, *Isabella Officials 1880-82*, p. 163; 202; 210 (December 6, 1880 and January 22, 1881).

181   Chalmers Letters, *Private Letters 1878-79*, p. 234 (April 24, 1878).

182   Chalmers Letters, *Private Letters 1878-79*, pp. 151; 167 (March 30 and April 5, 1878).

183   Chalmers Letters, *Isabella Officials 1880-82*, p. 162 (December 6, 1880).

184   Chalmers Letters, *Isabella Officials 1880-82*, p. 172 (December 15, 1880)(punctuation added).

185   Chalmers Letters, *Private Letters 1880-81*, p. 538 (December 16, 1880).

186   Chalmers Letters, *Isabella Officials 1880-82*, pp. 176-77 (December 18, 1880).

187   Chalmers Letters, *Private Letters 1880-81*, p. 543 (December 24, 1880)(punctuation added).

188   Chalmers Letters, *Isabella Officials 1880-82*, p. 184 (December 28, 1880). At least one of those suits was apparently filed by the Vulcan Powder Company, which was owed at least $3,000. Chalmers Letters, *Isabella Officials 1880-82*, pp. 183; 192-93 (December 25, 1880 - January 17, 1881).

189   Chalmers Letters, *Isabella Officials 1880-82*, pp. 193-95 (January 17, 1881)(emphasis in original).

190   Chalmers Letters, *Private Letters 1880-81*, pp. 655 and 722 (February 15 and March 7, 1881).

191   Chalmers Letters, *Private Letters 1880-81*, pp. 727-28; 794 (March 25 and April 22, 1881).

192   Lewis was born September 20, 1881, at the Exchequer Mill. *See* "Births/Marriages/Deaths" Index, compiled by Kim Summerhill (Skinner)(manuscript containing extracts from various newspapers 1864-1886, at Alpine County Museum), p. 12 (*citing Monitor Argus* of September 26, 1881).

193   Chalmers Letters, *Private Letters 1880-81*, p. 805 (April 27, 1881).

194   Chalmers Letters, *Private Letters 1880-81*, p. 819 (May 6, 1881); Chalmers Letters, *Private Letters 1881-84,* pp. 5; 44 (June 29 and July 26, 1881).

195   Chalmers Letters, *Private Letters 1881-84*, pp. 7-9 (June 29, 1881).

196   Chalmers Letters, *Private Letters 1880-81*, p. 761 (April 11, 1881).

197   *See* note 177, *supra.*

198   Chalmers Letters, *Isabella Officials 1880-82*, pp. 500; 546 (January 12 and 25, 1882).

199   Chalmers Letters, *Private Letters 1880-81*, pp. 314; 315; 321, 325 (April 7 and 10, 1882).

200   Letter from Chalmers to D. Bari dated August 28, 1891 (original at Alpine County Museum).

201   Correspondence from Gordon Harland dated July 2, 2010, in the files of the author.

202   Obituary in *Aberdeen Daily Journal*, March 5, 1904.

203   Correspondence from Gordon Harland dated July 6, 2010 (*quoting Reno Evening Gazette* of May 16, 1904).

204   *Modesto Bee article* by Warren Williams, September 2, 1979 (copy at Alpine Museum).

205   The Chalmers house was sold by Mrs. Chalmers on November 8, 1913, to Mrs. R.K. Whitmore of Ceres, California. *See* Book "I" of Alpine County Official Records, page 438 (Indenture dated November 8, 1913 and recorded November 11, 1913). Interestingly, the deed recites a down payment of just $10, with another $400 being payable in one year from the date of sale.

206   *Oakland Tribune*, December 29, 1913.

207   *Record Courier*, January 16, 1914.

Chapter 10 Footnotes:

1   *Chronicle*, June 15, 1878.

2   William M. Maule, "A Contribution to the Geographic and Economic History of Carson, Walker and Mono Basis" (U.S. Forest Service 1938), at p. 45, *citing Chronicle* of August 15, 1868.

3   *Chronicle*, June 10, 1871 (enumerating arriving flocks of between 800 and 10,000 animals; most were owned by men, but one troupe of 3,000 sheep belonged to "Mrs. Clara Parker").

4   *Chronicle*, July 22, 1871. A similar 135,000 sheep were grazing in Alpine in 1870. "Upper Carson Watershed Report" (June 2004), Section 5.1.7 (Agriculture), *available on-line*.

5   *Chronicle*, July 13, 1878.

6   *Chronicle*, June 29, 1878.

7   Upper Carson Watershed Report, supra, at Section 5.1.7.

8   *Chronicle*, May 27, 1871.

9   *Chronicle*, March 23, 1878. The new trespass law apparently passed. *See Chronicle*, March 30, 1878.

10   *See* www.Calaverashistory.org, "Emigrant Road/Big Tree and Carson Valley Turnpike/Alpine Highway," *citing* the San Andreas Independent (July 2, 1859). Dennis would later acquire a ranch in Bear Valley, which he sold in 1864 to Harvey Blood.

11   *Monitor Gazette*, June 11, 1864.

12   *Chronicle*, June 6, 1868.

13   *Chronicle*, January 7, 1871 (delinquent tax notice for C. Kirby, owner of a butcher shop in the town of Silver Mountain and a slaughter house below town on Silver Creek).

14   *Alpine Miner*, July 6, 1867. According to its advertisement, the Empire Meat Market operated by C.H. Kilgore ran a meat wagon every Saturday to Mount Bullion and Monitor.

15   *Chronicle*, August 19, 1871 (advertisement).

16   *Chronicle*, August 31, 1872 (also noting that Smith had "a quantity of mohair on hand," and sold skins made into "robes" for $15 apiece).

17   Chalmers Letters, *Private Letters 1871-72*, p. 224 (August 16, 1871). Davidson was to "feed, tend, and shear" the sheep until re-delivered to Sloan at "Davidson's Ranch, Utah Territory," suggesting that Davidson owned pasture land as far away as Utah. The contract included something of an insurance clause for Sloan, requiring that any dead animals be replaced "out of the said increase before division."

18   *Chronicle*, February 23, 1867.

19   *Chronicle*, February 23, 1867. A barrel factory was established at Woodfords in 1874 to craft (among other things) wooden butter tubs for the Hope Valley dairies. W. Turrentine Jackson, <u>Report on the History of Grover Hot Springs State Park Area and Surrounding Region of Alpine County</u> (Division of Beaches & Parks, Department of Parks and Recreation, State of California 1964), at p. 57 (*citing Alpine Chronicle*, January 10, 1874).

20   William M. Maule, *supra*, at p. 45, *citing Chronicle* of June 12, 1869.

21   *Chronicle*, November 2, 1872.

22   Peter Browning, <u>Place Names of the Sierra Nevada from Abbot to Zumwalt</u> (Wilderness Press 1991), at p. 120.

23   Chalmers Letters, *Exchequer Officials 1870-73*, p. 541 (June 27, 1872). *See also* p. 515 (December 15, 1871), stating "I have 10 cattle in good order at Snow Shoe Thompson's Ranch," and offering to sell them for $1,000).

24   *Chronicle*, September 30, 1871.

25   *Chronicle*, September 21, 1872 (indicating that hay was selling for $20 per ton "on the ranches"; $25 a ton at Markleeville, and $30 at Silver Mountain); *see similarly* October 21, 1876 (hay at Silver Mountain for $22 to $25 a ton).

26   *Chronicle*, July 22, 1871 and August 19, 1871.

27   Chalmers Letter, *Private Letters 1878-81*, p. 346 (August 31, 1880); and pp. 727-28 (March 25, 1881).

28   *Chronicle*, August 3, 1878.

29   *Chronicle*, August 3, 1872 (indicating that Thomas Orgon was successfully raising berries, apples, peaches, nectarines, watermelons, corn, potatoes, beans, onions, tomatoes, rhubarb, "in fact, almost every vegetable known.").

30   Chalmers Letters, *Private Letters 1868-69*, pp. 58; 92 (April 29 and June 29, 1868).

31   Chalmers Letter, *Private Letters 1868-69*, p. 159 (September 14, 1868).

32   *Monitor Gazette*, October 15, 1864.

33   Henry Eno, <u>Twenty Years on the Pacific Slope</u> (Yale University Press 1965), p. 143.

34   H. Eno, <u>Twenty Years on the Pacific Slope</u>, p. 143.

35   *Chronicle*, August 5, 1876.

36   Chalmers Letters, *Private Letters 1868-69*, p. 58 (April 29, 1868).

37   *Chronicle*, August 5, 1876.

38   *Chronicle*, July 1 and 22, 1876 (legal notice inserted by District Attorney Thomas Orgon, advising dam owners and managers that fish ladders were required at all dams, or "the penalties of the law will be strictly enforced against all offenders.").

39   *Chronicle*, October 19, 1872. To encourage the collection of fines, the state legislation provided that half of any penalties collected would be paid to the District Attorney prosecuting the case, while the other half would go to the county's school fund.

40   *Chronicle*, April 27, 1878.

41   *Chronicle*, July 29, 1876.

42   *Chronicle*, September 7, 1878.

43   *Chronicle*, March 18, 1871.

44   *Chronicle*, March 9, 1867; *see also* February 23, 1867, noting many of the townsfolk in Markleeville were out of wood, after a heavy storm.

45   *Chronicle*, September 21, 1872.

46   In earlier years, it appears that logs were floated whole to Nevada. By around 1870, however, it was noted that the cordwood for the last three years was being "split here, instead of at destination, Empire City." *Chronicle*, March 18, 1871. In some years, it appears that wood was cut beginning as early as May, and continuing over the summer. *Chronicle*, February 23, 1867.

47   "Upper Carson Watershed Report" (June 2004), Section 5.1.6 (Logging), *available on-line*.

48   "Oral history of Eddie Williams" (transcript at the Alpine County Museum), describing timber operations in the Dixon Creek/Wolf Creek area in the early 1870s. According to Williams, timber operations there served the Silver Mountain area, where logs would be hauled out and used locally. A similarly constructed "key" dam may well have been used for drives bound for Empire.

49   Harrell had a sawmill in Centerville near a sawmill being operated by Richardson Brothers. *See* Alpine County Assessment Roll of 1865 (Alpine County Archives); *see also* W. T. Jackson, *supra*, p. 28.

50   W.M. Maule, *supra*, at p. 29.

51   *Alpine Heritage: One Hundred Years of History, Recreation, Lore in Alpine County, California, 1864-1964*, published by the Alpine County Museum (Revised edition May 1987), at p. 39 (photo caption).

52   In 1878, for example, the *Chronicle* noted on July 6 that the wood drivers had reached Mt. Bullion the previous evening; and by the following week, they were at Young's Bridge. *Chronicle*, July 6 and 13, 1878. *See also* "Upper Carson Watershed Report" (June 2004), Section 5.1.6 (Logging), *supra* (indicating that a single drive might take 21 days).

53   *Monitor Gazette*, November 26, 1864.

54   A total of 14 million board-feet of lumber made its way down river in 1866, according to the Upper Carson Watershed Report, *supra*. *See similarly Chronicle*, May 11, 1867, estimating a drive of 6 million feet of "saw logs" ready to be floated down the Carson River to Empire City, Nevada.

55   *Chronicle*, December 1, 1866 ("Woodchoppers are at work near town"); and March 23, 1867 (caption noting that woodchoppers were "at it again" near Markleeville).

56   "Morgan, Ayers & Co. of the Middle Fork Lumber Co." reportedly had woodchoppers at work in what Maule speculates was Pleasant Valley Creek area. *See* W.M. Maule, *supra*, at p. 42, *quoting Chronicle* of December 1, 1866.

57   *Chronicle*, September 21, 1872.

58   *Chronicle*, September 28, 1872.

59   *Chronicle*, August 24, 1872, estimating that over 100 men would be cutting wood near Silver Mountain City the following winter.

60   W.M. Maule, *supra*, at p. 38, *quoting Douglas County Banner* of November 29, 1865.

61   *Chronicle*, August 31, 1872. Added the paper, "It is said that the Bank of California has a finger in this pie." *See similarly Chronicle*, September 7, 1872, indicating that Elliot & Co., "who have taken up Carson Canyon water rights for fluming purposes," were planning to build a sawmill devoted to producing flume lumber.

62   *Chronicle*, December 7, 1872, noting that the Spratt Brothers were "well-known wood contractors" with 60 men at work "slaying timber – 45 near Markleeville, and 15 near Silver Mountain." As elsewhere, these "wood chutes" were probably greased with tallow. *See* "Oral History of Harry Hawkins" (Alpine County Museum), at p. 22.

63   W.M. Maule, *supra*, at p. 38, *quoting Chronicle* of January 11, 1873.

64   *Chronicle*, February 2, 1878 (delinquent tax sale notice concerning the Alpine Wood & Lumbering Company, whose assets included a sawmill and flume); Nancy Thornburg, "Going West For The Mining," a typescript summarizing the life of William McElwee Thornburg (2010).

65   *Monitor Gazette*, November 26, 1864.

66 *Chronicle*, June 15, 1867.

67 *Carson Valley News*, July 21, 1876.

68 "Upper Carson Watershed Report" (June 2004), Section 5.1.7 (Agriculture), noting that brush fires reportedly set by shepherds in 1887 spread to nearby timber.

69 Owners of a footbridge over the Middle Fork sued the timber company Morgan, Ayres & Co. for damages to the bridge in 1866, only to have their suit dismissed by the state Supreme Court on appeal. *Chronicle*, October 20, 1866. The "Upper Carson Watershed Report" similarly mentions damage to bridges, roads, buildings, and land lower down in the valley. *Supra*, at Section 5.1.6 (Logging).

70 The "fine" Markleeville garden owned by Weiss & Fritz suffered flooding in 1872 from a "boom" across the river at the foot of Main Street, "thereby backing the water up and causing the river to cut through the garden. It was feared that their stable and outhouses would be carried away." *Chronicle*, May 11, 1872.

71 *Chronicle*, March 18, 1871.

72 *Chronicle*, August 31, 1872.

73 "Every foot of timber land in the vicinity of Silver Mountain has been located for the purpose of supplying the Virginia market with wood; and like locations have been made in every section of the county. The entire length and breadth of Carson Canon has been so located, and the water right taken up by two different companies for fluming purposes." *Chronicle*, August 31, 1872.

74 *Chronicle*, April 27, 1872 (noting that two different parties claimed and then started clearing the same parcel of land).

75 *Chronicle*, August 24, 1872.

76 *Chronicle*, April 20, 1872, estimating 20,000 to 25,000 cords; *see similarly* July 20, 1872, mentioning two separate drives passing through town of of 4,500 and 21,000 cords.

77 *Chronicle*, September 7, 1872.

78 *Chronicle*, September 14, 1872.

79 *Chronicle*, January 5, 1878 (death of Lewis Anderson, "aged about thirty years"); June 29, 1878 (death of Frank E. Young, "about 34," of Maine).

80 In 1878, a logger's "laborer's lien" was finally allowed by the State legislature. Opined the *Chronicle*, "Such a bill should have been passed years ago." *Chronicle*, March 30, 1878.

81 Chalmers Letters, *Private Letters 1871-72*, pp. 136 and 140 (June 18, 1871).

82 Elizabeth Ann Howatt's 1968 thesis, "Historical Geography of Alpine County" (U.C. Berkeley), indicates that the quantity of wood cut in 1873 was quadruple the usual amount; she also attributes the drop in wood prices to increased use of coal. *See also* Rossiter W. Raymond, <u>Mining Statistics West of the Rocky Mountains</u>,1874 (transcription of portion of the report pertaining to Alpine County, at Alpine County Museum), p. 10, indicating a price of $3/cord, delivered, at either mill or mine.

83 *Chronicle*, July 22, 1876 (noting that one Henry Chace [*sic*] had been criminally indicted for "cutting wood on public lands.") As late as 1877, the wood business was significant enough to pit even states against each other; Nevada granted an "exclusive franchise" to float wood down the Carson River to a gentleman named Crow (or Crowe), only to have the California courts indignantly intervene. *Chronicle*, December 15, 1877.

84 *Chronicle*, August 3, 1878; *see similarly* May 18, 1878, noting "several lots of wood have been attached in Alpine County and the outlook is bad for the choppers," due to "stagnation" of the Virginia City wood market.

85 W.M. Maule, *supra*, at p. 38, *citing Territorial Enterprise* of August 8, 1880; *see also* "Upper Carson Watershed Report" (June 2004), Section 5.1.6 (Logging), indicating that in the 1880s, logging "declined markedly."

86 W.M. Maule, *supra*, at pp. 40-44, includes an extensive list of local sawmills.

87   W.M. Maule, *supra*, at p. 40, *citing* the *Record-Courier* of September 11, 1925 (indicating that the Careys operated their mill in partnership with Daniel Woodfords and a Mr. Peabody, probably Luman [or Lyman] Peabody).

88   W.T. Jackson, *supra*, p. 50.

89   W.M. Maule, *supra*, at p. 40 (mentioning the Buist & Pearson mill); *see also* Alpine Assessment Roll of 1865 (Alpine County Archives), entry for G.E. Berry, describing property "running up to and opposite Robinson's Saw Mill."

90   W.T. Jackson, *supra*, p. 52.

91   *See* Alpine Assessment Roll of 1864 (Alpine County Archives), entry for William Brock.

92   *Chronicle*, February 15, 1868 (delinquent tax notice against J.H. Jacobs's one-half interest in "Sander's millsite" in Silver Mountain, and also his half-interest in the millsite on Murphy's Canyon Creek); *see also* similar delinquent tax notice in *Chronicle*, March 26, 1870, mentioning Sanders' mill site near 8th Street.

93   Quitclaim deed from Henry Mercer conveying a one-quarter interest in a mill site "to the northeast of the grave yard" in Silver Mountain to William Mercer, dated August 29, 1864 (original at Alpine County Museum); *see also* recorded version of same deed in Book "A" of Alpine County Official Records, p. 19.

94   Conveyance of mill site from James White to John Proffit, Book "A" of Alpine County Official Records, p. 30 (August 19, 1864).

95   Alpine Assessment Roll of 1867 (Alpine County Archives).

96   Chalmers Letters, *Private Letters 1871-72*, pp. 159 and 230 (July 4 and August 17, 1871)(noting that this sawmill was "1 mile out" from Silver Mountain). Mill sites were "located" and claimed along a river where the motive power would be sufficient to turn a water-wheel. Although claim papers were filed to hold a promising mill site, actual mills were never erected at many locations.

97   *Monitor Gazette*, July 16, 1864; Alpine Assessment Roll of 1865 (Alpine County Archives), entry for "Richardson & Bro."; *see also* W.T. Jackson, *supra*, p. 28 (*citing Monitor Gazette* of July 9, 1864). This may have been the operation at Centerville Flat able to produce 8,000 to 10,000 feet of lumber per day. *See* W.M. Maule, *supra*, at p. 40.

98   Alpine Assessment Roll of 1865 (Alpine County Archives), entry for "Richardson & Bro." indicating its location was "near Harell's Saw Mill."

99   W.M. Maule, *supra*, at p. 40, noting that the Luther ranch was identified in the plat survey as early as 1862.

100   *Chronicle*, June 16, 1866 (delinquent tax notice).

101   W.T. Jackson, *supra*, pp. 31-32, indicating that the two earlier sawmills were about four miles outside of Markleeville, and that a third sawmill was being built at about this time in closer proximity to town. The Hungerford Sawmill was identified as early as 1864 on Theron Reed's map. *See* W.M. Maule, *supra*, at p. 41.

102   *See Chronicle*, December 1, 1866, in which a Constable's Sale is noticed; *Chronicle*, March 9, 1867 (indicating the sawmill roof caved in due to snow, but machinery was uninjured); *Chronicle* February 15, 1868 (delinquent tax notice, indicating a 320-acre tract, a figure which suggests that a portion of the property had been sold). The Alpine Wood & Lumbering Co. also operated a sawmill on Pocket Mill Creek, and was similarly behind in taxes in 1878. *Chronicle*, February 2, 1878.

103   W.M. Maule, *supra*, at p. 41. Maule indicates that this operation was just southwest of the original Hot Springs Ranger Station and ran continuously from at least 1866 to 1878, producing 15,000 to 20,000 board feet daily.

104   W.M. Maule, *supra*, at p. 40. *See also* mention of an assessment on the Curtz & Griffith sawmill being "stricken" from the assessment rolls in 1878, perhaps because it was no longer functioning. *Chronicle*, August 10, 1878.

105   The Bemis Mill was considered "a fine mill" and was able to produce from 25,000 to 35,000 board-feet per day. Described as a "portable" saw mill, it was moved to Mrs. Hawkins' ranch about 1878, and eventually

became the Cohen Sawmill. W.M. Maule, *supra*, at p. 41; *Chronicle*, May 4, 1878. *See also* ephemera at Alpine Museum identifying Isadore Cohen (also sometimes spelled "Isador Cohn") as proprietor of the Cohen Sawmill in 1898 and 1902. Lumber from Bemis's mill was transported as far away as Bodie. *Chronicle*, October 12, 1878.

106   W.M. Maule, *supra*, at p. 41 (indicating that Koenig's operation ran from 1907-1914).

107   *Chronicle*, February 23, 1867, and April 6, 1872.

108   The Minnesota Sawmill was located on the East Fork of the Carson River, six miles from Monitor and four miles from Silver King, and was described as "new" in September, 1864. *Monitor Gazette*, September 10 and 17, 1864.

109   Chalmers Letters, *Private Letters 1868-69*, p. 319 (March 15, 1869)(indicating Chalmers had acquired both the Hanson and Lecony mill sites).

110   W.M. Maule, *supra*, at p. 29.

111   The "Silver King Mills and Lumbering Company" had seven acres with a mill on the south side of the East Carson River about a mile north of the town of Silver King, and advertised "the lowest price for cash." *See* W.T. Jackson, *supra*, p. 45; Alpine Assessment Roll of 1864 (Alpine County Archives), entry for D.D. Matson, Agent; *see also Monitor Gazette*, May 20, 1865.

112   Bancroft Scraps (Bancroft Library), p. 51. Another source estimates a total of 45 sawmills in Alpine by the mid-1860s, a figure that seems too large both for the populace and for local lumber needs. *See* "Upper Carson Watershed Report" (June 2004), Sec. 5.1.6 Logging, *available on-line*. As for the price of the lumber output of these mills, Chalmers reports the going rate was $24.25 per 1,000 board-feet at Monitor in mid-1871, but Chalmers himself had been willing to provide the lumber for the Tarshish Mill at $21 and was low-balled by Curts & Griffith, at just $20. Chalmers Letters, *Private Letters 1871-72*, p. 221 (August 13, 1871).

113   *Chronicle*, September 7, 1872. Interestingly enough, the exclusive purpose of this sawmill was apparently to produce lumber for a flume down Carson Canyon.

114   The Frevert (or "Friebert") mill was managed by Thomas Audrain. *See* W.M. Maule, *supra*, at p. 41, and *Chronicle* September 9, 1876.

115   W.M. Maule, *supra*, at p. 41.

116   "Upper Carson Watershed Report," Sec. 5.1.6. One of these lumber mills may have been the Thornburg Sawmill, built by William M. Thornburg. According to family history, this mill was constructed around 1884 "in Thornburg Canyon about three miles from Hot Springs Creek" to produce "flume lumber" to construct timber flumes. "Going West For The Mining," a typescript summarizing the life of William McElwee Thornburg, compiled by Nancy Thornburg (2010).

117   W.M. Maule, *supra*, at p. 12.

118   *See* Homesteads Book "A", p. 44, homestead dated July 5, 1865 for Daniel Davidson (Alpine County Archives), identifying the homestead land as "beginning about 25 chains below Davidson's Mill."

119   Rossiter W. Raymond, Mineral Resources West of the Rocky Mountains,1872 (transcription containing Chalmers' report pertaining to Alpine County, copy at Alpine County Museum), p. 5.

120   Chalmers Letters, *Exchequer Officials 1873-74* (Bancroft Library), p. 205 (November 26, 1873).

121   *Chronicle*, September 30, 1876. The capacity of this shingle machine was reportedly 25,000 shingles in 24 hours.

122   *Chronicle*, October 14, 1876.

123   Rossiter W. Raymond, Mineral Resources West of the Rocky Mountains, 1870 (transcription containing Chalmers' report pertaining to Alpine County, copy at Alpine County Museum), p. 5; *see similar claim in* the 1872 Mineral Resources transcript, p. 5.

124   R.W. Raymond, Mineral Resources, 1872, *supra*, at p. 5; *see similarly* Chalmers Letters, *Private Letters 1871-72*, p. 533-535 (March 21, 1873).

125   Rossiter W. Raymond, <u>Mineral Resources West of the Rocky Mountains</u>,1873 (transcription containing Chalmers' report pertaining to Alpine County, copy at Alpine County Museum), p. 8.

126   *Chronicle*, July 29, 1876.

127   W.W. Harris advertised his services as a "watchmaker and jeweler," promising not only "great care exercised in repairing watches and valuable jewelry" but also "quartz specimen and bullion work executed with neatness and dispatch." *Alpine Miner*, July 6, 1867 and *Chronicle*, May 30, 1868.

128   The 1864 Assessment Roll indicates George J. Harris's store was near the Fiske Hotel (Block 2), and included a stock of merchandise worth $1,200. Amador Assessment Roll of 1864 (Alpine County Archives), entry for George J. Harris. *See also* <u>Diary of Addison Curtiss</u> (original in Amador County archives), entries for May 25 and June 4, 1864, noting that a "pair of duck overalls" at "Harris's store" set him back $2.25, while new boots were $7 at "Frank Smith & Co."

129   Jacob Struben had a "shoe shop" in Silver Mountain in 1865; *see* Alpine Assessment Roll of 1865 (Alpine County Archives), entry for "Jacob Strubin [*sic*]". C. Bechlet similarly had a cobbler's store in Markleeville, located on Main Street between Montgomery and Water Streets (*see* April 23, 1864 *Chronicle, reprinted in* <u>Maule</u> history).

130   *Silver Mountain Bulletin*, October 13, 1866.

131   Wichelhausen served as the "exclusive agent" for the San Francisco Bulletin, the Sacramento Union, and the Virginia Enterprise. *Alpine Miner*, July 6, 1867.

132   <u>Diary of O.S. Adams</u> (Dustman collection), entries for August 14 through October 15, 1867.

133   *Chronicle*, May 14, 1870 (advertisement disclosing that "Blind Tom" was more formally Thomas Johnson).

134   W.T. Jackson, *supra*, p.50.

135   Alpine Assessment Roll of 1865 (Alpine County Archives), entry for "H. Swinerton."

136   Alpine Assessment Roll of 1865 (Alpine County Archives), entry for "Sauquet's", showing he was taxed on $800 worth of merchandise for his store plus his $500 real estate; by the July 1870 census, his personal property alone was worth $2000. *See also* 1877 map of Silver Mountain, drawn by L.L. Hawkins.

137   *See* advertisement for "Wangenheim & Blum" in *Monitor Gazette*, June 11, 1864, noting that "S. Wangenheim" was based in San Francisco, while his local partner "J. Blum" was in Markleeville; *see also Chronicle*, June 16, 1866 (ad by "Sol. Wangenheim," with no mention of Blum); and *Alpine Miner*, July 6, 1867 (Wangenheim alone). By 1869, the store may have been sold to John Weis, who supplied Chalmers with goods (including wooden water buckets) for many years. *See* Chalmers Letters, *Private Letters 1868-69*, pp. 289; 296 (February 8 and 20, 1869); *see also Alpine Argus*, August 8, 1885 (suggesting Weis's store was also near the corner of Montgomery and Main).

138   *Silver Mountain Bulletin,* December 22, 1866 (acquired Harris's store); *Chronicle*, February 25, 1871 (advertisement showing store in Monitor was operated by E.F. Gibson while Reinstein remained in San Francisco). Reinstein and partner Gibson would lose $6,000 in merchandise in the 1872 Monitor fire; unlike many others they had taken out insurance, but only to the tune of $1,000. W.T. Jackson, *supra*, p. 41 (*quoting Alpine Miner* of April 6, 1872); *Chronicle* April 6, 1872.

139   Receipt dated December 1, 1871 showing the location of Reinstein & Gibson at Monitor (original document at Alpine County Museum, Thornton folder). By this time, the firm's Silver Mountain location had appparently folded. *See infra* at note 156.

140   Chalmers Letters, *Private Letters 1868-69*, p. 159 (September 14, 1868); *see similarly Chronicle*, July 13, 1872, noting the arrival of the "first fruit team of the season"; and *Chronicle* of October 28, 1876, noting that the "last fruit team" was expected to arrive over the Big Trees Road, with goods for the rest of the season coming only via Carson.

141   Frank Dastague operated the Pioneer Meat Market at the corner of Main and Third as early as 1866, a location which later became Love's Meat Market. *Silver Mountain Bulletin*, October 13, 1866 (Sheriff's sale of

property of Dastague); *see also Chronicle,* January 7, 1871 (delinquent tax notice re Kirby's butcher shop and slaughterhouse); Alan H. Patera, "Silver Mountain California," <u>Western Places: A Chronicle of Western Settlement</u>, Vo. 1, No. 3 (September, 1992), at p. 51 (reproducing ad for Love's meat market, at the corner of Main and Third Streets); and <u>Bancroft Scraps</u> (Bancroft Library), p. 54 (letter from "I.M.," probably published in the SF Weekly Bulletin of May 29, 1863), indicating that two butcher shops were operating in "Konigsburg" in May 1863.

142   H. Eno, <u>Twenty Years on the Pacific Slope</u>, p. 143-44 (April 24, 1866)(punctuation added).

143   Chalmers Letters, *Imperial Officials 1867-70*, p. 341 (July 1, 1869).

144   Chalmers Letters, *Private Letters 1868-69*, p. 296 (February 19, 1869)(ordering from Gibson's Silver Mountain store); and *Imperial Officials 1867-70*, p. 314 (May 6, 1869)(ordering kegs of powder, resin soap, and pick handles from Gibson).

145   The Pioneer Bakery is mentioned in a tax delinquent notice against J.G. Perrins. *Chronicle,* February 15, 1868. William Kent also operated the Silver Mountain Bakery & Restaurant along with a boarding house, offering meals for 50 cents, and lodging for another 50 cents. *Silver Mountain Bulletin,* December 22, 1866.

146   Addison Curtiss mentions taking breakfast at a "French Restaurant" kept by a woman – and separately mentions the French Hotel, run by a Mrs. Scott. <u>Addison Curtiss Diary,</u> entry for May 6, 1864.

147   Frank Betchmann ran the Silver Mountain Livery Stable on Main Street (probably between 2nd and 3rd), for example. *Chronicle,* October 20, 1866 (Betchmann); and May 31, 1873 (Silver Mountain Stable operated by John J. Rice). *See also Chronicle,* February 8, 1868, indicating a new stable had "lately been inaugurated up town."

148   Dr. J.T. Harrison of San Jose and partner George Pomeroy proposed to open a combination "drug store and assay office" at Silver Mountain as early as April, 1864. *See Mining & Scientific Press,* April 2, 1864.

149   *Silver Mountain Bulletin,* October 13, 1866; February 16, 1867. James A. Owens was one of the early incorporators of the Buckeye No. 2 Gold & Silver Mining Company in May, 1863 (*see* Certificate of Incorporation, Amador County archives, Document ID 5264.A15), and served as an initial Trustee for the Alta Company, formed to work the Pennsylvania Ledge, in June, 1863 (Certificate of Incorporation, Amador County archives, Document ID 5264.A5).

150   *Alpine Miner,* July 6, 1867.

151   Gates' location was known as "Gates' Corner" or the "Silver Mountain Pioneer Drug Store and Mill-men's Depot." *Silver Mountain Bulletin,* December 22, 1866; *see similarly copy of the April 23, 1864 Chronicle reprinted in* W.M. Maule, *supra.* The proprietor was referred to as "Dr." Gates in the *Chronicle* of June 15, 1867.

152   *Chronicle,* December 15, 1877 (between 4th and 5th Streets).

153   Silver Mountain merchant F.H. Smith evidently complained in a July 9, 1864 letter to a San Francisco backer that business in his dry goods store was not as favorable as he'd hoped (Letter from Royal Fisk to F.H. Smith dated July 16, 1864, at Bancroft Library), and an "exodus" from town was reported after the excitement in Spring, 1864 had waned. *Miner,* October 20, 1866.

154   Sauquet's store at the corner of 6th and Main still shows up on the 1877 plat of Silver Mountain. Sauquet was elected a director of the Pennsylvania G&SM Co. in 1878 and remained active in mining affairs into the 1880s. (*Chronicle,* August 31, 1878; *see also* Chalmers Letters, *Private Letters 1881-84*, pp. 31; 38 (July 15-22, 1881) (mentioning Sauquet, who apparently held mining interests).

155   *Chronicle,* May 30 and June 6, 1868 (late ads by Wangenheim, showing his store still at Main and Montgomery, Markleeville); the roof of the building owned by "Gates Brothers of Sacramento" fell in, "making it a complete wreck." *Chronicle,* December 30, 1871.

156   *Chronicle,* September 17, 1870 (Reinstein selling out his stock of goods in Silver Mountain); he apparently was still operating a store in Monitor with Gibson, however, which was consumed by the fire of 1872 (*Chronicle,* April 6, 1872).

157   <u>Diary of O.S. Adams,</u> entries for April 13 and 15, 1867.

158   <u>Diary of O.S. Adams</u>, entry for November 10, 1867.

159   *Chronicle*, September 21, 1878. An earlier article suggested that Alpine was the "second highest taxpaying" county in the State. *Chronicle*, February 17, 1872.

160   *Chronicle*, August 12, 1876.

161   *Chronicle*, November 3, 1866.

162   *Chronicle*, December 31, 1870. The "Dog Tax of 1866" netted the County quarterly income of all of 94 cents for the period ending September 3, 1866. *Chronicle*, November 3, 1866.

163   *Chronicle*, June 25, 1870.

164   *Chronicle*, April 20, 1878.

165   *Chronicle*, June 22, 1878, noting that the match tax was to be abolished effective January 1, 1879. In addition to all the taxes mentioned, there were also road tolls paid to private road contractors for the privilege of using the roads, described in Chapter 5.

166   *Bulletin*, May 25, 1867.

167   *Chronicle*, December 7, 1867.

168   *Chronicle*, June 4, 1870.

169   *See* Cynthia G. Fox, "Income Tax Records of the Civil War Years," Prologue Magazine, Winter 1986 (Vol. 18 No. 4), *available online at* www.archives.gov/publications/prologue/1986/winter/civil-war-tax-records. html.

170   *Chronicle*, July 9, 1870 and March 30, 1872 (spelling corrected).

171   Cynthia G. Fox, "Income Tax Records of the Civil War Years," *supra*. Interestingly enough, the U.S. Supreme Court declared the income tax unconstitutional in 1895, prompting a legislative rescue for the "odious" income tax in the form of the Sixteenth Amendment in 1913. *Id.*

172   *Chronicle*, April 6 and 20, 1872 (estimating Alpine's take at about $1,000 per year, and also noting that the State Board of Equalization was ignoring the new law); *see also Chronicle*, August 12, 1876 (listing quarterly income from the Migratory Stock Tax of $1,176.63). Sheep owners in San Joaquin and other counties also found that intervening counties like Calaveras attempted to impose their *own* assessment on sheep passing through, destined for Alpine. *Chronicle*, July 13, 1878.

173   Book "B" of Board of Supervisors Minutes, p. 425 (July 10, 1889).

174   Chalmers Letters, *Imperial Officials 1867-70*, p. 284 (March 8, 1869)(placing the blame for the proposal on Frank Jones). There is no indication that such a license tax was in fact adopted.

175   *Monitor Gazette*, March 25, 1865 (listing Justice Court complaints filed by the District Attorney to collect unpaid property taxes from 1864).

176   Chalmers Letters, *Imperial Official 1867-70*, pp. 368-68 (duplicate page number in original) (August 16, 1869).

177   *Bulletin*, March 23, 1867. It was unclear, however, (as the *Bulletin* pointed out) whether two or more partners working a mine together, or a company working the mine through a corporation, could claim the same exemption.

178   Chalmers Letters, *Private Letters 1871-73*, p. 411 (June 27, 1872).

179   Letters from F.A.S. Jones to James Jones, dated April 20 and May 29, 1865 (Jones Letters, Alpine County Museum)(both mentioning that the tax rate was $3.50 per $100 assessed valuation, payable in gold).

180   Chalmers Letters, *Private Letters 1868-69*, p. 116-117 (August 24, 1868); *Imperial Officials 1867-70*, pp. 134-135 (double-numbered)(September 21, 1868).

181   Jones Letters, *supra*, April 20 and May 29, 1865. The *Chronicle* argued (unsuccessfully) in favor of permitting county warrants to be used to pay county taxes, asserting that "the delinquent list would be materially reduced." *Chronicle*, November 10, 1866.

182   The issue of whether to tax an unproducing mine when it represented a mere hole in the ground was subject to considerable debate. The *Chronicle* came out in favor of taxing these exploratory ventures; the competing *Miner* abstained for a time, then similarly came out in favor of taxation. *Chronicle*, June 6 and 13, 1868 (contending that the Alpine assessor's valuation on undeveloped claims "will be but nominal").

183   Chalmers made this argument to the *Mining & Scientific Press*, among others, urging them to print his letter. *See* Chalmers Letters, *Imperial Officials 1867-70*, p. 428-37; 442 (October 5-19, 1869).

184   Chalmers Letters, *Private Letters 1868-9*, p. 116-117 (August 24, 1868); *Imperial Officials 1867-70*, p. 134-135 (double-numbered)(September 21, 1868).

185   Chalmers wrote to the County Assessor in White Pine, Nevada and in 10 California counties, inquiring about their method of taxing unproductive mines. Chalmers Letters, *Imperial Officials 1867-70*, pp. 428-37; 442 (October 5-19, 1869).

186   Chalmers wrote to Gregory Yale for a legal opinion (as he informed the California Attorney General), and even contacted Nevada's Senator Mullen for assistance. Chalmers Letters, *Imperial Officials 1867-70*, pp. 161; 166 (October 14 and 26, 1868); p. 181 (December 7, 1868)("I spoke from 11 o'clock to 5 against the assessment on our claims, but without avail."); and p. 246 (February 15, 1869).

187   Chalmers Letters, *Imperial Officials 1867-70*, p. 181 (December 7, 1868). Fellow mine owners Coulter and Pilkington apparently joined with Chalmers in this bribe. The final tax of $24.37 on the Imperial's mining claims (on a $750 valuation) he paid "under protest." (*Imperial Officials 1867-70*, p.175 (November 13,1868).

188   Letter from Lewis Chalmers to the Board of Equalization at Markleeville, dated July 21, 1876 (original at Alpine County Museum).

189   Chalmers Letters, *Isabella Officials 1878-80*, p. 259 (June 9, 1879).

190   *Chronicle*, February 2, 1867.

191   *See Chronicle,* March 30, 1867, and *Alpine Miner*, July 6, 1867, indicating earlier timber tolls were 37-1/2 cents on cordwood. The tolls struck down as an illegal burden on interstate commerce in Carson River Lumbering Co. v. Patterson, 33 Cal. 334 (1867) were $1 per cord for firewood floated down the river, and $1 per thousand feet of saw logs. *See also Chronicle*, August 10, 1878, reflecting assessed values of $3/cord on "all wood in the big 'drive,'" likely referring to the personal property value "on the ground" rather than a toll on floated wood.

192   *See, for example, Chronicle*, October 20, 1866, reporting that District Court Judge Reed had ruled in favor of the County on the tax issue. *See also* H. Eno, Twenty Years on the Pacific Slope, pp. 78-79.

193   Of this amount, $1,900 was received in the form of a promissory note, which the *Chronicle* pointed out was illegal, because the statute required payment in coin. *Chronicle*, October 13, 1866. An auditor's report for the quarter ending September 3, 1866 suggests the wood tax collections (at least for that quarter) came to only $1,766.60. *Chronicle*, November 3, 1866.

194   *Chronicle*, February 15, 1868. The Folger brothers early disapproved of the tax, recognizing "If the Court should decide against the validity of the Act in question, the County would have to refund it together with damages and interest." *Chronicle*, June 29, 1867 and September 2, 1871. The newspapermen also urged the Supervisors to pass resolutions against a new "Carson River Franchise Act," noting that "everybody receives a portion of the woodchopper's dollar." *Chronicle*, February 15 and 22, 1868.

195   Carson River Lumbering Co. v. Patterson, 33 Cal. 334 (1867).

196   *Chronicle*, July 20, 1872.

197   *Chronicle*, February 22, 1868.

198   *Chronicle*, August 10, 1878.

199   *Chronicle*, June 4, 1870.

200   *Chronicle*, May 18, 1878 and August 3, 1878 (noting the "stagnation" of the wood business); *and see also Chronicle*, August 5, 1876 (citing a decline in the assessment roll to just $453,111, representing a valua-

tion drop of $200,000 from the previous year "caused by decrease of wood business," and observing ironically that 200,000 cords of wood would have yielded a "paltry" county tax of $6,000).

Chapter 11 Footnotes:

1   *Silver Mountain Bulletin*, April 13, 1867.

2   *Silver Mountain Bulletin*, April 13, 1867; *see also Chronicle*, April 6, 1867 (reporting lower figures of $667 in silver and $72 in gold).

3   *Alpine Miner*, May 11, 1867; *see also* W. Turrentine Jackson, Report on the History of Grover Hot Springs State Park Area and Surrounding Region of Alpine County (Division of Beaches & Parks, Department of Parks and Recreation, State of California 1964), at p. 38. *See similarly* Rossiter W. Raymond, Mineral Resources West of the Rocky Mountains, 1873 (transcription of Lewis Chalmers's report pertaining to Alpine County, at Alpine County Museum), p. 24, noting that a load of ore was worked by the Freiburg process at Dall's Mill in Washoe Valley, yielding $400/ton. This presumably was the same 7,000 pounds of ore milled at Washoe's Ophir mill, which produced either $300 or $350/ton, depending on the reporting source.

4   *See Silver Mountain Bulletin*, May 4, 1867 for the $300 figure; Henry Eno suggests that the yield was somewhat higher, at over $350/ton. Henry Eno, Twenty Years on the Pacific Slope (Yale University Press 1965), p. 162.

5   *Chronicle*, June 29, 1867.

6   Rossiter W. Raymond, Mineral Resources West of the Rocky Mountains, 1873, p. 24. This money may have been intended for a mill; in April, the Superintendent was apparently trying to purchase a mill. *See Chronicle*, April 6 and 13, 1867.

7   H. Eno, Twenty Years on the Pacific Slope, p. 162.

8   Historian William M. Maule puts the figure at 200. *See* Maule's "A Contribution to the Geographic and Economic History of Carson, Walker and Mono Basins" (U.S. Forest Service 1938), at p. 27, quoting *New York Times* article of April 30, 1872 and Pacific States Business Directory of 1878. *See also* Bancroft Scraps (Bancroft Library), p. 52, suggesting that the population of Silver Mountain was 300 circa 1867-71. This would have been a sizeable drop from Henry Eno's estimate of "about 350" inhabitants at the county seat in April, 1866. H. Eno, Twenty Years on the Pacific Slope, p. 143 (April 24, 1866). The ever-hopeful *Chronicle*, however, noted the population of the county was "steadily on the increase." *Chronicle*, February 8, 1868.

9   *Chronicle*, September 17, 1870.

10   *Chronicle*, September 24, 1870.

11   *Chronicle*, October 15, 1870.

12   *Chronicle*, December 17, 1870.

13   *Chronicle*, December 31, 1870.

14   *Chronicle*, June 24, 1871.

15   *Chronicle*, April 8, 1871.

16   *Chronicle*, April 15, 1871.

17   *Chronicle*, September 30, 1871.

18   *Chronicle*, September 21, 1872.

19   *Chronicle*, July 8, 1871.

20   *Chronicle*, July 15, 1871. By 1871, the Ogden's Saloon was operating in the Court House building (*Chronicle*, August 10, 1872), indicating the landslide likely descended near Union and Fourth.

21   *Chronicle*, July 22, 1871.

22   *Chronicle*, May 14, 1870.

23   Former sheriff D.N. McBeth was grading a lot in Monitor for a lavish new hotel in March, 1871, later said to be worth $2,000. *Chronicle*, March 25, 1871 and April 6, 1872.

24   W.T. Jackson, *supra*, p. 40.

25   Prospectus for the Globe Mine (1872)(California State Library, California History Room, Rare Book Collection). The entire county population for 1870 was just about 650 inhabitants, using the 1870 Official Census as a guide.

26   Bancroft Scraps, p. 52; William B . Clark, Mines and Mineral Resources of Alpine County, California (Calif. Division of Mines and Geology 1977), p. 5 (estimating Monitor's population at 300 in 1872). *But see* Chalmers Letters, *Private Letters 1871-73*, p. 541 (March 21, 1873), estimating the Monitor population in early 1873 at just about 200.

27   *See Chronicle*, April 6 and 13, 1872; *see also* W.T. Jackson, *supra*, pp. 40-41.

28   *Chronicle*, August 24; September 7 and 14, 1872. *See similarly Chronicle* of December 7 and 28, 1872, reporting "full loads of passengers" coming in by stage, reminiscent of the "good old days of 1863-4," and an "increasing" population.

29   For an excellent discussion of "The Crime of 1873" and demonetization, *see* website of professor François Micheloud, www.micheloud.com.

30   *See* www.micheloud.com.

31   The *Chronicle* regularly reported the exchange rate for greenbacks. In October, 1870, for example, it reported that greenbacks "are crawling up – but not into our pockets," with a conversion rate of 89½ cents (*Chronicle*, October 8, 1870). And in November, 1870, the quoted rate was "from 90 to 90¼ cents." (*Chronicle*, November 26, 1870).

32   For a fascinating look at the apocryphal tale of the supposed efforts by London banker Ernest Seyd to bribe Congress into passing the 1873 Coinage Act, *see* http://en.wikiquote.org/wiki/Ernest_Seyd, calling Seyd's supposed "secret confession" that he acted as an agent for the Bank of England to procure passage of the bill "almost certainly a hoax."

33   *See* www.micheloud.com.

34   At the election on October 20, 1875, the vote was 129 votes for Markleeville as the county seat, versus just 35 for Silver Mountain. *See* Book "B" of Supervisors Minutes, pp. 8-11 (Minutes of October 25, 1875).

35   Book "B" of Alpine County Supervisors' Minutes, pp. 12-14 (Book "B", Minutes of November 1, 1875); sale of the buildings was ordered again on May 7, 1877, fixing a sale date of July 16, 1877 (Book "B", pp. 40-43); but the sale of the old Silver Mountain jail was again postponed in the minutes of August 8, 1877 until November, 1877 (Book "B", p. 47).

36   Eliza Withington captured the event with her stereoscopic camera; the *Chronicle* mentions her presence in Silver Mountain in the August 26 and September 2, 1876 issues.

37   *Chronicle*, July 29, 1876.

38   *Chronicle*, October 7, 1876 – and at $603, still $103 over the "not to exceed" cap placed by the Supervisors at their February 7, 1876 meeting.

39   *Chronicle*, July 29, 1876. The same article noted that patents had been obtained on the Lady Franklin and Silver Cloud claims. The September 16, 1876 *Chronicle* similarly reported that the Lady Franklin mine was preparing to resume operations, after having been "idle since 1866."

40   Work on the Isabella was eventually suspended in December, 1880, after completing nearly 5,000 feet of tunnel. *See* Chalmers Letters, *Isabella Officials 1880-82*, pp. 202-210 (January 22, 1881).

41   *Chronicle*, December 23, 1876. Fearson & McClay advertised rooms that were "large, airy and light." *Chronicle*, September 30 and October 7, 1876.

42   *Chronicle,* January 5, 1878.

43   *See, e.g., Chronicle*, August 31 (reporting a "stampede for Bodie") and October 12, 1878.

44   Alan H. Patera, <u>Western Places: A Chronicle of Western Settlement</u>, Vo. 1, No. 3 (September 1992), at p. 53. A map of buildings in Bodie circa July, 1880 identifies Robert Love as the proprietor of the "City Market" on Main Street near the corner of Mill Street, and Love's home on Green Street near Fuller (Map ©1991 by Brownell Merrell, at Bodie Museum).

45   *Chronicle*, August 31 and September 14, 1878. *See also* May 18, 1878, predicting local voting would be light for a number of reasons, including that "Bodie has made inroads upon our voters."

46   A.H. Patera, <u>Western Places</u>, *supra*, at p. 47.

47   *Chronicle*, October 12, 1878.

48   *Chronicle*, October 12, 1878.

49   Chalmers wrote: "Last Saturday, the town of Silver Mountain was almost annihilated by fire" and "the Post Office [and] Postmaster's house are in ashes." Chalmers Letters, *Isabella Officials 1880-82*, p. 607 (February 23, 1882). *See also* Mabel Love, <u>History of the Alpine County Schools</u> (unpublished manuscript, at Alpine County Museum), p. 7.

50   Each piece of the building was reportedly numbered as the building was disassembled; it was then reassembled exactly as before, even re-using some of the nails, according to reports. W.T. Jackson, *supra*, p. 86-87; *Alpine Heritage: One Hundred Years of History, Recreation, Lore in Alpine County, California, 1864-1964*, published by the Alpine County Museum (Revised edition May 1987), at p. 13 (photo caption); *see also* family history concerning this event by Grover's granddaughter, Phyllis Grover Guerra, noting that Grover was forced to use all his expertise as a teamster to navigate the "deplorable" road, but "no one was afraid as long as Grover held the reins." (*Oakland Tribune Knave*, January 18, 1959). The Hot Springs Hotel was renamed the "Alpine Hotel" about 1900.

51   In February, 1882, Chalmers noted that there were only 3 adults in Silver Mountain, with 27 by contrast living at his Exchequer Mill, where he received a "daily large mail." Chalmers Letters, *Isabella Officials 1880-82*, pp. 607; 718 (February 23 and April 13, 1882); A.H. Patera, <u>Western Places</u>, *supra*, at p. 47 (indicating mail service to Silver Mountain was halted July 24, 1883, and sent instead to Silver Creek).

52   *Genoa Courier*, March 25, 1892, stating that Rice, who had died at Genoa, was "one of the oldest residents of Alpine County and the last inhabitant of Silver Mountain."

53   Frank Wedertz, <u>Mono Diggings</u> (Community Printing and Publishing, 2001), p. 140.

54   William B. Clark, <u>Mines and Mineral Resources of Alpine County</u>, *supra*, at p. 28. Clark also estimates county-wide total gold and silver production through 1977 at $3 to $5 million, "with gold and silver being in about equal amounts in value." *Id.* at pp. 13; 14.

55   Chalmers Letters, *Private Letters 1871-73*, pp. 43 and 50 (May 1 and May 22, 1871); and p. 535 (March 21, 1873).

56   The rough-hewn log enclosure now holding the iron cells was first constructed in downtown Markleeville behind the old courthouse (near the site of the present-day Chamber of Commerce building) in 1876. The entire building, cells and all, was later skidded up Schoolhouse Hill to its present location on the Alpine Museum grounds.

INDEX